LIFE IN POVERTY
NEIGHBOURHOODS

"Do poor neighbourhoods make their residents poorer?"

In contemporary European and American urban policy and politics and in academic research it is typically assumed that spatial concentrations of poor households and/or ethnic minority households will have negative effects upon the opportunities to improve the social conditions of those who are living in these concentrations.
Since the level of concentration tends to be correlated with the level of spatial segregation the 'debate on segregation' is also linked to the social opportunity discussion.

This book explores the central question in urban and housing studies, "Do poor neighbourhoods make their residents poorer?" Does the neighbourhood structure exert an effect on the residents (behavioural, attitudinal, or psychological) even when controlling for individual characteristics of the residents? This issue has offered a locus for multi-disciplinary investigations on both sides of the Atlantic, and this volume demonstrates the rich geographical, sociological, economic and psychological dimensions of this issue.

This book is a special issue of the journal *Housing Studies*.

Jürgen Friedrichs is Professor of Sociology in the Research Institute for Sociology, University of Cologne, Germany. **George Galster** is Clarence Hilberry Professor of Urban Affairs, College of Urban, Labor and Metropolitan Affairs, Wayne State University, Detroit, USA. **Sako Musterd** is Professor of Urban Geography in the Department of Geography and Planning of the University of Amsterdam, The Netherlands.

LIFE IN POVERTY NEIGHBOURHOODS

European and American Perspectives

Edited by Jürgen Friedrichs, George Galster and Sako Musterd

Routledge
Taylor & Francis Group

LONDON AND NEW YORK

First published 2005
by Routledge
2 Park Square, Milton Park, Abingdon, Oxon, OX14 4RN

Simultaneously published in the USA and Canada
by Routledge
270 Madison Ave, New York NY 10016

Routledge is an imprint of the Taylor & Francis Group

Transferred to Digital Printing 2009

© 2005 Routledge

Typeset in Palatino by Infotype Ltd, Eynsham, Oxfordshire

British Library Cataloguing in Publication Data
A catalogue record for this book is available
from the British Library

Library of Congress Cataloging in Publication Data

ISBN10: 0-415-35363-7 (hbk)
ISBN10: 0-415-56835-8 (pbk)

ISBN13: 978-0-415-35363-2 (hbk)
ISBN13: 978-0-415-56835-7 (pbk)

CONTENTS

Editorial

Neighbourhood Effects on Social Opportunities: The European and American Research and Policy Context

JÜRGEN FRIEDRICHS, GEORGE GALSTER & SAKO MUSTERD

In contemporary European and American urban policy and politics and in academic research it is typically assumed that spatial concentrations of poor households and/or ethnic minority households will have negative effects upon the opportunities to improve the social conditions of those who are living in these concentrations. Since the level of concentration tends to be correlated with the level of spatial segregation the 'debate on segregation' is also linked to the social opportunity discussion. The central question is "Do poor neighbourhoods make their residents poorer?" (Friedrichs, 1998), i.e. does the neighbourhood structure exert an effect on the residents (behavioural, attitudinal or psychological) even when controlling for individual characteristics of the residents?

The issue of neighbourhood effects on social opportunities of residents possesses rich geographical, sociological, economic and psychological dimensions, and as such has offered a locus for multi-disciplinary investigations on both sides of the Atlantic. Such diversity is amply demonstrated in this Special Issue of *Housing Studies*, with economists, geographers, planners and sociologists, hailing from Germany, the Netherlands, UK and USA, represented among the contributors. These diverse perspectives often intersect in two realms: spatial relationships and selective household mobility.

The spatial focus of neighbourhood effect studies is clear, for example, in economic geographical studies about the spatial mismatch between demand and supply on the labour market (Kasarda *et al.*, 1992). The thesis here is that economic restructuring has led to a situation in which the peripheral locations of suitable jobs for unskilled workers and inner-city residential locations of these potential workers have grown too far from each other to enable matching on a daily basis; this would aggravate the social conditions of those who live in inner-city areas. The spatial element is also evident in the research underpinnings of American housing policy aimed at changing the locations of low-income or minority households (Briggs, 1997; Del Conte & Kling, 2001; Katz *et al.*, 2001; Ludwig *et al.*, 2001; Rosenbaum, 1995; Rosenbaum *et al.*, 2002). These American policies for changing the spatial distribution of the disadvantaged are related to European ideas about 'mixed neighbourhood policies' that nowadays receive considerable attention and critiques (Atkinson & Kintrea, 2001; Kearns,

2002; Musterd *et al.*, 1999, Musterd *et al.*, this issue; Ostendorf *et al.*, 2001). As an illustration, in this issue van Beckhoven & Van Kempen address the urban restructuring effects in two Dutch cities, focusing on the social relations and interactions of residents. They conclude that the neighbourhood restructuring plays only a limited part in the life of most of the residents.

Urban researchers from multiple disciplines also intersect each other when they pay attention to selective residential migration processes in relation to neighbourhood effects. One of the crucial issues in this regard is the increasing concentration of poverty in certain areas, which is exacerbated by middle-class households moving out to more affluent neighbourhoods. In many American cities the flight of these households towards suburban neighbourhoods expresses a process of 'leaving the cities behind' (cf. Thomas, 1991; Wilson, 1987). As an effect, the service structure in poor inner-city neighbourhoods declines as the local tax base erodes. Vicious circles are expected to develop in extreme cases, implying a clear, pernicious neighbourhood effect. For example, one might start with the development of concentrations of poor inhabitants (frequently poor immigrants or ethnic minorities), followed by an erosion of public facilities and services, residential abandonment and rising crime, lack of opportunities and therefore again the attraction of those with the weakest positions. Racial factors may overlay class factors in creating a dual-feature segregation that intensifies poverty and constrains outward opportunity (Massey & Denton, 1993).

However, the fact that these kinds of mobility processes are encountered in American cities does not imply there are necessarily special neighbourhood effects. In their paper Kearns & Parkes pay attention to mobility in relation to neighbourhoods in the UK context. Their focus is on home and neighbourhood perceptions and residential mobility behaviour. They include poverty, anti-social behaviour and crime as key variables affecting perceptions and mobility. Nevertheless, their conclusion is that there is "no evidence to support the notion of a distinctive culture in deprived UK areas", rather, "residents in poor areas were responding to negative residential conditions in the same way as the rest of the population". It is also interesting to see that in several European cities the levels of segregation and separation are much lower compared to American experiences. This may imply that neighbourhood effects are less significant in Europe.

Moreover, unlike the American experience, usually it is not the inner city that collects the largest problems. Instead it is the outer areas, such as the *banlieue* in Paris (cf. Wacquant, 1993) and other large French cities, or post-war social housing complexes on the fringes in cities such as Amsterdam, Berlin, Glasgow, Stockholm and Naples, which are characterised by serious concentrations of social problems. One factor contributing to such concentrations is the social housing allocation policy in many European cities. In Germany, for example, poor or 'problematic' families are allocated to social housing dwellings by non-profit housing associations. These dwellings are predominantly located in the peripheral housing estates, thereby increasing the spatial concentration of distressed households.

In sum, the field of neighbourhood effects and social opportunities is currently an exciting one, characterised by spirited, multi-disciplinary debates. Unfortunately, one set of debates has been conducted within North America and another within Europe, often with little commonality. It is the goal of this Special Issue to bridge this gap, and offer ways of thinking about this issue that will help advance the discussion in both regions. This issue offers four illustrations of exemplary recent European research on neighbourhood effects, followed by two

American-authored papers, one by Galster, offering a new methodological strategy and the other by Briggs, who both offers comments on the European papers by putting the neighbourhood effect debate into a dynamic city-wide, nation-wide and global nested framework; and links the European papers to potential policy arenas.

The Editorial now proceeds by providing a Trans-Atlantic overview of the neighbourhood effects debates. Specifically, the review is organised around the questions: How large are neighbourhood effects? How can these effects be measured precisely? How do these effects transpire? Directions for future research on the topic are then suggested.

How Much, How, and How do we Know? A Trans-Atlantic Overview

Neighbourhood effects have been the source of American scholarly enquiries for over half a century. An early manifestation was the discussion on the proper 'social mix' of a neighbourhood (e.g. Gans, 1961; Sarkissian, 1976), but in this literature the effect was assumed to exist but not specified nor explored empirically. American empirical interest in the issue arguably was kindled by the seminal work of William Julius Wilson (1987), who claimed that the socially isolated environments of concentrated poverty neighbourhoods encouraged 'underclass' behaviours in US cities. Since then there has been a dramatic increase in the number of scholarly studies produced in the USA that investigate the impact of the residential neighbourhood on a variety of outcomes for youth and adults. The burgeoning findings of this multidisciplinary literature have spawned several comprehensive review articles (see especially Briggs, 1997; Ellen & Turner, 1997; Galster, 2002; Galster & Killen, 1995; Gephardt, 1997; Johnson et al., 2001; Leventhal & Brooks-Gunn, 2000; Sampson et al., 2002).

Geographers are among the first who should pay attention to the study of neighbourhood effects. However, as the dissertation of De Vos (1997) shows, it was only some three decades ago when geographical neighbourhood effect studies first emerged in Europe. Most of these studies addressed voting behaviour and only some dealt with other issues. Kevin Cox, Ron Johnston and Kelvin Jones were among the most active European researchers to address the neighbourhood effects. Only recently geographers started to pay attention to the impact of the social environment on social mobility in particular. Andersson (2001) and Musterd et al. (2001), for example, carried out large-scale longitudinal empirical research in Sweden and the Netherlands. They used datasets consisting of several millions of individuals and households who could be followed in their social career and in various socio-spatial settings, controlling for other influences on social careers. They found some independent but not very strong neighbourhood effects and had to conclude that additional research should be carried out before stronger answers can be provided. The review by Friedrichs (1998) also suggests that relatively few European sociologists have focused on this issue.

The vast majority of work in both the US and Europe has addressed the question, 'How much independent effect do neighbourhoods have?' Multiple methods have been employed to answer this 'How much?' question, and a healthy ferment is bubbling about which are most appropriate and where the most fertile advancements might lie, as will be seen below. Relatively few studies have addressed the question, "How does this neighbourhood effect occur?", one of the first being the methodological analysis by Erbring & Young (1979).

How Much Neighbourhood Effect?

The American literature on size of impact generally has concluded that the neighbourhood environment makes a non-trivial, independent difference for a variety of outcomes, although the impact is not nearly as decisive as parental or individual characteristics, or macro-economic conditions (Brooks-Gunn *et al.*, 1997; Haveman & Wolfe, 1995; Jargowsky, 1997). The measured impact clearly varies according to what sort of outcome is being considered, the age of the person being affected and how neighbourhood is measured. In Europe it appears that neighbourhood effects may be comparatively muted because of significantly different housing supply and social welfare systems that jointly limit the variation of neighbourhood conditions and ameliorate or compensate for these differences through other support programs (Atkinson & Kintrea, 2001; Musterd, 2002). Even this most general consensus is hardly unanimous, how-ever, with some arguing the measured impacts are over-stated and other claiming just the opposite.

Some have argued that most measured neighbourhood effects are biased upward because of selection effects (Evans *et al.*, 1992; Plotnick & Hoffman, 1999; Tienda, 1991). They argue that parents will self-select certain kinds of neighbour-hood environments with the intent of bettering themselves and their families. Yet, because typically the variables that measure such motivations are absent from the non-experimental, longitudinal databases analysed, a substantial de-gree of the apparent statistical association between neighbourhood conditions and various outcomes is, in fact, due to these unmeasured parental characteris-tics that led to the differential selection of the observed neighbourhood charac-teristics. Analogous forms of selection biases plague neighbourhood impacts measured from evaluations of US poverty deconcentration programmes, both quasi-experimental designs, as in the Gautreaux and Yonkers programs (e.g. Briggs, 1998; Rosenbaum, 1995), or random-experimental designs, as in the Moving to Opportunity (MTO) demonstration (Del Conte & Kling, 2001; Katz *et al.*, 2001; Ludwig *et al.*, 2001).

On the other hand, it has been argued that previous studies create downward biases in the measured neighbourhood effect (Brooks-Gunn *et al.*, 1997). First, they note that implicit in the selection argument above is the notion that a large number of parents *believe* that neighbourhood is important and act accordingly, thus belying the conclusion of no impact. Second, 'neighbourhood' is typically measured in US studies at the census tract, a relatively homogeneous area of 4000 inhabitants, on average. Such tracts might be too large in scale to measure accurately the variables of 'local neighbourhood' that actually are affecting residents. Third, readily available demographic and socio-economic data typi-cally employed as indicators may serve as poor proxies for the essence of 'neighbourhood' that may crucially affect outcomes, and may evince limited variation in the databases conventionally analysed (Brooks-Gunn *et al.*, 1997). Finally, as argued by Leventhal & Brooks-Gunn (2000) and Sampson *et al.* (2002), past studies have typically focused on the direct effects of neighbourhood only, not how neighbourhood might also influence outcomes through intervening variables that conventionally are treated as controls. Galster in this issue, for example, suggests that neighbourhood may influence outcomes through related choices of tenure and mobility, and through longer-run changes in household income and wealth.

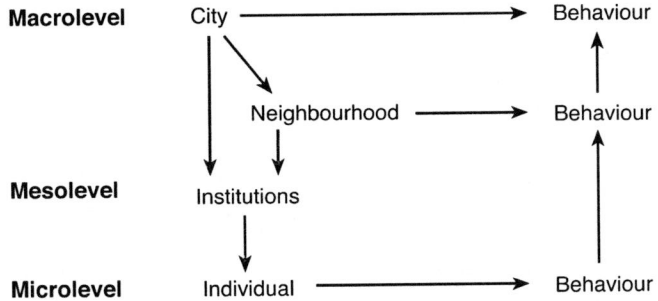

Figure 1. A multi-level model of neighbourhood effects.

The difficulties to specify neighbourhood effects on individuals arise from the complex structure in which the individual is embedded. This structure can be formalised in a multi-level model, shown in Figure 1. Neighbourhoods may be influenced by macro-level (city) changes, such as the aforementioned de-industrialisation. This will not only change the opportunities for residents to find a job, but as well result in the perception that many households in the neighbourhood are unemployed or eventually living from transfer payments only. Furthermore, the impact of the neighbourhood on the residents is not only direct, but also indirect via social institutions, such as the quality of schools, police and peer groups, further by the public and private facilities like shops and for recreation available in the area. It is, therefore, difficult to account for a neighbourhood effect on, say, the school drop out rate, if we do not control for both individual and school variables.

How do we Know?

There are two basic methodological approaches to the measurement of neighbourhood effects. Although these are described and critiqued in fuller detail in Haveman & Wolff (1995), Gephardt (1997), Leventhal & Brooks-Gunn (2000), Sampson *et al.* (2002) and Galster (this issue), in brief they are:

- Neighbourhood Case Study: individuals' attitudes, behaviours, life trajectories and social interrelationships are examined through archival, survey and/or ethnographic methods in one or more neighbourhoods with notable characteristics (typically associated with extreme deprivation and social exclusion); sometimes results are contrasted to those in other types of neighbourhoods; Van Beckhoven & Van Kempen (this issue) and Friedrichs & Blasius (this issue) are illustrative.
- Statistical Analysis of Non-Experimental, Longitudinal Databases: individuals are observed over time in different residential contexts, and multivariate statistical techniques are used to uncover correlations between these contexts and behaviours or outcomes for these individuals, controlling for background and other individual characteristics; Musterd *et al.* (this issue) and Kearns & Parkes (this issue) are illustrative.

Each approach has distinct strengths and weaknesses (Duncan *et al.*, 1997; Haveman & Wolfe, 1995). Both approaches share in common the challenge of responding to the aforementioned issue of selection biases. Without a convincing methodological response, both approaches remain highly vulnerable to the charge that not only the magnitude of the measured association between neighbourhood and individual outcomes is erroneous, but also causation itself may be absent. Finding such a convincing response has been the object of much greater attention by US than European scholars. The seminal analysis here is by Manski (1993, 1995), and the rapidly evolving literature during the subsequent decade has been summarised by Haurin *et al.* (2002). Several responses have emerged. First, instrumental variables might be substituted for the direct measures of neighbourhood found in non-experimental, longitudinal databases. In this issue Galster proposes an advance along this front based on the recognition of the simultaneity of neighbourhood and other choices affecting outcomes. Second, siblings can be studied over time in ways that fixed effects associated with common, but unobserved, parental characteristics can be differenced out, leaving the independent impacts of varying residential environments more visible. Third, if the outcomes in question involve non-linear responses to neighbourhood characteristics (such as threshold relationships or binary decisions like housing tenure or participation in the labour force), there are means of identifying unambiguously the independent neighbourhood effect (Brock & Durlauf, 2001). Fourth, social experiments might be designed whereby the allocation of subjects to neighbourhoods is done through random assignment procedures, such as the MTO demonstration in the US.

How are Neighbourhood Effects Transmitted?

Since the seminal paper by Jencks & Mayer (1990), there have been expanding theoretical discussions about the mechanisms of neighbourhood effects, in particular those related to neighbourhood institutions (such as schools), as inserted in Figure 1. However, there has been comparatively little empirical work: the paper by Friedrichs & Blasius in this issue is a welcome exception. There appears to be an emerging consensus that neighbourhood effects could transpire through one or more of the following mechanisms (Friedrichs, 1998; Gephardt, 1997; Leventhal & Brooks-Gunn, 2000; Sampson *et al.*, 2002):

- Neighbourhood resources: reputation of place, local public services and informal organisations, accessibility to jobs, recreation, health and other key services.
- Model learning via social ties and interrelationships: nature of interpersonal networks, peer groups, etc.
- Socialisation and collective efficacy: commonality of norms, sense of control of local public space.
- Resident perceptions of deviance, such as crime, drug dealing, physical decay of buildings and general state of disorder.

The first point refers to characteristics of places that often may be defined independently of the characteristics of residents. For example, the potential role of inadequate local public services in retarding social advancement is straightforward. The aforementioned spatial mismatch theory is based on the idea that access to jobs is insufficient; accessibility also plays a key role in the idea that inner-city poor residents are being cut off from proper institutions and services. The origin and role of the reputation of a place is more complicated because stigmatisation can occur on the basis of perceptions from outside of the neighbourhood's social composition. For example, a neighbourhood might become stigmatised on the basis of the percentage of unemployed people living there, therefore making it more difficult for those residents to find jobs.

Another dimension that may help to understand neighbourhood effects is the extent, type and quality of the social networks to which people belong. Although this is related to the socialisation dimension (see Andersson, 2001), the development of networks along certain lines (age, gender, class, ethnicity) may independently stimulate or reduce peoples' opportunities to discover new ways of life or employment options, and may or may not prevent people from becoming trapped in a weak social position. They learn by models available in the neighbourhood (cf. Thornberry *et al.*, 1994).

Socialisation is a dimension that refers to the (visual or verbal) interaction between people in the neighbourhood and the idea that these people, via their interaction, adopt each other's behaviours and attitudes, for example, via the acceptance of group norms and through social contagion. In this issue, Friedrichs & Blasius address these hypothetical explanations with a focus on explaining acceptance of and tolerance towards deviant behaviour in poverty neighbourhoods.

Finally, not only effects due to interaction must be included but also the residents' perceptions of the neighbourhood, e.g. visible deviant behaviour or the extent of physical decay. Examples are the 'broken windows' proposition by Wilson & Kelling (1982) or the recent study by Ross *et al.* (2001), who show that 'perceived disorder' among persons with low personal control leads to distrust other residents.

The relationships among these types of causal connections are difficult to decipher since the corresponding 'variables' are of different types and may require separate research projects to be measured adequately. Therefore, it is difficult to estimate the relative weight of these explanations, especially given the scant amount of empirical work. The review by Sampson *et al.* (2002) finds that all have been linked in one study or another to criminal activity, often as mediating factors between neighbourhood structural characteristics like concentrated poverty. Leventhal & Brooks-Gunn's review (2000) finds that the strongest evidence regarding child and youth outcomes relates to norms and collective efficacy, especially peers who serve as mediators of neighbourhood effects. A similar institutional effect (cf. Figure 1) was reported by Haynie (2001) who found strong effects of the density of the peer network structure on peer delinquency.

Considerations in Framing a Research Agenda

Knowledge about the size and mechanism of the impact of the neighbourhood is rapidly growing. However, crucial questions remain unanswered. These questions require a research agenda. This final section provides some organising elements that may play a useful role in constructing such a research agenda.

Even when we focus attention on the neighbourhood environment's effects on individuals, there remains considerable latitude. Effects can be varied, individuals can be varied and environments can be varied. Effects, as 'dependent' variables, may refer to the social mobility opportunities of people, but whose social mobility? Should the attention be focused on children's progress in particular, since their steps in life may be decisive for the rest of people's lives? Or would it also make sense to investigate the effects of environments on the lives of adults, unemployed, immigrants, etc. But even then various interpretations of social mobility are possible. The focus can be on improving the labour market position (from unemployed to employed; from poor to rich; from unstable jobs to stable jobs); but can also be on the social capital dimension (the size and quality of one's social network), or on school participation (level of participation). Instead of focusing on social outcomes, we also may want to highlight outcomes in other spheres, such as health development, deviant behaviour, criminal behaviour, and the like.

Independent variables can be distinguished at various levels, as indicated in Figure 1. It makes sense to distinguish between six types of variables, each with a different implicit spatial scale: individual characteristics; household characteristics; endogenous neighbourhood variables; exogenous neighbourhood variables; metropolitan area characteristics and welfare state regimes. Among the most important individual characteristics are variables such as age, gender, ethnicity, socio-economic position and dynamics and educational attainment and dynamics. Household type in demographic and socio-economic terms is also most important. The lifestyle of these households, their urban orientations (or not) and their spatial mobility levels seem to be most relevant to understand variations in 'effects'. With regard to the neighbourhood variables, we suggest distinguishing between endogenous (factors originating within neighbourhoods) and exogenous (factors originating outside of neighbourhoods) ones. Endogenous variables are, for example, related to theories regarding socialisation and social control. They further include characteristics like the proportion of socially 'weak' households, the physical attributes and housing structure conditions, and the neighbourhood's situation (location) in the metropolitan area. Exogenous variables are, for example, related to perceptions from outside and can, thus, contribute to the ideas related to stigmatisation. Here we should think of perceptions of service levels and physical conditions and of valuation by financial institutions, for example. At the metropolitan area level of explanations the dominant economic structure or historically grown, path-dependent structure appears to be important, as well as the level of political fragmentation of the area, the area's attraction to immigrants and the overall level of segregation of the population. The state level, finally, seems relevant as well, since various levels of policy intervention and the types of intervention may have large impact upon the social arena in metropolitan areas.

The questions that may be deduced from these categories can be addressed in various ways. We may distinguish between studies that address perceptions or actual behaviour; that investigate simple cases, or multiple cases; that use self-constructed spatial units, or statistical units; that use cross-sectional or longitudinal data; small-scale or large-scale neighbourhoods; samples or populations. Wide and long and longitudinal datasets seem to offer the best opportunities to carry out innovative research projects aimed at analysing and controlling for multiple environment effects specified in our model on individual opportunities (individual, household, neighbourhood, metropolitan area and state levels simultaneously); or following certain age cohorts over time; or including the change of environments during the process of social mobility; or to allow for better tests of non-linear relations between neighbourhood compositions and social effects. There are a growing number of studies on 'neighbourhood effects', but there is still a long way to go before a sufficiently high level of knowledge is attained to fundamentally evaluate the actual impact of neighbourhoods. As long as this goal has not been reached, urban and housing policies that aim to change the neighbourhood compositions in order to gain more positive social effects, are taking the plunge into largely uncharted waters (Galster, 2002; Galster & Zobel, 1998; Ostendorf *et al.*, 2001).

Acknowledgements

The idea for compiling this special issue on 'poverty neighbourhood effects' arose from the European Network for Housing Research working group on poverty neighbourhoods. That working group had organised a workshop within the larger European Network of Housing Researchers conference on Housing Cultures, Convergence and Diversity, which was held in July 2002 in Vienna. This edition of *Housing Studies* has been co-ordinated by ourselves in collaboration with the two editors of the journal. All papers have been subjected to the usual peer review processes of *Housing Studies*.

References

Andersson, R. (2001) Spaces of socialization and social network competition: a study of neighbourhood effects in Stockholm, Sweden, in: H.T. Andersen & R. Van Kempen (Eds) *Governing European Cities: Social Fragmentation and Urban Governance*, pp. 149–188 (Aldershot, Ashgate).
Atkinson, R. & Kintrea, K. (2001) Disentangling area effects: evidence from deprived and non-deprived neighbourhoods, *Urban Studies*, 38, pp. 2277–2298.
Atkinson, R. & Kintrea, K. (2002) A consideration of the implications of area effects for British housing and regeneration policy, *European Journal of Housing Policy*, 2(2), pp. 1–20.
Atkinson, R., Kintrea, K., Austin, M. & Baba, Y. (2001) Disentangling area effects: The contributions of place to household poverty, *Urban Studies*, 38, pp. 2277–2298.
Beckhoven, van & Kempen van (this issue).
Briggs, X. de Souza (1997) Moving up versus moving out: neighborhood effects in housing mobility programs, *Housing Policy Debate*, 8, pp. 195–234.
Briggs, X. de Souza (1998) Brown kids in white suburbs: Housing mobility and the many faces of social capital, *Housing Policy Debate*, 9, pp. 177–221.
Brock, W. & Durlauf, S. (2001) Interactions-based models, in: J. Heckman & E. Learner (Eds) *Handbook of Econometrics* (Vol. 5), pp. 3297–3380 (Amsterdam, North-Holland).
Brooks-Gunn, J., Duncan, G. & Aber, J. (Eds) (1997) *Neighborhood Poverty: Vol. I, Context and Consequences for Children* (New York, Russell Sage Foundation).
De Vos, S. (1997) *De omgeving telt.* PhD thesis (Amsterdam, Instituut voor Sociale Geografie, Universiteit van Amsterdam).
Del Conte, A. & Kling, J. (2001) A synthesis of MTO research on self-sufficiency, safety and health, and behavior and delinquency, *Poverty Research News*, 5(1), pp. 3–6.
Duncan, G., Connell, J. & Klebanov, P. (1997) Conceptual and methodological issues in estimating causal effects of neighborhoods and family conditions on individual development, in: J. Brooks-Gunn, G. Duncan & J. Aber (Eds) *Neighborhood Poverty: Vol. I, Context and Consequences for Children*, pp. 219–250 (New York, Russell Sage Foundation).
Ellen, I. G. & Turner, M. A. (1997) Does neighborhood matter? Assessing recent evidence, *Housing Policy Debate*, 8, pp. 833–866.
Erbring, L. & Young, A. A. (1979) Individuals and social structure, *Sociological Methods and Research*, 7, pp. 396–430.
Evans, W., Oates, W. & Schwab, R. (1992) Measuring peer group effects: A study of teenage behavior, *Journal of Political Economy*, 100(5), pp. 966–991.
Friedrichs, J. (1998) Do poor neighbourhoods make their residents poorer? Context effects of poverty neighbourhoods on residents, in: H.-J. Andress (Ed.) *Empirical Poverty Research in Comparative Perspective* (Aldershot, Ashgate).
Galster, G. (2002) Trans-Atlantic perspectives on opportunity, deprivation and the housing nexus, *Housing Studies*, 17(1), pp. 5–12.
Galster, G. & Killen, S. (1995) The geography of metropolitan opportunity: A reconnaissance and conceptual framework, *Housing Policy Debate*, 6(1), pp. 7–43.
Galster, G. & Zobel, A. (1998) Will dispersed housing programs reduce social costs in the US? *Housing Studies*, 13, pp. 605–622.
Gans, H. J. (1961) The balanced community: homogeneity or heterogeneity in residential areas, *Journal of the American Institute of Planners*, 27, pp. 176–184.
Gephart, M. (1997) Neighborhoods and communities as contexts for development, in: J. Brooks-Gunn, G. Duncan & J. Aber (Eds) *Neighborhood Poverty: Vol. I, Context and Consequences for Children*, pp. 1–43 (New York, Russell Sage Foundation).
Haurin, D., Dietz, R. & Weinberg, B. (2002) The impact of neighborhood homeownership rates: A review of the theoretical and empirical literature, (Columbus, OH: Department of Economics, Working Paper, Ohio State University).
Haveman, R. & Wolfe, B. (1995) The determinants of children's attainments: A review of methods and findings, *Journal of Economic Literature*, 33, pp. 1829–1878.

Haynie, D. L. (2001) Delinquent peers revisited: does network structure matter? *American Journal of Sociology*, 106, pp. 1013–1057.

Jargowsky, P. A. (1997) *Poverty and Place, Ghettos, Barrios and the American City* (New York, Russell Sage Foundation).

Jenks, C. & Mayer, S. (1990) The social consequences of growing up in a poor neighborhood, in: L. Lynn & M. McGeary (Eds) *Inner-city Poverty in the United States*, pp. 111–186 (Washington, DC, National Academy Press).

Johnson, M., Ludwig, J. & Ladd, H. (2001) The benefits and costs of residential-mobility programs for the poor, *Housing Studies*, 17(1), pp. 125–138.

Kasarda, J. D., Friedrichs, J. & Ehlers, K. E. (1992) Urban industrial restructuring and minority problems in the US and Germany, in: M. Cross (Ed.) *Ethnic Minorities and Industrial Change in Europe and North America* (Cambridge, Cambridge University Press).

Katz, L., Kling, J. & Liebman, J. (2001) A moving to opportunity in Boston: Early results of a randomized mobility experiment, *Quarterly Journal of Economics*, 116, pp. 607–654.

Kearns, A. (2002) Response: from residential disadvantage to opportunity? Reflections on British and European policy and research, *Housing Studies*, 17, pp. 145–150.

Leventhal, T. & Brooks-Gunn, J. (2000) The neighbourhoods they live in: the effects of neighborhood residence on child and adolescent outcomes, *Psychological Bulletin*, 126, pp. 309–337.

Ludwig, J., Duncan, G. & Hirschfield, P. (2001) Urban poverty and juvenile crime: Evidence from a randomized housing-mobility experiment, *Quarterly Journal of Economics*, 116(2), pp. 655–679.

Manski, C. (1993) Identification of endogenous social effects: The reflection Problem, *Review of Economic Studies*, 60, pp. 531–542.

Manski, C. (1995) *Identification Problems in the Social Sciences* (Cambridge, Harvard University Press).

Massey, D. S. & Denton, N. A. (1993) *American Apartheid* (Cambridge, Harvard University Press).

Musterd, S. (2002) Response: mixed housing policy: a European (Dutch) perspective, *Housing Studies*, 17, pp. 139–143.

Musterd, S., Priemus, H. & Van Kempen, R. (1999) Towards undivided cities: the potential of economic revitalisation and housing redifferentiation, *Housing Studies*, 14, pp. 573–584.

Musterd, S., Ostendorf, W. & de Vos, S. (2001) Armoedeconcentraties en sociale effecten in dynamisch perspectief; de relatieve concentratie van huishoudens met een zwakke sociaal-economische positie en de effecten daarvan op hun sociale mobiliteit: de ontwikkeling tussen 1989 en 1994 (Amsterdam, AME).

Ostendorf, W., Musterd, S. & de Vos, S. (2001) Social mix and the neighbourhood effect. policy ambitions and empirical evidence, *Housing Studies*, 16, pp. 371–380.

Plotnick, R. & Hoffman, S. (1999) The effect of neighborhood characteristics on young adult outcomes: Alternative estimates, *Social Science Quarterly*, 80(1), pp. 1–18.

Rosenbaum, J. E. (1995) Changing the geography of opportunity by expanding residential choice: lessons from the Gautreaux Program, *Housing Policy Debate*, 6, pp. 231–269.

Rosenbaum, J. E., Reynolds, L. & Deluca, S. (2002) How do places matter? The geography of opportunity, self-efficacy and a look inside the black box of residential mobility, *Housing Studies*, 17, pp. 71–82.

Ross, C. E., Mirowski, J. & Pribesh, S. (2001) Powerlessness and the amplification of threat: neighborhood disadvantage, disorder, and mistrust, *American Sociological Review*, 66, pp. 568–591.

Sampson, R., Morenoff, J. & Gannon-Rowley, T. (2002) Assessing 'neighborhood effects': Social processes and new directions in research, *Annual Review of Sociology*, 28, pp. 443–478.

Sarkissian, W. (1976) The idea of social mix in town planning: an historical review, *Urban Studies*, 13, pp. 231–246.

Thomas, J. M. (1991) The cities left behind, *Built Environment*, 17, pp. 218–231.

Thornberry, T. P, Lizotte, A. J., Krohn, M. D., Farnworth, M. & Joon Jang, S. (1994) Delinquent peers, beliefs, and delinquent behavior: a longitudinal test of interactional theory, *Criminology*, 32, pp. 47–83.

Tienda, M. (1991) Poor people and poor places: Deciphering neighborhood effects of poverty outcomes, in: J. Haber (Ed.) *Macro-Micro Linkages in Sociology*, pp. 244–262 (Newbury Park, Sage).

Wacquant, L. J. D. (1993) Urban outcasts: stigma and division in the black American ghetto and French urban periphery, *International Journal of Urban and Regional Research*, 17, pp. 366–383.

Wilson, J. Q. & Kelling, G. L. (1982) Broken windows, the police and neighborhood safety, *The Atlantic Monthly*, March, pp. 29–38.

Wilson, W. J. (1987) *The Truly Disadvantaged; The Inner City, the Underclass, and Public Policy* (Chicago, University of Chicago Press).

Social Norms in Distressed Neighbourhoods: Testing the Wilson Hypothesis

JÜRGEN FRIEDRICHS[1] & JÖRG BLASIUS[2]

[1]Research Institute for Sociology, University of Cologne, Germany; [2]Seminar for Sociology, University of Bonn, Germany

[Paper first received 16 January 2003; in final form 15 March 2003]

ABSTRACT   Poverty or distressed neighbourhoods are assumed to have a negative impact on their residents, e.g. on deviant behaviour. This context effect is reviewed, in particular the work of Wilson (1987). Based upon his assumptions, the paper analyses the impact of distressed neighbourhoods on the acceptance of deviant behaviour by their residents in a sample of four neighbourhoods in Cologne, Germany. Findings support some of Wilson's propositions, in particular the impact of the neighbourhood on the acceptance of deviant behaviour, even when individual variables are controlled. In contrast, the assumed impact of exposure to neighbourhood on deviant norms, measured by time spent in the neighbourhood and total network size, are supported only in bivariate but not multivariate analyses. It is found, however, that total network size and annoyance about deviance are negatively related to acceptance of deviance.

KEY WORDS: distressed neighbourhoods, poverty, social norms

Introduction

Over the last 15 years there has been a growing interest in the effects of neighbourhood characteristics on the attitudes and behaviour of their residents. It was, in particular, the work of Wilson, *The Truly Disadvantaged* (1987) that influenced the debate about (negative) context effects of poor neighbourhoods on their residents, i.e. when controlling for individual characteristics. Yet, the discussion is much older and can be dated back to the study of Shaw & McKay (1942) on delinquency in urban areas. It is also linked to the question of which social mix or population heterogeneity has an impact on neighbourhood stability and behaviour of residents (Gans, 1961a, 1961b; Sarkissian, 1976). Generally, the authors assume a (limited or 'balanced') social mix to have positive effects on residents, whereas homogeneity has negative consequences.

While these assumptions in principle apply to all types of neighbourhoods, empirical studies have almost entirely focused on distressed or disadvantaged neighbourhoods, exhibiting low heterogeneity and predominantly low-class residents. One obvious reason for this restriction is the fact that with increasing poverty in highly industrialised countries the spatial concentration of poverty rose, resulting in an increase in the number of poverty areas in large cities (cf.

McCulloch, 2001; Small & Newman, 2001, p. 25), and this topic becoming a major theme of theory and research, as indicated by, for example, the contributions in Andress (1998), or the European UGIS project <www.ufsia.ac.be/ugis>.

Furthermore, policy contributed to the interest in neighbourhood effects: diverse national and regional programmes are directed towards distressed neighbourhoods in European countries (e.g. the German programme The Social City or the French programme Politique de la Ville), and the Gautreaux and the Moving to Opportunity (MTO) programmes in the US (cf. Galster & Zobel, 1998; Goetz, 2002; Johnson *et al.*, 2002; Rosenbaum, 1995), are all spatially targeted, and implicitly take a negative neighbourhood effect as given.

The crucial question thus becomes: do poor neighbourhoods make their residents poorer? (Friedrichs, 1998). The following analysis addresses this question. First, the theoretical problem is stated in greater detail and several propositions to be tested are derived. The following section presents data from an empirical study of four distressed neighbourhoods in Cologne, Germany. The third section presents the research methodology with respect to the measurement of deviant social norms and behaviour. The following sections are devoted to testing propositions, which are mainly drawn from the influential study of Wilson (1987). In the final section, results are discussed with respect to the context effect assumption and some directions for further research are outlined.

Theory

Studies on neighbourhood effects rest upon a multi-level model involving at least a macro level, typically, the spatial unit 'neighbourhood', and a micro level, typically the individuals or residents. Further, a context effect has to be specified, linking neighbourhood characteristics to individual behaviour; these are addressed below.

Based on a rich set of empirical data, Wilson (1987) finds deprived Chicago neighbourhoods exhibit higher rates of deviance from the norms of mainstream society, as well as higher rates of deviant behaviour such as school drop-outs, teenage pregnancy and crime. He further reported physical deterioration of buildings in distressed neighbourhoods (cf. Skogan, 1990). (For further evidence, see Skogan, 1990, and a recent review Sampson *et al.*, 2002, p. 465.) He assumes the high rates of deviance to be due to the impact of living in an area of high poverty. Wilson further argues that deviant neighbourhood norms become dominant norms in the neighbourhood because of the restricted opportunities of their residents, eventually causing an increasing social isolation of the area and its residents from the urban fabric.

Most of Wilson's propositions are formulated in implicit form. Based on a detailed explication of his propositions (Friedrichs, 1998), the following hypothesis are drawn for the purpose of the analysis here:

(1) The neighbourhood has an impact on the behavioural patterns in so far as observed patterns serve as models for social learning.
(2) Disadvantaged neighbourhoods have a larger segment of persons exhibiting behaviour and norms deviating from the mainstream society.
(3) The deviance from the mainstream society is not perceived as deviant by neighbourhood residents.

(4) Deviant norms and behaviour spread among residents become dominant, held by the majority of residents.

(5) The more restricted the opportunities of the neighbourhood's residents (including perceived discrimination), the more resigned and socially isolated from the rest of the city they become.

The context effects Wilson assumes can be specified by different 'mechanisms' distinguished in the literature (Buck, 2001; Erbring & Young, 1979; Jencks & Mayer, 1990; Leventhal & Brooks-Gunn, 2000; Small & Newman, 2001, p. 33; Tienda, 1991). The two most important seem to be: (a) the socialisation model, which posits the presence of available role models and supervision to be important; and (b) the contagion model, assuming a diffusion of perceived negative behaviour patterns (e.g. of peers) in the neighbourhood to spread among residents (Leventhal & Brooks-Gunn, 2000, pp. 309–310). In a strict sense, in the latter model (denoted as 'group norms' model by Erbring & Young) a norm or 'climate' in the context is supposed to influence (indirectly) the individuals, i.e. the types and extent of deviant behaviour perceived in the neighbourhood. Whereas these models or mechanisms imply indirect effects, the 'social contagion' model embraces both 'environmental cues' and interaction among individuals, such as persuasion, competition or contagion. Thus, it is also observation of deviant behaviour and interaction with (deviant) residents that account for the adoption of deviant norms and behaviour. However, the common element in both models specifying the context effects is social learning.

Social learning (Akers *et al.*, 1979; Akers, 1985; Bandura & Walters, 1963) can be viewed as the most general explanation to account for the imputed effect of contextual traits of the neighbourhood on the behaviour of its residents. It comprises both the interaction and the normative adjustment hypotheses. It implies for the contagion model that there must be some individuals or households serving more than others as behavioural models. The presence of such 'role models' is supposed to have positive effects on the residents, be it simply persons having a regular employment or persons adhering to middle-class norms. This assumption is supported by empirical evidence from several studies. Crane (1991) finds that even a share of 5 per cent higher status residents (e.g. managerial and professional workers) in a lower-class neighbourhood leads to a reduction of high school drop-out rates and teenage pregnancies. Brooks-Gunn *et al.* (1993) obtained similar results regressing these variables on the share of high-income families in the neighbourhood.

Yet, it must also be considered that even if positive role models are absent in the neighbourhood they are available outside the neighbourhood and may counterbalance the negative local models. This necessitates the introduction of the social network of residents as a mediating (meso level) condition (cf. Sampson & Groves, 1989, pp. 779–781, 799). In the framework of Feld's theory (Feld, 1981), the neighbourhood is not the only focus of interaction available to the residents. Not all of the residents are restricted to the neighbourhood focus, with all other foci, such as kinship, voluntary associations and place of work being either irrelevant or located as well in the neighbourhood. Therefore, it is assumed that association with local persons may have a positive effect on accepting deviant norms, whereas total network size may be assumed to result in higher rejection of deviant norms.

Wilson's propositions can be related to the more formally stated theory of 'structural effects' by Blau (1960, 1974), whereby the distribution of nominal (e.g. ethnicity) and graded (e.g. income) parameters in a given context conditions the behaviour of the members. For example, if there is a high share of unemployed persons or persons receiving public assistance in a neighbourhood, then there is a high likelihood for a given resident in a random encounter to hit upon a person with these characteristics. Or, to use Wilson's 'restricted marriage pool' hypothesis, young girls in distressed neighbourhoods face a limited choice of employed young males, hence there is a higher probability of associating with an unemployed male. Furthermore, if she gives birth to a child there is a high probability that he will not be able to support the family and he will eventually leave the mother and child. This, in turn, increases the probability that the single mother will have to apply for public assistance. It is for this reason, we conceive of neighbourhoods as an opportunity structure (Galster & Killen, 1995), or, in the words of Hernes (1977, pp. 517): the "macro level provides a context for individual choices by its reward structure, incentives and constraints".

From the complex set of propositions specifying the neighbourhood context effects, five hypotheses are tested in this empirical study. Since deviant norms and behaviour are crucial to Wilson's analysis and many studies have found neighbourhood poverty to be related to crime or, more generally, deviant behaviour (e.g. Haynie, 2001; Krivo & Peterson, 1996; Sampson & Groves, 1989; Sampson *et al.*, 2002), acceptance of deviant behaviour was chosen as the dependent variable, measured by judgements of a set of situations describing deviant behaviour. The hypotheses tested were:

(1) Acceptance of deviance increases with the extent of neighbourhood distress.
(2) Acceptance of deviance increases with exposure to neighbourhood, either (2.1) by share of time spent in the neighbourhood or by (2.2) share of local network persons of all network persons.
(3) Acceptance of deviant behaviour decreases with total network size.
(4) The higher the perceived rate of deviance, the higher the sense of powerlessness.
(5) Subjective powerlessness is positively related to acceptance of deviant behaviour.

Sample and Data

In 1996 and 1997 a series of studies were conducted in Cologne neighbourhoods (Friedrichs & Blasius, 2000). These studies addressed two major topics. First, to describe the lifestyles of different population groups and to test Bourdieu's hypothesis of a 'culture of necessity' of lower-class households (Blasius & Friedrichs, 2003) and second, to test several hypotheses drawn from Wilson's work on the contextual effects of neighbourhoods on their residents. This survey was conducted in four deprived areas with different but above city average rates of recipients of public assistance.

Based on official statistics (among others, the proportion of persons receiving social transfer payments), the expertise of social workers from qualitative interviews, and by inspection of the neighbourhoods, four neighbourhoods were chosen in which 'poverty' seems to be concentrated on different levels. In terms of stratification, the two neighbourhoods Bilderstoeckchen and Kalk-South can be assigned to the upper-lower classes, Kalk-North belongs to the middle-lower classes and Koelnberg to the lower-lower classes.

The four areas can be briefly characterised. Bilderstoeckchen is located in the north–northwest of Cologne, 5 km from downtown, next to a circular main street and a road leading to a highway. The neighbourhood is well connected to the downtown by public transport. Building structures originate from the 1950s and 1960s, with a majority of three-to-four storey multi-family structures. The area has 14 000 inhabitants of which 24.4 per cent are foreign-born.

Kalk is an inner-city area, located on the right side of the River Rhein. It is a traditionally working-class area; most residential buildings have three storeys and were built in the 1930s and 1950s. Kalk is well connected to downtown by public transport; it has 21 200 inhabitants of which 23.5 per cent are foreign-born. The district can be subdivided into several neighbourhoods; two of them were chosen, which for simplicity are denoted as Kalk-North and Kalk-South. Kalk-North includes a large part of an old railway-employees residential area, residential buildings are multi-family, and in poor physical condition. Kalk-South has a similar building structure, but in better condition. In contrast, the fourth neighbourhood, Koelnberg, is a peripheral area in the southwest of Cologne. It has 3900 inhabitants of which 83.2 per cent are foreign-born. It is a housing estate, consisting of several high-rise buildings, completed in the early 1980s. As the data show, Koelnberg is the most deprived neighbourhood among the four areas studied.

In the four distressed neighbourhoods a total of $n = 430$ persons with German citizenship were interviewed face-to-face by means of a standardised questionnaire; the response rate was 47.3 per cent. For a short characterisation of the sample, Table 1 shows the most important socio-demographic characteristics of the respondents. Compared to the US literature, the four distressed areas exhibit low poverty rates, if the 40 per cent poverty rate criterion used to denote poverty neighbourhoods or 'ghettos' is applied (Brooks-Gunn *et al.*, 1993; Jargowski, 1997; Wilson, 1991).

To describe the neighbourhoods, several socio-demographic characteristics are used, listed in Table 1. Looking at marital status, the relatively high percentage of singles in Kalk-South and Koelnberg is striking, furthermore there is a somewhat higher percentage of divorced inhabitants in Bilderstoeckchen and Koelnberg. The four distressed neighbourhoods also differ by age structure. In Kalk-South, the proportion of 26–35-year-olds is above average, in Kalk-North this holds for the elderly (65 years and older). In Koelnberg, the proportion of 18–25-year olds and of 36–45-year olds are significantly higher than the average of the lower classes, while the respondents 56 years and older are clearly below average.

There are relatively large differences among the areas with respect to the years of schooling. In Kalk-South and Bilderstoeckchen, the proportion of inhabitants with 13 and more years of schooling is above average whereas the proportion of inhabitants with nine years of schooling is particularly high in Kalk-North. With reference to the equivalent income, Koelnberg is the neighbourhood where the proportion of respondents with the two lowest income groups is by far the highest. (The equivalent income is the weighted net-income of a household: the first adult receives a weight of 1.0, all other adults 0.8, 15–18-year olds receive a weight of 0.9, 8–14-year olds 0.7 and the youngest 0.45.) With respect to income, the other three neighbourhoods differ little, but in the postulated direction, Bilderstoeckchen is the least distressed one, followed by Kalk-South and Kalk-North.

In Koelnberg, many residents are dependent on transfer payments, whereas there are comparatively few in Bilderstoeckchen. Thus a rank order is arrived at of the four neighbourhoods that confirms the earlier reported degree of distress: Bilderstoeckchen, Kalk-South, Kalk-North, Koelnberg. This order also holds for two other indicators, housing benefits and unemployment benefits. Neighbourhoods appear in this order in the Tables.

Further, with the exception of a children's allowance, which is paid in Germany independently of the economic status of the households, the same holds for all types of transfer income: the values increase with the degree of distress in the neighbourhood. The most distressed residential area, Koelnberg, has the highest values, the less distressed areas, Bilderstoeckchen and Kalk-South, have comparatively low values and Kalk-North has values in between. The respondents were also asked to indicate whether they intended to move out of the neighbourhood and if so, whether they had actively searched, for example, by reading accommodation advertisements in newspapers or visiting estate agents. Results indicate that the share of respondents willing to move increases with the level of neighbourhood distress. Thus, all areas exhibit the three characteristics of the social disorganisation model by Shaw & McKay (1942), Leventhal & Brooks-Gunn, (2000), pp. 309, 326, 328) which assumes low SES, high fluctuation and ethnic heterogeneity to promote deviant behaviour.

Research Methodology

The questionnaire comprised questions pertaining to the action space, time budget, social network and attitudes towards deviant behaviour of the residents. To assess the attitudes, the respondents were presented with a set of eight situations involving different forms of deviant behaviour. These items were intended to correspond to some of the forms of deviance listed in Wilson's analysis as well as covering a wider range of deviant behaviour to be observed in every day life. The final set of eight items or situations were retained from a larger set of 12 such situations after a pretest of 30 persons. The full-length version of the items is as follows:

> Please, think of the following situations, evaluate these and tell me whether this has occurred in your neighbourhood.

A. Children play in front of your house. An elderly neighbour living on the first floor shouts at the children and beats one of them because the children do not calm down and go away.
B. In a pub, a woman is sexually molested by a drunken man.
C. In a supermarket, you see an elderly woman stealing a packet of cheese and putting it into her handbag.
D. Youngsters meet at a street corner. You see them shouting at a foreign-born woman.
E. You often hear a neighbour beating his children.
F. An acquaintance of yours lives with her three children on public assistance. She gets a well-paid cleaning job in a nearby office. She takes the job without informing the public assistance office.

Table 1. Socio-demographic characteristics of the four distressed neighbourhoods

Variable	Bilder-stöckchen	Kalk-South	Kalk-North	Koelnberg	Total
Marital status[1]					
Married	59.6	47.9	53.6	45.2	51.9
Single	13.8	21.8	17.0	23.8	18.9
Living with a partner	8.3	13.4	6.3	19.0	11.3
Divorced	12.8	9.2	9.8	10.7	10.6
Widowed	5.5	7.6	13.4	1.2	7.3
Age[2]					
18–25 years	7.4	7.6	7.1	13.1	8.5
26–35 years	15.7	23.5	18.8	14.3	18.4
36–45 years	20.4	26.1	17.0	36.9	24.3
46–55 years	14.8	9.2	8.9	15.5	11.8
56–64 years	23.1	16.0	18.8	9.5	17.3
65 years and older	18.5	17.6	29.5	10.7	19.6
Education[3]					
9 years of school	48.6	55.5	68.2	52.8	56.4
10 years of school	31.8	17.6	18.7	33.7	24.9
13 years of school	19.6	26.9	13.1	13.5	18.7
Equivalent income (DM per month)[4]					
Less than 1000	16.0	15.0	23.0	44.8	22.7
1000 to 1499	23.4	27.4	28.0	31.3	27.3
1500 to 1999	20.2	23.9	20.0	13.4	20.1
2000 and more	40.4	33.6	29.0	10.4	29.9
Transfer income					
Children's allowance[5]	25.9	20.3	17.9	45.5	26.3
Housing benefit[6]	6.4	8.4	13.5	34.9	14.5
Maintenance allow.[7]	6.5	8.5	2.7	6.1	6.0
Unemploym. benefit[8]	0.9	7.0	8.1	8.5	6.0
Unemploym. support[9]	6.5	1.7	8.9	20.7	8.6
Social welfare[10]	8.3	4.2	12.5	37.3	14.0
Intention to move[11]					
None	52.3	41.4	33.9	22.5	38.2
Yes, but no activity	28.4	27.9	28.8	22.5	27.2
Yes, activity	19.3	30.6	37.3	55.1	34.7
n	109	120	112	89	430

Notes:
1: Chi^2 = 25.8, $p < 0.05$, Cramer's V = 0.14
2: Chi^2 = 32.1; $p < 0.01$, Cramer's V = 0.16
3: Chi^2 = 18.3, $p < 0.01$, Cramer's V = 0.15
4: Chi^2 = 34.9. $p < 0.001$, Cramer's V = 0.18
5: Chi^2 = 23.0, $p < 0.001$, Cramer's V = 0.23
6: Chi^2 = 37.5, $p < 0.001$, Cramer's V = 0.30
7: Chi^2 = 3.5, n.s.
8: Chi^2 = 6.9, n.s.
9: Chi^2 = 22.8, $p < 0.001$, Cramer's V = 0.23
10: Chi^2 = 50.2, $p < 0.001$, Cramer's V = 0.35
11: Chi^2 = 32.1, $p < 0.001$, Cramer's V = 0.19

G. A friend of yours tells you that her 15-year-old daughter is pregnant.
H. You frequently see somebody standing drunk in front of a kiosk [a small shop selling newspapers and alcoholic beverages].

Table 2. Judgement, perception and annoyance by neighbour-hood

Item		Bilderst.	Kalk-S	Kalk-N	Koelnberg	Total
A. Neighbour	a	98.1	98.3	88.1	97.7	95.4
shouts at children	b	18.1	17.2	15.1	36.6	21.0
	c	100.0	78.6	85.7	96.2	91.0
B. Sexual	a	100.0	99.2	99.1	94.3	98.4
molestation	b	14.1	28.8	12.3	35.9	22.3
	c	100.0	94.7	77.8	91.7	91.8
C. Elderly	a	29.5	39.3	38.7	37.5	36.3
woman steals	b	40.0	37.0	31.3	34.3	35.5
cheese	c	34.5	48.0	37.5	34.6	38.5
D. Youngsters	a	100.0	98.3	94.3	87.2	95.5
shout at foreign-	b	37.9	51.6	36.3	59.2	45.2
born women	c	93.9	95.5	88.9	83.7	90.5
E. Neighbour	a	94.3	98.3	93.7	94.2	95.2
beats his children	b	26.7	21.6	17.6	29.0	23.3
	c	95.5	90.5	92.3	90.5	92.2
F. Female public	a	41.7	29.8	40.2	31.0	35.8
assistance fraud	b	48.6	31.1	27.1	28.1	33.8
	c	42.4	33.3	50.0	42.9	41.8
G. Teenage	a	46.2	50.4	47.7	43.2	47.2
pregnancy	b	29.2	18.1	16.9	27.0	22.6
	c	23.1	14.3	26.7	12.5	19.7
H. Drunk in	a	64.5	63.0	62.0	64.0	63.3
public	b	81.9	76.1	67.7	80.2	76.5
	c	54.3	57.0	46.8	52.4	53.0

Notes:
(a) % reporting attitudes to deviant behaviour as 'very bad' and 'bad'
(b) % reporting the occurrence of deviant behaviour ('sometimes' and 'often')
(c) % reporting they were 'annoyed' by deviant behaviour

For all items respondents were asked:

(1) To judge the situation on a four-point scale from 'very bad' to 'not bad at all'.
(2) Whether this behaviour had occurred in the neighbourhood: 'yes, often', 'yes, seldom', 'no', 'don't know'.
(3) Whether it annoyed them (the response categories are: 'annoys me', 'I do not care').

Thus, there are three measures for each respondent for each item, referred to as judgement, perception and annoyance (Table 2).

Table 2 shows that judgements of deviant behaviours vary strongly across the items. More than 95 per cent of the respondents judge the items 'neighbour shouts at children', 'sexual molestation', 'youngsters shout at foreign-born female' and 'neighbour beats his children' as 'very bad' or 'bad'. In contrast, approximately 35 per cent give this judgement for the items 'elderly woman steals cheese' and 'female public assistance fraud'. If the items are subdivided into two groups, one including items such as 'neighbour shouts at children', measuring a kind of violence or force attached to deviant behaviour, and a second group including items such as 'elderly women steals cheese', measuring a kind of tolerance, one can see that 'tolerance' is much more accepted in all four neighbourhoods than 'force'. It is concluded that deviance involving 'force' is more strongly and more uniformly rejected than deviance involving 'tolerance'.

Turning to the *perceived* occurrence of deviant behaviour (rows abbreviated with 'b'), Table 2 shows that on the items measuring forceful deviant behaviour, the percentage of respondents in the most distressed areas, Koelnberg is higher than average. This indicates that in the most distressed neighbourhoods the opportunity of meeting different forms of violence is much higher than in the less distressed neighbourhoods.

Annoyance about deviant behaviour was asked only in those cases where respondents reported a perception of a given deviant behaviour. Annoyance was relatively high for those items involving force and relatively low for the others; the variation between the areas was low and not related to the extent of distress. To summarise Table 2, occurrence of deviant behaviour is not related to annoyance.

Space of Deviant Behaviour

There now follows a description of the structure of the eight items of deviant behaviour in a latent space (or, when referring to Bourdieu, 1984, 'social space'). As shown, there are two different kinds of norms, with four questions measuring 'force' and with the other four 'tolerance'. These questions can be subdivided in the latent space along a single dimension which mirrors the difference between the two sets of items with 'force and non-tolerance' on the one hand versus 'tolerance and non-force' on the other hand (in short, 'force' vs. 'tolerance'). Further, there should be a dimension measuring the 'degree of acceptance of deviant behaviour' (in short, 'acceptance of deviant behaviour') with a high level of acceptance on the one hand and a low level of acceptance on the other.

Respondents often using the categories 'not bad at all' or 'less bad' for most of the items should receive a high positive value on the dimension 'acceptance of deviant behaviour', respondents using mainly 'very bad' for all items should receive a high negative value. Independent of the level on 'deviance', on the dimension 'force vs. tolerance' respondents will receive a high positive value if they agreed more with items on 'tolerance' than with items on 'force'. On the other hand, respondents will receive a high negative value if they agreed more with the items on 'force' than those on 'tolerance'. In the case that both dimensions have merit, the latent space can be described with two dimensions: 'acceptance of deviant behaviour' and 'force versus tolerance'; further, each respondent can be located in the two-dimensional space using their scores on the latent variables.

Considering the ordered categorical properties of the items, non-linear principal components analysis (NLPCA) is applied (see Gifi, 1990; Heiser & Meulman, 1994) which can be understood as principal components analysis with ordered categorical data. In NLPCA the number of dimensions has to be chosen in advance; two were chosen here, since two latent variables were expected ('acceptance of deviant behaviour' and 'force vs. tolerance'). To visualise the structure of the items in the latent space the biplot methodology is used (Gower & Hand, 1996).

Results

To visualise the structure of responses the eight biplot axes are shown (Figure 1). The axes are calibrated at the category points and labelled next to the category 'very bad'. The negative part of dimension 1 symbolises a relatively low acceptance of all forms of deviant behaviour, i.e. all eight items are positively associated with dimension 1 (see the common direction of the eight vectors on dimension 1). Dimension 1 explains 25.8 per cent of the total variation, which is denoted 'degree of acceptance of deviant behaviour'. The factor loadings of this latent variable (not shown) range from 0.336 (teenage pregnancy) to 0.610 (youngsters shout at foreign-born female). Respondents with negative values, i.e. responding to most of the questions with 'very bad' receive a high negative score, respondents with positive values, i.e. responding to many of the questions with 'not bad at all' receive a positive score.

With respect to dimension 2, which explains another 20.3 per cent of the total variation, the four items indicating a relatively high 'tolerance' are found to be positively associated and the four items indicating a relatively high 'force' negatively associated. With respect to the communality of the items, i.e. the amount of explained variance the items have in the two-dimensional space, the percentages range from 0.325 (for teenage pregnancy) to 0.616 (for elderly woman steals cheese).

Figure 1 exhibits a clear distinction between the two sets of variables along the vertical dimension: the items indicating 'tolerance' (and non-forceful deviant behaviour): F, C, G, and H, and the items indicating 'force' (and non-tolerant deviant behaviour): D, B, A and E. The items belonging to 'force' point towards the bottom, the items belonging to 'tolerance' towards the top, i.e. respondents that accept relatively more forceful than tolerant forms of deviant behaviour are in the negative part of dimension 2.

Within the two sets of items there are only very small subdivisions. In the set of 'force' items 'A' and 'E' are quite close to each other (both have in common that they measure violence against children) as well as items 'B' and 'D'. In the set on 'tolerance', item 'H' is little separated, 'drunken people' are evaluated closer in the direction of 'force' than 'public assistance fraud' and 'early pregnancy'. Both sets of items are almost uncorrelated in the two-dimensional space (the angles between the biplots are approximately 90 degrees). Independent from the level of deviance, it can be concluded that respondents differentiate among the two kinds of deviant behaviour: 'force' and 'tolerance'. A significant number of respondents accept some 'force' and do not accept 'tolerance', another group of respondents accepts some 'tolerance' and does not accept 'force'.

The scores of the respondents on the two dimensions will be used for further analyses. Within an ANOVA-approach several variables were used to compute the mean-values of the two latent variables. Using this information, a map can be drawn that includes the categories of the following variables: marital status, years of schooling, size of networks, network typology, sex, equivalent income, age groups, paid work, unpaid work, transfer income (with categories no transfer income, unemployed and social welfare), and neighbourhood (Figure 2).

Interpreting the 'social space' of deviant behaviour, it is found that living with a partner includes a high deviance, caused mainly by a high degree of 'tolerance'. In contrast, no unpaid work, living in Koelnberg, or having no or only one

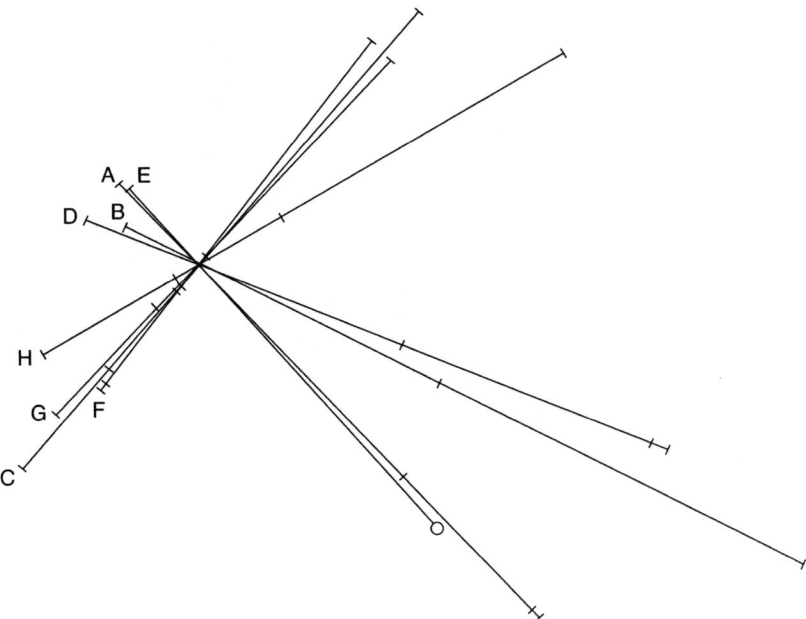

Figure 1. Biplot axes.

network person (N1) are associated with high deviance, predominantly caused by a high acceptance of 'force'. Similar holds true for persons 65 years and older and for persons with small social networks (TA, TC, N2, N3), irrespective whether their network members live inside or outside the neighbourhood. In contrast, a high number of network persons (especially N4, N6, TD), and those respondents receiving a rather high equivalent income is associated with low deviance.

With respect to the four neighbourhoods, a trajectory is found from Bilderstoeckchen via Kalk-South, Kalk-North to Koelnberg. The less distressed areas, Bilderstoeckchen and Kalk-South are relatively close to each other, both can be described as low on 'deviance'. Kalk-North is on average on 'deviance', with respondents tending slightly towards 'force'. Koelnberg, the most distressed neighbourhood, can clearly be assigned with high degree on 'deviance' which is mainly caused by a high acceptance of forceful deviant behaviour.

These results give a first indication of which variables are associated with the latent variable 'degree of deviant behaviour' for a later test of Wilson's hypotheses. However, Figure 2 shows the associations of single variables (variable categories) with 'deviant behaviour' and with 'force vs. tolerance'. For the statistical test there has to be control for those variables associated with 'deviant behaviour' to see whether the effects of the neighbourhood remain.

Time–Budget and Network Effects

In the explication of Wilson's arguments it was suggested that time spent in the neighbourhood would have an impact on the acceptance of deviant behaviour. The reasoning behind this proposition was that the more exposed a person is to the neighbourhood, the higher the propensity to accept deviance. Exposure was measured by the share of time (out of 24 hours) spent in the neighbourhood.

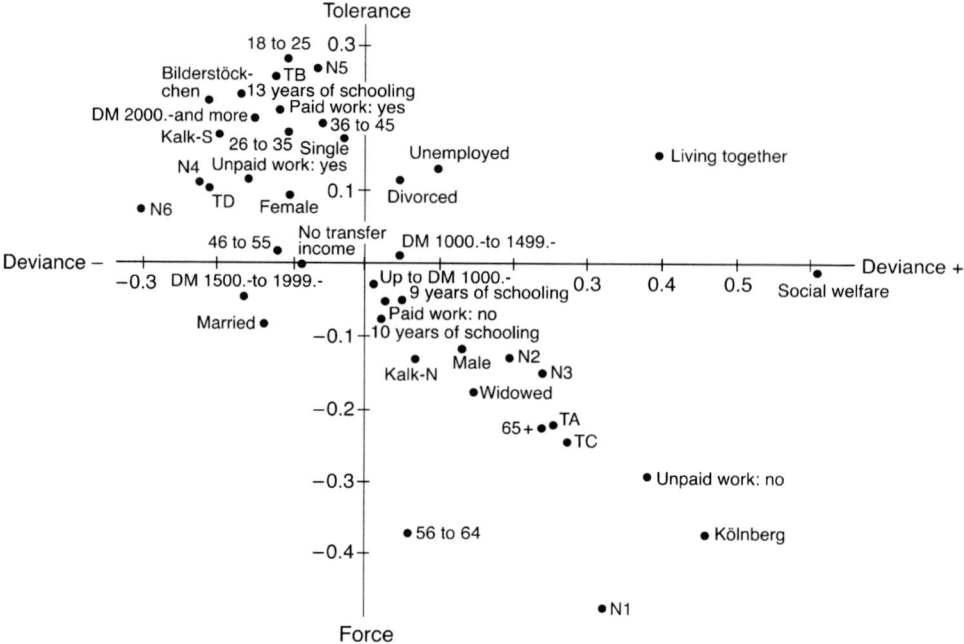

Figure 2. The social space of deviant behavior.
Abbreviations: N refers to the network persons, with N1 = no or one person, N2 = two persons, N3 = three persons, N4 = four or five persons, N5 = six to nine persons, N6 = 10 or more persons; T refers to the network typology, with TA = total number of network persons low and number network persons in the neighbourhood (nb.) low, TB = total high and nb. low, TC = total low, nb. high, TD = total high, nb. high.

However, the empirical results showed low and not significant correlation coefficients with the dependent variables 'deviance' and 'tolerance–force' (Tables not shown). Therefore, this proposition is rejected. The findings do not support the proposition that higher exposure to the neighbourhood leads to more acceptance of deviant norms. It should be noted, however, that for the two most distressed neighbourhoods, Kalk-North and Koelnberg, a low positive correlation was found of share of time spent in the neighbourhood and acceptance of 'force'.

A set of propositions pertains to the social network. If the neighbourhood is conceptualised as an opportunity structure, a predominantly local network would foster a differential association with the residents holding deviant norms. However, the correlations are low: share of network persons in the neighbourhood with the latent variable 'acceptance of deviant behaviour' yields $r = -0.08$ (n.s.), and with the latent variable 'tolerance vs. force', $r = -0.10$ ($p < 0.05$), i.e. the higher the share of persons in the neighbourhood, the higher the tendency towards 'force and non-tolerance'. Evidently, the association with local residents has no impact on the acceptance of deviance, as indicated by the low and negative correlation coefficients.

Turning to the total network size, findings differ in the expected direction, supporting the initial propositions. The correlation with 'acceptance of deviance

Table 3. Network typology, by neighbourhood (%)

Network-type	Bilderst.	Kalk-S.	Kalk-N.	Koelnberg
1: Total small, Nb. small	23.4	28.6	35.7	42.5
2: Total large, Nb. small	27.1	26.9	17.9	18.4
3: Total small, Nb. small	8.4	11.8	11.6	18.4
4: Total large, Nb. large	41.1	32.8	34.8	20.7
Total	100.0	100.1	100.0	100.0
n	107	119	112	87

Notes: Total refers to total number of network persons; Nb. = Number of network persons in neighbourhood. Total small = 0–3 persons, large = 4 and more persons; Nb. small = 0–1 person(s), large = 2 and more persons in neighbourhood. Chi^2 = 20.4; df = 9; $p < 0.01$; Cramer's V = 0.13.

behaviour' score is $r = -0.12$ ($p < 0.01$), i.e. the higher the number of network persons, the lower the acceptance of 'deviant behaviour', and 'tolerance vs. force' is $r = -0.22$ ($p < 0.001$), i.e. the higher the number of network persons, the lower the acceptance of 'force' and the higher the acceptance of 'tolerance'. Hence, it is not the local network but the total number of network persons that leads residents to reject deviant behaviour, and forceful deviant behaviour in particular. If total network size is interpreted as an indicator of the availability of role models different from those prevailing or even dominating the neighbourhood, these findings are in accord with the more general assumptions on the crucial significance of 'alternative' role models for the rejection of (or resistance to) deviant behaviour.

A further examination was made of whether the interaction of both variables, size of local network and total network size has an effect on the two deviance scores. Cross-tabulating the two dichotomised network variables yields four groups; their distribution over the four neighbourhoods is shown in Table 3.

There are significant differences between the four neighbourhoods, the strongest contrast being between Bilderstoeckchen and Koelnberg. Since the four neighbourhoods are ordered according to the extent of deprivation, it is expected shares of group 1 and group 3 will increase from Bilderstoeckchen to Koelnberg. This is indeed the case, the increase in shares is constant.

If the assumed neighbourhood effect exists, it is further expected that residents in group 2 should reject deviant behaviour more strongly than persons in group 3. The empirical results in Table 4 support this hypothesis. Persons with larger networks and few alteri in the neighbourhood exhibit a lower acceptance of deviant behaviour than those residents with small networks and many of them residing in the area. (Positive values indicate higher acceptance of deviance.) Thus, in cases of small networks, the neighbourhood has the strongest impact on residents belonging to group 3. On the basis of the ANOVA results, the groups can be ordered by the extent of approval of deviant behaviour: group 4, group 2, group 1, group 3. Rejection of deviant behaviour varies by total number of network persons, but not by the share residing in the neighbourhood. In more general terms, the more contacts a resident has (presumably with persons outside the area), the more deviant behaviour is rejected, the closer he or she is to the 'mainstream society', the less she or he is 'isolated, in the sense of Wilson. The main contrast is group 1 and 3 vs. group 2 and 4. Further, it may

Table 4. 'Deviance' by network typology, analyses of variance

Network-type	Mean	Std. Dev.	n	
1: Total small, Nb. small	0.189	1.12	136	$F = 4.7$
2: Total large, Nb. small	− 0.107	0.78	975	$p < 0.01$
3: Total small, Nb. large	0.241	1.24	214	$eta^2 = 0.03$
4: Total large, Nb. large	− 0.189	0.91	0	

Notes: For definitions of types, see Table 3.

be assumed that contact with persons outside the neighbourhood reduces the propensity to associate with persons residing in the neighbourhood, who may hold deviant norms.

There is now an explanation of the latent variable 'acceptance of deviant behaviour'. As independent variables, the number of total network persons, the percentage time spent in the neighbourhood, years of schooling and age are used, and as dummy variables transfer payment (0 = No, 1 = Yes) and three neighbourhood variables with the fourth (Bilderstoeckchen) serving as reference category (for all three variables: 1 = the certain neighbourhood, 0 = Bilderstoeckchen). In addition to these variables, four latent variables (with mean values 0 and standard deviations 1) were constructed on the basis of either multiple correspondence analysis or non-linear principal components analysis: (1) the condition of dwelling, measured on the basis of five variables describing the condition of the carpet, cleanliness of the dwelling etc. (the higher the value on this latent variable, the worse the condition of the dwelling); (2) skills, referring to the judgement of respondents of her or his capability to perform manual tasks such as sewing, ironing, repairing cars, attending children (the higher the value on 'extent of skills', the lower the ability); (3) and (4) 'composition of cultural and economic capital' and 'capital volume' are measured by a number of variables introduced by Bourdieu (1984), on the basis of four lists of items: the way of dressing, the preferred place for buying furniture, style of furniture in the living room, and the kind of meals served for guests. Multiple correspondence analysis was used to construct a latent space with dimensions 'composition of capital' (a positive value indicates a relatively high cultural capital and a relatively low economic capital), and 'capital volume' (the higher the value, the higher the capital volume).

When the neighbourhood has an effect on the 'acceptance of deviant behaviour', as postulated by Wilson (1987), then Koelnberg, the most distressed area, should have a (strong) positive effect on the dependent variable. Kalk-North should also have a positive effect, but less strong than Koelnberg (this neighbourhood is more distressed then Bilderstoeckchen, but less distressed then Koelnberg). Kalk-South should have no effect since its level of distress is similar to that of Bilderstoeckchen. The results for this regression model are given in Table 5.

Table 5 shows three variables have a significant effect on 'acceptance of deviance' $(T > |1.96|)$. First, the higher the capital volume, the lower the acceptance of deviant behaviour, i.e. with increasing cultural and/or economic capital, respectively, the 'acceptance of deviant behaviour' decreases. Second, in accordance with the propositions and the assumptions of Wilson (1987), positive effects are found from the neighbourhoods Kalk-North and Koelnberg on deviance,

Table 5. 'Deviance', multiple regressions

Variable	b	T
Total network persons	− 0.003	− 0.19
Pct. time spent in nb.	− 0.002	− 0.92
Condition of dwelling	0.094	1.78
Extent of skills	0.054	1.01
Composition of cultural and economic capital	0.033	0.58
Capital volume	− 0.147	− 2.76
Transfer payments	− 0.139	− 1.04
Years of schooling	0.034	0.46
Age	0.004	1.06
Kalk-South	0.061	0.47
Kalk-North	0.275	2.07
Koelnberg	0.536	3.45
Ajd. R^2	0.09	

whereby the one from the more distressed neighbourhood is higher. From this solution it is concluded that the neighbourhood distress is positively correlated to acceptance of deviance. Therefore even when controlling for other variables, such as age, composition of capital, capital volume, extent of skills and transfer income, the effects of the neighbourhoods remain significant. Third, although not significant, a negative correlation was found between the quality of the condition of dwellings and the acceptance of deviance.

An Extension of the Analyses

In a final step, there is a look at hypotheses 4 and 5 relating neighbourhood structure to powerlessness and powerlessness to the acceptance of deviant behaviour. Here, reference is made to the recent interpretation of neighbourhood effects by Ross *et al.* (2001), related to the premises of Wilson. To account for mistrust in neighbourhoods, they developed a complex set of propositions. Their 'structural amplification model' specifies that neighbourhood disadvantage (correlated with individual disadvantage) is indirectly related to mistrust in the neighbours via neighbourhood disorder and the subjective feeling of powerlessness. Residents with poor resources observe neighbourhood disorder, be it physical decay or deviant behaviour. Those having low command of resources, i.e. being in a disadvantaged position themselves, will perceive themselves as powerless (to change conditions) and, in turn, develop mistrust in the neighbourhood and their co-residents. Ross *et al.* (2001) posit "perceived neighbourhood disorder, which is common in disadvantaged neighbourhoods where disadvantaged individuals live, influences mistrust directly and indirectly by increasing perceptions of powerlessness among residents, which then amplify neighbourhood disorder's effect on mistrust" (p. 569). Thus, the contagion (or group norm) hypotheses receives further attention.

The data do not allow for a full test of these hypotheses. However, a test of a simplified model is possible, and those hypotheses specific to the immediate purposes are listed. It is assumed that social disorder leads to a sense of

Table 6. Mean values of 'acceptance of deviant behaviour' and of 'tolerance vs. force' scales§ on perception of deviant behaviour in the neighbourhood

Deviant Behaviour	Perception of Occurrence	n	'Acceptance of Deviant Behaviour'	'Force vs. Tolerance'
A. Neighbour shouts	Often	23	0.40	− 0.07
at children	Seldom	47	0.01	0.06
	Never	264	− 0.05	0.09
B. Sexual	Often	17	0.22	− 0.66
molestation	Seldom	44	0.22	− 0.05
	Never	213	0.04	0.06*
C. Elderly women	Often	48	0.10	− 0.43
steals cheese	Seldom	59	0.15	0.02
	Never	194	− 0.05	0.16**
D. Youngsters shout	Often	69	− 0.6	− 0.16
at foreign-born	Seldom	83	0.00	0.04
women	Never	184	− 0.04	0.02
E. Neighbour beats	Often	26	0.03	− 0.31
his children	Seldom	55	0.05	− 0.15
	Never	266	− 0.06	0.08
F. Female public	Often	47	− 0.26	0.00
assistance fraud	Seldom	47	0.05	− 0.06
	Never	184	− 0.03	0.14
G. Teenage	Often	10	− 0.46	0.05
pregnancy	Seldom	63	0.02	− 0.09
	Never	250	0.02	0.06
H. Drunk in public	Often	224	− 0.05	− 0.05
	Seldom	75	0.18	− 0.06
	Never	92	0.01	0.14

Notes:
§ 'Acceptance of deviant behaviour': higher values indicate higher acceptance. 'force vs. tolerance': negative values indicate higher acceptance of 'force' than of 'tolerance'.
* $p < 0.05$, ** $p < 0.01$. (Calculations exclude responses 'don't know'.)

powerlessness, and this, in turn, to a higher acceptance of deviant behaviour. 'Disorder' was operationalised by perceived deviant behaviour in a neighbourhood, 'powerlessness' as annoyance by deviant behaviour, and 'deviant behaviour' by acceptance of deviant behaviour. First, the three hypotheses are tested by analyses of variance and the results are presented in Tables 6 and 7.

Examination of Table 6 shows that none of the eight perceptions of deviant behaviour in a neighbourhood is significantly related to the acceptance of deviant behaviour, i.e. the attitudes towards norms are independent from the perception of the respective forms of deviant behaviour. The perceptions are further uncorrelated with the differentiation between the items indicating 'tolerance' and those indicating 'force'. However, among those reporting to have observed deviant behaviour often (in contrast to the other two groups) acceptance of 'neighbour shouts at children' is higher, but lower for 'female public assistance fraud' and 'teenage pregnancy'. A somewhat similar pattern can be found for forceful deviant behaviour: differences between perceived extent of deviance are not significant, but those observing deviance often more strongly reject forceful forms of deviance.

In contrast to the perception of deviant behaviour, the results for respondents

Table 7. Mean values of 'acceptance of deviant behaviour' and of 'tolerance vs. force' scales§ on annoyance with deviant behaviour in the neighbourhood

Deviant behaviour	Annoyance	n	'Acceptance of deviant behaviour'	'Force vs. tolerance'
A. Neighbour shouts	Annoyed	61	0.06	− 0.08
at children	Not annoyed	6	1.40**	0.66**
B. Sexual	Annoyed	56	0.11	− 0.36
molestation	Not annoyed	5	1.75**	1.33***
C. Elderly women	Annoyed	40	− 0.35	0.23
steals cheese	Not annoyed	64	0.56***	− 0.40**
D. Youngsters shout	Annoyed	133	− 0.15	− 0.07
at foreign-born	Not annoyed	14	1.25***	0.41
women				
E. Neighbour beats	Annoyed	71	− 12	− 0.32
his children	Not annoyed	6	1.78***	1.02***
F. Female public	Annoyed	41	− 0.55	0.62
assistance fraud	Not annoyed	57	0.26***	− 0.53***
G. Teenage	Annoyed	14	− 0.81	0.13
pregnancy	Not annoyed	57	0.15**	− 0.15
H. Drunk in public	Annoyed	151	− 0.27	0.04
	Not annoyed	134	0.35 ***	− 0.16

Notes: § 'Acceptance of deviant behaviour': higher values indicate higher acceptance, 'force vs. tolerance': negative values indicate higher acceptance of force than of tolerance.
*$p < 0.05$, ** $p < 0.01$, *** $p < 0.001$. (Calculations exclude responses 'don't know'.)

annoyed or not annoyed by a given behaviour exhibit significant differences (Table 7). Although the number of respondents who are not annoyed by deviant behaviour involving violence is small for some items, persons annoyed accept most forms if deviant behaviour much less and as well do accept less forceful deviant behaviour than those not annoyed; the differences are (highly) significant for all items.

To account for an interaction effect of disorder and powerlessness, the variables 'perception' and 'annoyance' were cross-tabulated (Tables not shown). Groups resulting from this classification were ordered on a continuum ranging from high protest to ignorance. This classification was run for each of the forms of deviant behaviour, separately for the deviance and the tolerance-force scores; the procedure used was analysis of variance. The results did not differ from those obtained in the former analyses: There is no interaction effect, only the annoyance accounts for differences in the acceptance of deviance or forceful deviant behaviour.

Overall, the analysis gives some support for the few propositions derived from the model suggested by Ross *et al.* (2001). The crucial variable seems to be whether a given deviant behaviour is judged as annoying, but not the sheer perception of deviant behaviour.

Discussion

The central objective was to explore the attitudes towards deviant behaviour in four neighbourhoods with a different extent of deprivation. From the literature on deprived neighbourhoods it was assumed the amount of deviant behaviour would be higher in the more deprived areas and the approval of deviant behaviour to be higher. To measure the different forms of deviant behaviour a series of everyday situations was constructed involving deviant behaviour in eight such situations. Although this is not yet a standardised scale the results have been encouraging for further use of this instrument. When scaling them by non-linear principal components analysis, two underlying dimensions were found: 'acceptance of deviant behaviour' and 'tolerance vs. force'. These scales were used as dependent variables in further analyses.

The findings support four of the five propositions stated in the 'theory' section. First, acceptance of deviant behaviour varies with a neighbourhood's extent of deprivation in the expected direction. Neighbourhood effects are found, although they are low, but this finding is in accord with the results Leventhal & Brooks-Gunn (2000, pp. 328–329) obtained from their review of the literature. Second, both measures of exposure, time spent in the neighbourhood and share of local network persons do not have the assumed positive effects on any of the two measures of deviance. Yet, there is a rank order of the neighbourhoods by mean values of acceptance of deviance, with Bilderstoeckchen exhibiting the lowest and Koelnberg the highest values, corresponding to the assumptions. This may indicate that the effects of exposure assumed by Wilson (1987) occur mainly in highly disadvantaged neighbourhoods, like those he studied. Third, the larger the total social network, the lower is the acceptance of deviant behaviour. Network sizes vary by neighbourhood: they are smaller in the more distressed neighbourhoods. However, when controlling for neighbourhood, the effect of network size on deviant behaviour disappears.

Finally, annoyance as a proxy for powerlessness is found to be positively related to both acceptance of deviance and forceful deviant behaviour. While not an adequate test of the model suggested by Ross *et al.* (2001), it is in accord with some of their findings.

Further research should be directed towards testing the hypotheses underlying this study by including a larger sample of neighbourhoods, including cases with higher rates of distress, namely, higher poverty rates, and objective indicators of deviance, e.g. crime rates, which were not available for the sample of neighbourhoods. Apart from such macro-micro level studies, it is suggested that a study in greater detail should be made of the (diffusion) process of adopting (and rejecting) deviant norms in a neighbourhood. Since the population in distressed areas is not homogeneous, a further study should assess which characteristics of residents are related to this process.

Correspondence

Jürgen Friedrichs, Research Institute for Sociology, University of Cologne, Greinstrasse 2, D-50939 Köln, Germany. Email: friedrichs@wiso.uni.koeln.de

References

Akers, R. L.(1985) *Deviant Behaviour: A Social Learning Approach*, 3rd edn (Belmont, CA, Wadsworth).
Akers, R. L., Kohn, M. D., Lanza-Kaduce, L. & Radisevich, M. (1979) Social learning and deviant behaviour: a specific test of a general theory, *American Sociological Review*, 44, pp. 636–655.

Andress, H.-J. (Ed.) (1998) *Empirical Poverty Research in a Comparative Perspective* (Aldershot, Ashgate).

Bandura, A. & Walters, R. H. (1963) *Social Learning and Personality Development* (New York, Holt, Rinehart and Winston).

Blasius, J. & Friedrichs, J. (2003) Les compétences pratiques–Font-elles partie du capital culturel? *Reveue francaise de sociologie*, 44, in print.

Blau, P. M. (1960) Structural effects, *American Sociological Review*, 25, pp. 178–193.

Blau, P. M. (1974) *Structural Contexts of Opportunities* (Chicago and London, University of Chicago Press).

Bourdieu, P. (1984) *Distinction. A Social Critique of the Judgement of Taste* (Cambridge, MA, Harvard University Press).

Brooks-Gunn, J., Duncan, G. J., Klebanov, P. K. & Sealand, N. (1993) Do neighborhoods influence child and adolescent development? *American Journal of Sociology*, 99, pp. 353–395.

Buck, N. (2001) Identifying neighbourhood effects on social exclusion, *Urban Studies*, 38, pp. 2251–2275.

Crane, J. (1991) The epidemic theory of ghettos and neighborhood effects on dropping out and teenage childbearing, *American Journal of Sociology*, 96, pp. 1226–1259.

Erbring, L. & Young, A. A. (1979) Individuals and social structure, *Sociological Methods and Research*, 7, pp. 396–430.

Feld, S. L. (1981) The focused organization of social ties, *American Journal of Sociology*, 86, pp. 1015–1035.

Friedrichs, J. (1998) Do poor neighbourhood make their residents poorer? Context effects of poverty neighbourhoods on residents, in: H.-J. Andress (Ed.) *Empirical Poverty Research in a Comparative Perspective* (Aldershot, Ashgate).

Friedrichs, J. & Blasius, J. (2000) *Leben in Benachteiligten Wohngebieten* (Dwelling in Distressed Areas) (Opladen, Leske & Budrich).

Galster, G. & Killen, S. P. (1995) The geography of metropolitan opportunity: a reconnaissance and conceptual framework, *Housing Policy Debate*, 6, pp. 7–43.

Galster, G. A. & Zobel, A. (1998) Will dispersed housing programs reduce social problems in the US? *Housing Studies*, 13, pp. 605–622.

Gans, H. J. (1961a) Planning and social life. Friendship and neighbor relations in suburban communities, *Journal of the American Institute of Planners*, 27, pp. 134–140.

Gans, H. J. (1961b) The balanced community: homogeneity or heterogeneity in residential areas? *Journal of the American Institute of Planners*, 27, pp. 176–184.

Gifi, A. (1990) *Nonlinear Multivariate Analysis* (Chichester, Wiley).

Goetz, E. G. (2002) Forced relocation vs. voluntary mobility: the effects of dispersal programmes on households, *Housing Studies*, 17, pp. 107–123.

Gower, J. C. & Hand, D. J. (1996) *Biplots* (London, Chapman & Hall).

Haynie, D. L. (2001) Delinquent peers revisited: does network structure matter? *American Journal of Sociology*, 106, pp. 1013–1057.

Heiser, W. J. & Meulman, J. J. (1994) Homogeneity analysis: exploring the distribution of variables and their nonlinear relationships, in: M. Greenacre & J. Blasius (Eds) *Correspondence Analysis in the Social Sciences. Recent Developments and Applications* (London, Academic Press).

Hernes, G. (1977) Structural change in social processes, *American Journal of Sociology*, 82, pp. 513–547.

Jargowski, P. A. (1997) *Poverty and Place: Ghettos, Barrios and the American City* (New York, Russell Sage).

Jencks, C. & Mayer, S. E. (1990) The social consequences of growing up in a poor neighborhood, in: L. E. Lynn & M. G. H. McGeary (Eds) *Inner-City-Poverty in the United States* (Washington, DC, National Academy Press).

Johnson, M. P., Ladd, H. F. & Ludwig, J. (2002) The benefits and costs of residential mobility programmes for the poor, *Housing Studies*, 17, pp. 125–138.

Krivo, L. J. & Peterson, R. D. (1996) Extremely disadvantaged neighborhoods and urban crime, *Social Forces*, 75, pp. 619–648.

Leventhal, T. & Brooks-Gunn, J. (2000) The neighborhoods they live in: the effects of neighborhood residence on child and adolescent outcomes, *Psychological Bulletin*, 126, pp. 309–337.

McCulloch, A. (2001) Ward-level deprivation and individual social and economic outcomes in the British Household Panel Study, *Environment and Planning A*, 33, pp. 667–684.

Rosenbaum, J. E. (1995) Changing the geography of opportunity by expanding residential choice: lessons from the Gautreaux Program, *Housing Policy Debate*, 6, pp. 231–269.

Ross, C. E., Mirowsky, J. & Pribesh, S. (2001) Powerlessness and the amplification of threat: neighborhood disadvantage, disorder, and mistrust, *American Sociological Review*, 66, pp. 568–591.

Sampson, R. J. & Groves, W. B. (1989) Community structure and crime: testing social-disorganization theory, *American Journal of Sociology*, 94, pp. 774–802.

Sampson, R. J., Morenoff, J. D. & Gannon-Rowley, T. (2002) Assessing 'neighborhood effects': social processes and new directions in research, *Annual Review of Sociology*, 28, pp. 443–478.

Sarkissian, W. (1976) The idea of social mix in town planning: an historical review, *Urban Studies*, 13, pp. 231–246.

Shaw, C. R. & McKay, H. D. (1942) *Juvenile Delinquency in Urban Areas* (Chicago, Chicago University Press).

Skogan, W. G. (1990) *Disorder and Decline. Crime and the Spiral of Decay in American Neighborhoods* (Berkeley, Los Angeles, University of California Press).

Small, M. L. & Newman, K. (2001) Urban poverty after *The Truly Disadvantaged*: the rediscovery of the family, the neighborhood, and culture, *Annual Review of Sociology*, 27, pp. 23–45.

Tienda, M. (1991) Poor people, poor places: deciphering the neighborhood effects on poverty outcomes, in: J. Huber (Ed.) *Micro-macro Linkages in Sociology* (Newbury Park, CA, Sage).

Wilson, W. J. (1987) *The Truly Disadvantaged* (Chicago, Chicago University Press).

Wilson, W. J. (1991) Studying inner-city social dislocations: the challenge of public agenda research, *American Sociological Review*, 56, pp. 1–14.

Living in and Leaving Poor Neighbourhood Conditions in England

ADE KEARNS & ALISON PARKES

Department of Urban Studies, University of Glasgow, Glasgow, Scotland

[Paper first received 20 December 2002; in final form 15 May 2003]

ABSTRACT *Current neighbourhood renewal and urban policies in the UK seek to improve neighbourhood conditions in poor areas and achieve greater residential stability. Using one of the few longitudinal housing datasets available in the UK, this paper analyses the influence of residential perceptions on house moving behaviour in poor and other areas. It is found that residential dissatisfaction is notably higher among residents of poor areas, and they respond to poor neighbourhood conditions in the same way as the general population. Dissatisfaction with the home itself, and unhappiness with disorder in the immediate surroundings both significantly increased the odds that someone would move home. Perceived neighbourhood decline was also found to increase the odds that someone wished to move home but to reduce the likelihood that they would actually do so. Residential mobility was found to be a particular problem for owner occupiers in declining neighbourhoods and for residents in deprived parts of inner London.*

KEY WORDS: neighbourhood, satisfaction, mobility, longitudinal

Poor Neighbourhoods: Issues of Condition, Choice, Stability and Culture

Neighbourhood Conditions

Since coming to power in the UK in 1997, the New Labour Government has re-discovered concentrated poverty and in particular what it terms 'scarred', 'poor' or 'deprived' neighbourhoods. In response, it has developed a National Strategy for Neighbourhood Renewal to tackle these areas (Social Exclusion Unit, 2001). The strategy itself has been described as practical, pragmatic and preventative, concentrating actions on supply-side and endogenous factors within poor neighbourhoods themselves (see Hall & Hickman, 2002; Tiesdell & Allmendinger, 2001). The strategy followed an extensive period of analysis and reflection in which 18 Policy Action Teams analysed different aspects of the problem; the nature of the challenge was both illuminating in its complexity and uncertain in its extent.

In its first consultation paper, the government's new Social Exclusion Unit described how "Over the last generation ... the poorest neighbourhoods have tended to become more run down, more prone to crime and more cut off from the labour market. The national picture conceals pockets of intense deprivation where the problems of unemployment and crime are acute and hopelessly tangled up with poor health, housing and education. They have become no go areas for some and no exit zones for others" (Social Exclusion Unit, 1998, p. 9). The paper went on to argue that: "In England as a whole, the evidence we have suggests that there are *several thousand* neighbourhoods and estates where condition is critical, or soon could be" (ibid., p. 9). By the time the final strategy document came out, the problem was redefined in the following way: "Over the past twenty years, *hundreds* of poor neighbourhoods have seen their basic quality of life become increasingly detached from the rest of society" (Social Exclusion Unit, 2001, p. 7), and there is a reference to the most deprived 10 per cent of wards in the country. In terms of the substantive focus, issues of worklessness, crime, skills/education and health were joined by an additional emphasis upon housing and the physical environment. This coincides with messages from researchers and political pundits that the 'street scene' or 'liveability agenda', safer, cleaner streets free from litter, graffiti, dog mess and anti-social behaviour, is an area of shame for the government vis-à-vis its European neighbours and will negatively influence the voters (Commission for Architecture and the Built Environment, 2002; Parker, 2001; Wintour, 2002). Neighbourhood conditions it seems, embracing both the physical and the social, have become more important both for deprived areas and in the country more generally.

Residential Choice

Turning from in-situ improvement to exit, the ability to move home in order to escape from poor home and neighbourhood conditions has been linked to better health (Ross *et al.*, 2000; Stokols & Shumaker, 1982) and also linked with improved housing and neighbourhood conditions (especially safety) in the US Gautreaux and Moving to Opportunity Schemes (Katz *et al.*, 2001; Rosenbaum & Harris, 2001). However, residential conditions need to be placed in the context of other factors that influence the ability and motivation to move, particularly the stage in the life cycle, socio-economic status and the availability of alternatives (Clark & Cadwallader, 1973; Landale & Guest, 1985; Lee *et al.*, 1994; Newman & Duncan, 1979; Speare, 1974). Not all groups find it equally easy to move out of poorer areas: for example, in the US there has been particular interest in the lower ability of blacks to move out of poor inner city areas (South & Crowder, 1997a and b). Owners may also become trapped in falling housing markets (Chan, 2001; South & Crowder, 1998).

But like neighbourhood improvement, increased housing choice is a current UK policy objective, with government promotion of choice-based social lettings policies (see Centre for Comparative Housing Research, 2002) and measures to support sustainable home ownership and raise standards in private rented housing (DETR, 2000a). In England, it appears that social renters are increasingly able to exercise some form of choice, as there is evidence of increasing mobility within the social housing sector (Burrows, 1999; Pawson & Bramley, 2000). Local authority re-let rates increased through the 1990s, although to a greater extent in the North compared to the South, where in high demand areas (London and the South East) there may not be so much choice available (Bate *et al.*, 2000). During the late 1990s net re-let rates for social housing in the South of England and

London declined, while continuing to rise in the North and Midlands (Bramley & Pawson, 2002).

Stability

However, increased mobility appears to be both a symptom and a cause of decline in deprived neighbourhoods. Low demand housing and neighbourhood abandonment is increasing (Bramley *et al.*, 2000; DETR Unpopular Housing Action Team, 1999; Holmans & Simpson, 1999), affecting both private and public sectors. Local authority low demand housing is concentrated in northern areas of England suffering economic decline and net outward migration, although there are pockets of unpopular housing in high demand areas such as London. Housing association stock is also affected (Ford & Pawson, 2001).

It should be acknowledged, however, that low demand for social housing also reflects the greater availability and attraction of low cost owner occupation (Bramley & Pawson, 2002). For example, in circumstances where modest economic recovery is combined with the ready availability of cheap owner occupied properties and transport links which facilitate decentralisation, low demand for social rented housing may reflect the fact that tenants have moved into the lower end of the owner occupied market, see for example Nevin *et al.*'s (2001) study of the M62 corridor.

The government's National Strategy Action Plan for neighbourhood renewal (Social Exclusion Unit, 2001) highlights the problem of deprived neighbourhoods 'stuck in a spiral of decline', saying "we should not have neighbourhoods where so many people's number one priority is to move out". In the official view, outward migration caused by a varying combination of economic decline, anti-social behaviour and poor reputation creates conditions (vacant properties and a population with few community ties) that favour rising crime: this in turn appears to fuel further out migration. Much of the evidence for this outline of the causes of low demand is derived from interviews with housing professionals, together with interviews of local residents in low demand case study areas (Bramley *et al.*, 2000). There is a lack of national statistical evidence to link individual residential dissatisfaction with moves, which longitudinal surveys can help address (see below). However, it can be noted that at one and the same time, the government wishes to promote greater residential choice but also needs to stabilise resident populations in deprived areas through improved conditions which will feed through into the choice to remain. Here, the government's neighbourhood renewal and urban policies intersect. In its urban policy, the government wants to "keep people in towns and cities" through a mixture of better neighbourhood environments and greater cultural and leisure opportunities (Urban Task Force, 1999). Related to this, the neighbourhood renewal strategy states that "the extent of deprivation in urban neighbourhoods has contributed to the outflow from cities to the edge of town" (Social Exclusion Unit 2001, p. 17).

Culture

One of the challenges facing programmes to enhance housing choices or to improve neighbourhood conditions might be that the residents of poor areas do not care enough about their conditions to be committed to improvement. As

Teitz & Chapple (1998) explain, the earlier culture of poverty thesis re-emerged in the 1980s as the notion of the underclass as "people whose behaviour departs from [mainstream] norms" (Ricketts & Sawhill, 1988, quoted in Teitz & Chapple, 1998). In their elaboration of area effects, Atkinson & Kintrea (2001) discuss how additional neighbourhood impacts which prevent people from escaping their situation include "socialisation processes in poor neighbourhoods" and low expectations of achievement. As Atkinson & Kintrea (2001) outline from US evidence, these cultural area effects include a 'ghetto culture' of short-term goals and deviant norms (Murray, 1996); the absence of middle-class role models (Wilson, 1987, 1996); and constraining forms of social capital (de Souza Briggs, 1998). Thus, both the identification of poor neighbourhood conditions, expressions of neighbourhood dissatisfaction, and attempts or desires to leave poor neighbourhoods behind might be absent or suppressed as a result of the culture of poor areas, where the abnormal becomes acceptable as the 'normal' (Ellen & Turner, 1997). However, some of the limitations of the evidence for deviant cultures in poor areas should be noted, namely: limited research on area effects in the British or European context (Atkinson & Kintrea, 2001, p. 2279); weaker evidence on ghetto populations than on the behaviours of welfare recipients more generally (Teitz & Chapple, 1998); and the inclusion of only small fractions of poor households or only small numbers of deprived neighbourhoods in recent poverty area research (Friedrichs, 1997).

Research Questions

One of the aims of this study was to explore the issues discussed above in the context of residence in UK neighbourhoods. Therefore a series of research questions was set to be examined through secondary analysis of one of the few available national, longitudinal housing datasets (see next section). The questions asked were:

- Are neighbourhood conditions perceived to be worse by residents in poor areas in the UK? Do residents in poor areas express higher levels of neighbourhood dissatisfaction?
- In general, do home and neighbourhood perceptions act as 'push factors' in forming residential dissatisfaction and an intention to move home? Which aspects of the residential experience matter most in this regard? Do anti-social behaviour and crime have most impact (as argued by Bramley et al., 2000 for low demand areas), or do environmental factors and neighbourhood facilities matter more (argued by Bramley et al., 2000 as of lesser importance).
- Do home and neighbourhood conditions as well as movement intentions influence actual house moves over the subsequent period? Thus, as well as possibly adversely affecting neighbourhood commitment, do residential perceptions influence actual behaviour?
- Are all groups equally able to escape poor neighbourhood conditions? Here, there is particular interest in the relative mobility of those in different tenures, with the focus on possible trapping of owner occupiers in deprived areas. There is also interest in the contrast between mobility in low demand northern areas and mobility among residents of unpopular housing in generally high demand London areas.
- Over and above the possible impact of neighbourhood conditions upon

Table 1. Tenure profile of EHCS longitudinal 1991–96 sample compared to the full 1991 sample

	Longitudinal sample	Full 1991 sample*
n	3366	19 111
Tenure	%	%
Owner occupied	55	67
Private rented	5	10
Local authority rented	29	20
Housing association rented	11	3
Total	100	100

*Source: *DoE (1993) English House Condition Survey: 1991.*

residential dissatisfaction and moving behaviour, does residence in a poor neighbourhood have any additional effects upon outcomes? In other words, is there any evidence that the deliberations and behaviours of residents in poor areas are different to those of the 'mainstream'?

Research Approach

The English House Condition Survey 1991–96

The research progressed through an analysis of the English House Condition Survey (EHCS) 1991 to 1996. The EHCS is a national survey of housing stock condition conducted every five years by the responsible government department (the Department for the Environment, Transport and the Regions (DETR) at this time), comprising twin physical and social surveys at each sampled property. The seventh such survey in 1996 comprised household interviews at 16 100 addresses, including a longitudinal sub-sample of 3366 interviews at repeat addresses from the 1991 survey (see Department of the Environment (DoE), 1993 and DETR, 1996). The longitudinal data-file was utilised, consisting of the 3366 household interviews conducted at the same addresses in 1992 (the social survey was a year later than the physical survey) and 1996. Analysis of the longitudinal sample profile indicated that it had a similar tenure split to the full 1991 sample (Table 1), although the private rented sector (PRS) and flatted accommodation appeared slightly under-represented in the longitudinal sample. This is likely to have the effect of underestimating overall mobility rates, as those in flats and the PRS were found to be relatively mobile groups.

Movers and Stayers

Since households were not directly asked whether or not they had been interviewed previously at the same address, it was identified whether or not the occupying household was the same in 1996 as in 1992 according to the respondent's answer to the question on length of residency asked in 1996: on this basis 749 new occupants were identified in the properties in 1996, compared with 1992. The analysis assumes that the previous occupants had moved home in the intervening period, but clearly it is possible that a small number had died in the four-year period, although it was not possible to tell this from the dataset. It is also not necessarily the case that those who moved house also changed their neighbourhood of residence. The EHCS longitudinal dataset gives no information on movers' destinations or distances moved as it is a survey primarily of houses, not households.

Analysis of the 1997–98 Survey of English Housing suggests that one in four house moves in England are within a mile of the previous address (23 per cent of those moving in the previous three years moved less than a mile, with a further 16 per cent moving 1–2 miles). Where respondents said that they had moved for area-related reasons, such as moving to a better neighbourhood, 15 per cent had remained within one mile of their previous address and a further 19 per cent within 2 miles, although this was fewer than among those who moved for other reasons (25 per cent moving within a mile and 15 per cent within two miles). Alongside this, it is known from the Scottish Social Attitudes Survey that half of people consider their 'local area' to lie within one mile of their home and two-thirds within two miles (Kearns & Parkes, 2003). Thus, it can be reasonably assumed that most people change neighbourhood at the same time as they move house, and those who move home for 'area' reasons are more likely to change neighbourhood than others. It can also be noted that the few studies which exist of people who frequently move house show that although such people tend to move short distances (Keenan, 1998) they tend to move not because of residential dissatisfaction but for reasons related to family formation problems stemming from childhood difficulties (Richardson & Corbishley, 1999). The issue of short distance moving is, however, one where the evidence is very limited and more research is necessary.

Having identified 'movers' and 'stayers' over the period, an examination was made of the views of their home and neighbourhood held by movers in 1992 in order to see whether their residential perceptions were associated with their subsequent housing behaviour. There was also a wish to see if residential perceptions were associated with movement intentions, since all respondents were asked in 1992 whether they 'expected or hoped to move home in the next five years'.

Residential Perceptions

In the EHCS, three types of question about the residential environment were asked of respondents. First, they were asked to say whether or not they were happy or unhappy with 15 features of their home; 13 features of the 'immediate surroundings'; and 8 features of the 'neighbourhood'. This split of the residential experience into three domains was unusual in the British experience, with the 'immediate surroundings' concentrating on issues of the environment, and the 'neighbourhood' on issues of amenities and facilities.

Second, respondents were asked about neighbourhood change, specifically whether or not their neighbourhood had become a 'better or worse place to live' in the past few years. Answers were recorded on a five-point scale, ranging from 'a lot better now' through 'much the same' to 'a lot worse now'. In the analysis that follows, those who thought that it had become either 'worse' or 'a lot worse' were amalgamated: they formed 22 per cent of the sample cases.

Third, respondents were asked their overall level of satisfaction with their

Table 2. Longitudinal EHCS sample by area types

Neighbourhood	%	Location	%	Region	%
Poor neighbourhood	10	Urban	33	Northern deprived industrial	7
Other neighbourhoods	90	Suburban	48	London deprived and inner-city estates	6
		Rural	19	Other areas	87
n = 3366					
	100		100		100

home, immediate surroundings and neighbourhood. Responses were coded on a five-point scale, from 'very satisfied' to 'very dissatisfied'. For the purpose of analysis, the two groups who were either dissatisfied or very dissatisfied were amalgamated and contrasted with the 'not dissatisfied'. The dissatisfied groups formed 6 per cent, 7 per cent and 4 per cent of cases for home, surroundings and neighbourhood respectively.

Location

Three area-type variables were used in the analysis. First, a variable was used to indicate whether the property was in a 'poor' area. Property surveyors were asked to code this in the 1996 physical survey, but there were around a fifth missing values in the longitudinal file, so the geo-demographic area classification was utilised, called ACORN (based on the 1991 Census) which is attached to the EHCS data file. Here, the lowest three ACORN groups, 15–17, have been combined to form the 'poor area' identifier. These comprise high unemployment council estates; council estates with high numbers of lone parents; and multi-ethnic areas with high unemployment and overcrowding. Second, and more successfully, surveyors classified each dwelling as being in an urban, suburban or rural area. Third, a regional variable was used based on the UK Office for National Statistics (ONS) classification of local authorities and health authorities which was also available with the dataset. Here, properties were identified that were in two areas of interest from the research on low demand housing: residents in inner-city estates and deprived areas in London, a high demand region; and residents in deprived industrial areas of northern England, a low demand region spanning the North, North West and Yorkshire and Humberside administrative areas. Table 2 gives the representation of these area type groups in the longitudinal sample, from which it can be seen in particular that residents in poor areas comprise 10 per cent of the sample.

Logistic Regression Modelling

A series of logistic regression models are constructed to identify significant predictors of three things: residential dissatisfaction in 1992; movement intentions in 1992; and actual mobility between 1992 and 1996. In addition to the locational variables described above, a series of background variables relating to the respondent and the dwelling itself are used for control purposes in the models. These control variables (age, income, household type, length of residence and accommodation type) had all been found in earlier research to be significantly associated with neighbourhood satisfaction (Parkes *et al.*, 2002).

For the purposes of the statistical modelling, the 37 residential perception items noted above were combined into nine residential dimensions as follows:

Home: condition; facilities; and suitability.
Surroundings: environment; disorder; and social.
Neighbourhood: access; facilities; people.

Each summary variable consisted of the standardised sum of the scores for the component variables (these ranged from 1: 'happy with' through 2: 'indifferent', to 3: 'unhappy with'), re-coded so that respondents with scores greater than one standard deviation from the mean were termed 'unhappiest' with each summary feature. Table 3 lists the 37 individual features contributing to each summary variable, and indicates the percentage of all respondents who were unhappy with each feature. The levels of unhappiness in the longitudinal survey sample were similar to those recorded in the full 1991 EHCS (DoE, 1993). In the full survey, it was also noted that respondents' answers were related to the surveyors' independent assessments of dwelling and environmental conditions: for example, unhappiness with heating was doubled for households with no central heating; and households in dwellings below the bedroom standard were twice as likely to be unhappy with the number of rooms in their home.

As there is no information in the survey on movers' destinations, the analysis neglects the 'pull' factors that influence moves. There is also the problem of the delay between the measurement of dissatisfaction (1992) and actual moving over the following four years: clearly, many unforeseen factors will moderate the influence of residential perceptions (Duncan & Newman, 1976; Kan, 1999). Residents may decide not to move if they can solve their residential problems through repairs and improvements (Deane, 1990) or neighbourhood change (Cox, 1983; Orbell & Uno, 1972).

Residential (Dis)Satisfaction

Table 4 shows the incidence of dissatisfaction with the home, immediate surroundings and with the wider neighbourhood. The incidence of each type of residential dissatisfaction in poor areas is roughly twice that in the country as a whole, and is also higher than among council tenants, or in urban areas. Furthermore, it can be seen that, particularly in poor areas, dissatisfaction with one's immediate surroundings is relatively higher than the other two types of residential dissatisfaction.

Table 5 shows the proportion of residents in all areas and in poor areas who fell into the 'unhappiest' group on each of the composite residential dimensions to be used in the logistic regression modelling. Here, it can be seen that there are three residential dimensions for which unhappiness is around twice as prevalent in poor areas as in other areas: first, home condition, within which unhappiness with the state of repair and general appearance of the dwelling are notably higher in poor areas than in other areas (12 and 13 point differences in incidence, respectively); second, surroundings disorder, within which unhappiness with car security and level of vandalism are markedly higher in poor areas (25 and 26 point differences); and finally, surroundings environment, within which un-

Table 3. Unhappiness with aspects of the residential environment, grouped by dimension

	% Unhappy		% Unhappy		% Unhappy
Home					
Condition		*Facilities*		*Suitability*	
General appearance	8	Bathroom	11	Number of rooms	11
Heating	15	Kitchen fittings	16	Size of rooms	7
Hot water provision	5	Amount of daylight	6	Layout of house	8
State of repair	16	Garage/parking	22	Size of kitchen	16
Running costs	16	Garden	12		
Decoration	12				
Surroundings					
Disorder		*Environmental*		*Social*	
Security from burglary	23	Level of rubbish, litter	25	Close neighbours	6
Security: car	21	General appearance	11	Privacy	5
Personal safety	10	Condition of paths/paving	28		
Level of vandalism/graffiti	19	Street lighting	13		
		Control of dogs	32		
		Level of traffic	24		
		Noise from industry, railway, aircraft	8		
Neighbourhood					
Access		*Facilities*		*People*	
Convenience for work	5	Shopping facilities	14	The people around here	3
Public transport	15	Doctor/dentist, etc	6	Closeness to family	10
		Local schools	4		
		Leisure facilities	21		

happiness with the level of rubbish and with the general appearance are markedly higher in poor areas (18 and 20 point differences in incidence). In addition, one-and-half times as many people in poor areas considered that their area had got worse in recent years, compared to in other areas. The rates of unhappiness on the composite items are also all higher in poor areas than in urban areas and among council tenants.

Housing Tenure and Location as Predictors

Previous research on the 1997–98 Survey of English Housing (Parkes *et al.*, 2002) has cautioned that although background variables associated with respondent

Table 4. Residential dissatisfaction 1991 (% tenants dissatisfied—col. %)

	All areas	Poor areas	Council tenants	Urban areas
Home	6	10	10	9
Surroundings	7	16	11	11
Neighbourhood	4	9	7	6

tenure and area type are associated with differences in residential dissatisfaction, they do not appear to explain much of the variation in individual respondents' dissatisfaction levels. Nevertheless, there is policy interest in the extent to which social renters and those living in relatively deprived areas suffer from residential dissatisfaction, and the extent to which they are able to escape from this by moving home.

Three area type variables were selected for analysis as described earlier: poor neighbourhood; urban/suburban/rural location as classified by surveyors during the physical inspection of the properties; and region. The regional variable picked out two groups of particular interest from the research on low demand housing: residents of deprived northern industrial areas and residents of inner-city London estates. This was done in order to investigate differences in mobility in relatively low demand and relatively high demand areas, respectively.

Logistic regression models were used to examine which of these background variables helped predict whether a respondent was unhappy with the various aspects of the residential environment, controlling for a number of other variables related to residential satisfaction, namely respondent age, length

Table 5. Unhappiness with the residential environment by area type and tenure (% in Unhappiest group)

	All areas	Poor areas	Urban areas	Council tenants
Home				
Condition	10	19	14	16
Facilities	9	12	12	10
Suitability	7	11	9	9
Surroundings				
Disorder	12	24	15	16
Environment	10	19	13	14
Social	6	8	6	8
Neighbourhood				
Access	9	6	8	6
Facilities	15	19	13	18
People	8	11	10	9
Worse place to live	22	31	25	26
n	*3366*	*326*	*1118*	*900*

of residence, household type, income and accommodation type. The results are given in Tables 6a and 6b.

Local authority tenure emerged as a consistent predictor of dissatisfaction, controlling for the other variables. Local authority tenants were significantly unhappier than owner occupiers, the most satisfied tenure, in respect of home condition, all three aspects of their surroundings and neighbourhood facilities. They were over 2.5 times more likely than owner occupiers to be dissatisfied with their home, surroundings and neighbourhood overall, and also significantly more likely than owners to report that their neighbourhood had become a worse place to live in. Housing association tenants also showed significantly higher overall surroundings and neighbourhood dissatisfaction and greater unhappiness with neighbourhood facilities, compared to owners. Private renters were more dissatisfied than owners with their home (including specifically its condition) and with their surroundings.

Area type variables were not as consistent predictors of dissatisfaction as tenure. After controlling for tenure, poor neighbourhood was a significant predictor of unhappiness related to surroundings disorder and environmental problems. Residents of poor neighbourhoods were also more likely (one-and-a-half times) to report that their neighbourhood had become worse. However, poor neighbourhood was not significantly associated with unhappiness with elements of the home.

Those in urban areas were more likely to be dissatisfied with their home (including more specifically, home condition and facilities) and with their surroundings than those in suburban areas. Urban respondents were less likely to be unhappy over neighbourhood features; indeed access and facilities were more the concern of those in rural areas.

Turning to the two specific regional categories included in the model, those in London deprived areas and inner-city estates were more dissatisfied with their home, especially its condition, than most of the rest of the sample population. Living in these areas did not, however, increase the probability of dissatisfaction with surroundings or neighbourhood, after controlling for the other background variables. In contrast, residents of deprived northern industrial areas showed greater overall dissatisfaction with the home, surrounding and neighbourhood, as well as specific unhappiness over home facilities, surroundings disorder and environmental problems and neighbourhood facilities. They were also more likely to think that their neighbourhood had got worse than the rest of the sample population. This more pervasive residential dissatisfaction in northern locations may be reflected in the fact that over the 1991–98 period 58 per cent of all dwellings demolished or closed by clearance orders in England were in the North East, North West and Yorkshire and Humberside regions. Given the high demand regional context in London and the South East, housing dissatisfaction in inner London is perhaps less likely to lead to statutory removal of properties and indeed only 4 per cent of all demolitions/closures in England in the 1990s were in London (source: < www.housing.odpm.gov.uk/statistics >).

In this section, it has been seen that the incidence of residential dissatisfaction is higher in poor areas than elsewhere, especially in the case of dissatisfaction with the immediate surroundings of the home. Indeed, poor area is a significant predictor of unhappiness with both disorder in the surroundings and with the surrounding environment, which is not surprising given that certain problems such as a poor general appearance and higher levels of vandalism are more

Table 6a. Tenure and area-type predictors of residential dissatisfaction, 1991

Odds Ratios: 1 indicates greater probability of residential dissatisfaction on column item.

Variable		Home			Surroundings			Neighbourhood		
		Condition	Facilities	Suitability	Disorder	Environment	Social	Access	Facilities	People
Tenure	Owner	1.00	1.00	1.00	1.00	1.00	1.00	1.00	1.00	1.00
	Private rent	2.23***						1.61*		
	Council rent	2.21***			1.83***	1.56**	1.78**		1.71***	
	HA rent								1.53*	
Location	Suburban	1.00	1.00	1.00	1.00	1.00	1.00	1.00	1.00	1.00
	Urban	1.37*	1.25*						0.70**	
	Rural				0.55**			1.94***	1.53***	
Poor Nhood	Not poor	1.00	1.00	1.00	1.00	1.00	1.00	1.00	1.00	1.00
	Poor				1.69**	1.59**				
Region	Other	1.00	1.00	1.00	1.00	1.00	1.00	1.00	1.00	1.00
	Northern dep.		1.55*						1.68**	
	London estates	1.81**			2.09***	1.99***				

Notes:
*p < 0.05, **p < 0.01, ***p < 0.001
Also controlled for: age; income; household type; length of residence; accommodation type.
Only statistically significant results shown.

Table 6b. Tenure and area-type predictors of residential dissatisfaction, 1991

Independent variable		Neighbourhood a 'worse place'	Home dissatisfaction	Surroundings dissatisfaction	Neighbourhood dissatisfaction
		Odds Ratios: 1 indicates greater probability of residential dissatisfaction on column item.			
Tenure	Owner	1.00	1.00	1.00	1.00
	Private rent		2.42**	1.94*	2.53***
	Council rent	1.25*	2.64***	2.55***	3.76***
	HA rent			2.01**	
Location	Suburban	1.00	1.00	1.00	1.00
	Urban		1.43*	1.47*	
	Rural				
Poor neighbourhood	Not poor	1.00	1.00	1.00	1.00
	Poor	1.47**			
Region	Other	1.00	1.00	1.00	1.00
	Northern deprived	1.53*	1.72*	2.46***	2.50***
	London estates		2.10**		

Notes:
*$p < 0.05$, **$p < 0.01$, ***$p < 0.001$
Also controlled for: age; income; household type; length of residence; accommodation type.
Only statistically significant results shown.

Table 7. Reasons for moving given by those who intended to move in 1992 (% of respondents—col. %; more than one reason could be given)

Reasons for moving	All movers	Poorest neighbourhoods	Owners	Private renters	LA renters	HA renters
Better house	56	58	59	33	58	58
More suitable area	24	40	22	17	32	27
Family reasons	24	20	22	21	29	28
Another job	9	1	10	26	2	8
n cases	*842*	*92*	*471*	*82*	*203*	*86*

prevalent in poor areas. However, council tenure and residence in deprived northern districts, more so than living in a poor area *per se*, were found to be consistent predictors of unhappiness with a combination of aspects of the home, surroundings and neighbourhood. It would seem that in the council housing sector and in deprived northern districts, problems in the immediate surroundings to do with disorder and a poor environment are compounded by inadequate homes and poor neighbourhood facilities. This is not necessarily the case in poor areas.

Movement Intentions

In 1992, 25 per cent of all respondents said that they 'expected or hoped' to move in the next few years, this being only slightly higher in poor areas at 28 per cent. Those who intended to move home were asked for their reasons (see Table 7). 'A better house' was the most common reason for moving (given by over half those who intended moving), followed by a move to a more suitable area and family reasons (each given by a quarter of respondents). Those living in the poorest neighbourhoods and local authority renters were more likely to give area reasons for moving compared to all respondents (including two-in-five residents of poor areas), but no more likely to mention a better home. Private sector renters were more likely than other tenures to mention a new job, and less likely to mention a 'better house' as reasons for moving.

A logistic regression model was developed to examine the relative influence of both background variables and residential perceptions on the respondent's desire to move home. A first block of background variables was entered into the model relating to the respondent's characteristics (age, income, household type and length of residence); dwelling (accommodation type, tenure); and location (whether in an urban, suburban or rural area; whether in a poor neighbourhood; and region). A second block of residential perception variables was a significant addition to the explanatory power of the model (see block Chi-square for perception variables in Table 8). The residential perception variables consisted of the nine composite measures relating to different aspects of the residential environment; neighbourhood decline; and the three overall dissatisfaction variables for the home, surroundings and neighbourhood.

Taking residential perceptions into account, the results show that younger persons (under 25s), single person households, flat dwellers and private renters are more likely than others to consider moving home. Income, living in a poor

Table 8. Logistic regression of moving intentions on background variables and residential perceptions

Variable		Odds ratios
		Moving intentions
Age	16–24	1.00
	25–44	0.61*
	45–59	0.26***
	60 +	0.17***
Household income		1.00
Household type	Single	1.00
	Small	0.87
	Large	0.68**
Length of residence		0.98**
Accommodation type	House	1.00
	Flat	1.48**
Tenure	Owner	1.00
	Private renter	1.80**
	LA renter	0.56***
	HA renter	0.65*
Poor area?	Not poor ACORN	1.00
	Poor ACORN	0.92
Location	Suburban	1.00
	Urban	1.00
	Rural	0.75*
Region	Other	1.00
	Northern deprived	1.30
	London inner-city estates	1.12
Perceptions (unhappiest with compared to rest)		
Home	Condition	0.69*
	Facilities	1.30
	Suitability	1.31
Surroundings	Disorder	1.31*
	Environmental	1.06
	Social	1.21
Neighbourhood	Access	1.15
	Facilities	0.91
	People	1.47*
	Worse place to live	1.30*
Overall Dissatisfaction	Home	2.66***
	Surroundings	2.25***
	Neighbourhood	1.18
n cases		3304
Initial –2 Log Likelihood		3733.4
– 2 Log Likelihood		3166.5
Model Chi-square		566.9***
Block Chi-square for perceptions		153.3***

*$p < 0.05$, **$p < 0.01$, ***$p < 0.001$

area and region were not in themselves significant predictors of moving intentions.

In relation to residential perceptions, those who were dissatisfied with their home or surroundings, those who were particularly unhappy with disorder

Table 9. Predicting movement intentions: interaction between tenure and dissatisfaction with home condition

Variable		Odds ratio
Tenure	Owner occupier	1.00
	Renter	0.65***
Unhappy with home condition		0.47**
Interaction between tenure and home condition		
Owners who are unhappy		1.00
Renters who are unhappy		2.09*

Notes:
*$p < 0.05$ **$p < 0.01$, ***$p < 0.001$
Also controlled for in logistic regression: other residential perceptions and background variables found to be significant in combined model of moving intentions.

aspects of their surroundings or with people in their neighbourhood and those who thought that their neighbourhood had become a worse place to live were all more likely to consider a move in 1992. Overall dissatisfaction with the home or with surroundings had the highest odds ratios, predicting in either case that a dissatisfied individual was more than twice as likely to consider moving as a satisfied one. Those who were unhappy with the condition of their home were less likely to consider a move, possibly because of concern over the marketability of property among owner occupiers (see below).

In order to see whether members of any particularly dissatisfied groups were more likely than others to display potential mobility, a series of interaction terms were entered into the model for examination. These terms covered potential interactions between a series of background variables (age, household type, accommodation type, tenure, poor neighbourhood, location and region) and those residential perceptions found to have significant effects (namely, home condition, neighbourhood people, worse place to live, dissatisfaction with home, and dissatisfaction with surroundings). The only significant interaction was between home condition and tenure. All rented tenures who were dissatisfied with home condition were significantly more likely to consider a move than dissatisfied owner occupiers, again indicating that poor home condition acts as a barrier to moving among owner occupiers (Table 9).

It has already been seen that living in a poor area increases the probability that a resident is unhappy with disorder in their surroundings and that they consider that their neighbourhood is getting worse as a place to live. These two factors in turn increase the probability that someone will have an intention to move home, thus reducing their residential attachment. However, living in a poor area does not in itself significantly affect the two factors which have the greatest influence upon movement intentions, namely overall dissatisfaction with the home and with the immediate surroundings.

Actual Mobility

Twenty-three per cent of the sample were classified as movers over the four-year period. This included 48 per cent of those who declared an intention to move home in 1992 (54 per cent of movers), as well as 14 per cent of those who in 1992 did not think they would move home. Actual mobility was higher among residents in poor areas compared with other areas: 31 per cent versus 22 per cent. A similar logistic regression model to that for movement intentions was created to examine influences upon actual mobility, before and after movement intentions themselves are taken into account, see columns 1 and 2 in Table 10.

The first thing to note is that residential perceptions appear to have less influence upon actual moves than upon movement intentions. The 'fall off' in the influence of specific perceptions proceeding from moving intentions to moving behaviour is to be expected (Landale & Guest, 1985; Lee *et al.*, 1994; Newman & Duncan, 1979). Additional factors related to unforeseen changes in employment or personal circumstances occurring in the period after respondents were asked about their moving intentions make it less likely that residential perceptions will be as closely associated with actual moves as with moving intentions. There was, however, no evidence in the longitudinal EHCS sample for differences in the effect of residential perceptions on those who moved relatively early (during 1992–93) and those who moved later (during 1994–96).

Other researchers have also found that overall dissatisfaction variables are stronger predictors of moving than more specific perceptions, and, as in the present case, that factors associated with the home are relatively important compared to those associated with the neighbourhood (Butler *et al.*, 1964; Deane, 1990; Landale & Guest, 1985; Newman & Duncan, 1979; Varady, 1983). To summarise the findings in column 1 of Table 10, after controlling for background variables related to respondent lifecyle stage, income, accommodation and area type, it was found that dissatisfaction with the home and to a lesser extent unhappiness with surroundings disorder (pertaining to crime, safety and vandalism) increased the probability that an individual would actually move home.

The models presented here support Bramley *et al.*'s (2000) finding that inadequate neighbourhood facilities such as shops, leisure centres and schools are overall relatively unimportant 'push factors' compared to problems in the area closer to the home itself. The specific effect of surroundings disorder on moving bears out the views expressed by housing professionals and residents of deprived areas in research on low demand housing (Bramley *et al.*, 2000). It also echoes the findings of US research on the effects of crime as a 'push factor' in migration (Morenoff & Sampson, 1997; Sampson & Wooldredge, 1986).

Renters remained significantly more mobile than owner occupiers after controlling for residential dissatisfaction (two to three times as likely to move), so differences in mobility of these tenure groups are more likely to reflect barriers to owner occupier mobility (such as the higher cost of moving for owners and lack of suitable alternatives), rather than differences in satisfaction levels. Other background variables had similar effects to those upon movement intentions. After taking background characteristics and residential perceptions into account, poor area did not itself significantly influence actual residential mobility. However, those living in London inner city and deprived estates were significantly less likely to move after controlling for residential perceptions, which was not the case in deprived northern districts. This may reflect barriers to moving created by pressures on social rented accommodation in a relatively high demand area such as London, as well as the constraint of higher house prices in London and the South East. This regional contrast is illustrated by the fact that

Table 10. Logistic regression of actual moves 1992–96 on background
variables and residential perceptions

		Odds ratios	
		Moving(1)	Moving(2)
Age	16–24	1.00	1.00
	25–44	0.40***	0.39***
	45–59	0.13***	0.16***
	60 +	0.20***	0.30***
Household income		1.00	1.00
Household type	Single	1.00	1.00
	Small	0.65***	0.65***
	Large	0.43***	0.47***
Length of residence		0.99**	0.99*
Accommodation type	House	1.00	1.00
	Flat	1.86***	1.76***
Tenure	Owner	1.00	1.00
	Private renter	3.23***	2.96***
	LA renter	1.43**	1.78**
	HA renter	2.32***	2.95***
Poor area?	Not poor ACORN	1.00	1.00
	Poor ACORN	0.96	0.99
Location	Suburban	1.00	1.00
	Urban	1.13	1.14
	Rural	0.94	1.03
Region	Other	1.00	1.00
	Northern deprived	1.13	1.06
	London inner city estates	0.68*	0.61*
Perceptions (unhappiest with compared to rest)			
Home	Condition	0.78	0.86
	Facilities	0.83	0.73
	Suitability	0.90	0.81
Surroundings	Disorder	1.35*	1.24
	Environmental	1.28	1.28
	Social	0.84	0.77
Neighbourhood	Access	0.92	0.87
	Facilities	1.02	1.05
	People	1.13	1.02
	Worse place to live	0.84	0.77*
Overall Dissatisfaction	Home	2.53***	1.97**
	Surroundings	1.25	0.93
	Neighbourhood	1.07	1.02
Intends moving '92			5.71***
n cases		3266	3265
Initial − 2 Log Likelihood		3470.6	3470.1
− 2 Log Likelihood		2965.8	2708.0
Model Chi-square		504.8***	762.1***
Block Chi-square for perceptions		40.5***	

Note:
*$p < 0.05$, **$p < 0.01$, ***$p < 0.001$

during the 1992–97 period, the number of social housing lettings rose in the three northern regions, from 152 400 in 1992–93 to 173 200 dwellings in 1996–97 (an increase of nearly 14 per cent), while lettings in London over the same interval fell by 7 per cent, from 67 000 to 62 300 dwellings (source: <www.housing.odpm.gov.uk/statistics>.

When mobility intentions were inserted into the combined logistic regression model of moving behaviour (see Table 10, column 2), an intention to move was associated with more than fives times the probability of moving compared with those who said they did not expect/hope to move. Controlling for moving intentions in this way, renters were again more likely to move than owner occupiers, and those in London deprived areas were less likely to move. However, negative residential perceptions such as being unhappy with disorder in the immediate surroundings (with the exception of housing dissatisfaction), were no longer associated with an increased probability of moving. This implies that the main influence of 1992 perceptions was on the formation of moving intentions, rather than on subsequent moves.

Only two residential perceptions had a persistent effect over the four-year period after controlling for original moving intentions: housing dissatisfaction and declining neighbourhood. Housing dissatisfaction expressed in 1992 made it almost twice as likely that an individual who did not consider moving in 1992 would in fact move in the next four years. Rating the neighbourhood as a worse place to live was associated with a significant decreased chance of actually moving when moving intentions were taken into account, despite being associated with a higher probability of having movement intentions in 1992. This may indeed reflect the problems of poor reputation and low demand in the owner occupied sector.

In relation to non-movers amongst those with an intention to move, there is a limited amount that can be said. It is not possible to tell whether other events have intervened for these households to reduce the importance of moving or to impose practical constraints upon moving. However, the analysis in Table 10 suggests that middle-aged and older residents with larger households in owner occupied houses are least likely to convert a movement intention into an actual move. A reasonable inference from this is that tolerance of unsatisfactory dwelling and neighbourhood conditions combined with residential inertia (the social, psychological and financial costs of moving home) may cause certain types of resident to remain in situ. This is, nonetheless, an area where further research is required to properly understand residential processes.

In the model of moving behaviour controlling for moving intentions, interactions between the background variables (as described in the previous section) and the three significant neighbourhood predictors of actual mobility (surroundings disorder, home dissatisfaction and declining neighbourhood) were explored. There was a significant interaction between local authority tenure and neighbourhood decline. It was found that while local authority tenants' mobility did not differ significantly overall from that of other tenures (combining the other tenures together), local authority tenants in areas of neighbourhood decline were almost twice as likely to move as those in other tenures in the same areas (see Table 11). While the effect on owners of neighbourhood decline and stigmatisation may be attributed to a fall in the marketability of their property, it is less straightforward to see why neighbourhood decline might restrict the mobility of private renters and housing association tenants, who were included

Table 11. Predicting moving behaviour 1992–96: interaction between housing tenure and neighbourhood decline

Variable		Odds ratio
Tenure	Not local authority renter	1.00
	Local authority renter	0.97
Neighbourhood worse		0.63**
Interaction between tenure and neighbourhood decline		
Other tenures in declining neighbourhood		1.00
LA renters in declining neighbourhood		1.84*

Note:
*$p < 0.05$, **$p < 0.01$

in the interaction effect with owners. The effect may be due to the relatively small sizes of the private and housing association sectors compared to the local authority rented sector in many areas, which may severely constrain the range of desirable alternatives if an individual wishes to move within the same sector.

Discussion and Policy Implications

To conclude, there will be a reflection upon some of the findings in relation to the research questions stated at the outset. First, it was found that the incidence of poor neighbourhood conditions was indeed higher in poor areas: this was true both for several of the composite dimensions of the residential experience and for overall dissatisfaction with the home, the immediate surroundings and the wider neighbourhood. However, after controlling for characteristics of the dwelling and the respondent, poor area remained a significant predictor of unhappiness with only two residential dimensions, namely surroundings disorder (covering issues of personal, home and car security and vandalism and graffiti), and the surrounding environment (covering issues of appearance, cleanliness and nuisances like dogs, traffic and the condition of the pavements). These results would support the targeting of special efforts to tackle crime and anti-social behaviour and to better clean and better manage streets and public spaces in poor areas: the former has received more attention in the National Strategy for Neighbourhood Renewal (through Crime and Disorder Reduction Partnerships and Neighbourhood Wardens) than the latter. The danger is that the 'streetscene' or 'liveability' agenda advocated by the Commission on Architecture and the Built Environment (CABE, 2002) could be seen predominantly as part of the urban renaissance drive and a response to the complaints of middle-class urbanites, rather than an equally pressing entitlement for residents of poor areas, who appear to suffer the most adverse effects from a poor quality local environment. Thus, the current interest in the 'public realm' in the UK has to extend beyond city centres and retail areas to reach out-of-the-way places and pockets of deprivation.

   After taking perceptions of residential conditions into account, poor area did not emerge as significantly associated with movement intentions nor actual mobility. Rather, regional location mattered more here, for it was found that residing in poorer parts of London was associated with significantly lower odds of actually moving home, suggesting that low availability of social housing is a particular constraint upon mobility in regions of high housing demand. Leaving poor residential conditions appears relatively easier in northern English regions of lower housing demand. It is perhaps time for more attention to be given to difficulties caused for renters and owners living in poor area conditions in London and the South East.

Overall dissatisfaction with the home itself was found to significantly increase (by more than twofold) the odds that someone would wish to move home and would actually do so over the subsequent few years, more so than dissatisfaction with the surroundings or neighbourhood. The design and state of repair of homes were found to have the most influence upon home dissatisfaction. Layout and size are particularly important, suggesting that if the government wishes to reduce the incidence of mobility intentions among UK residents, then the design and adaptability of homes has to improve to match people's needs, especially as household structures are becoming more flexible and as the population gets older and perhaps more infirm. This is a big challenge for UK housing policy, since house designs in the UK are not generally very variable and house sizes in the UK are amongst the smallest in Europe (Haffner & Dol, 2000) with little attention being paid to space standards in government regulations (see DTLR, 2001). Furthermore, the traditionally 'tight' matching of household types and sizes to dwelling sizes within social housing sector allocations policies may have a further effect upon subsequent residential dissatisfaction. Early evidence from flexible allocations policies (Cope, 2000) and community lettings suggests that in some circumstances such approaches can reduce residential turnover (Griffiths *et al.*, 1996), but it is not possible to tell whether this is due to the relaxation of household:dwelling matching criteria or other aspects of the lettings approach. The analysis here does strongly indicate, however, that the attainment of a goal of neighbourhood stability may depend as much on UK housing strategies as upon neighbourhood strategies.

Having said this, two aspects of the neighbourhood were found to influence residents' desire to move home after taking background and dwelling characteristics into account. First, being unhappy about local disorder and about local people increased the odds that someone would wish to move home. This is not only an issue of effective neighbourhood management and control, but may also be a problem for the government's objective of creating 'mixed communities' (see Urban Task Force, 1999). There is not a majority in the UK in favour of mixing communities by income, class or housing tenure, with owner occupiers being particularly opposed and people in rented housing areas more in favour (for example see Kearns & Parkes, 2003). Additionally, studies of mixed communities in the UK have concluded that they may produce conflict rather than a sense of community, either because they are enforced or because the British are now much more familiar with homogenous communities (see Cole *et al.*, 1997). Thus, without adequate and sensitive local management, the creation of mixed communities could result in resentment between the less and better off, thus exacerbating local problems of security and disorder which produce movement intentions. Recent research on nine housing estates where owner occupation has been introduced to achieve tenure diversification supports these concerns about potential friction and disorder:

> With increased contact, more evidence of tension between tenures appeared to emerge. At one level, this could be put down to differences in lifestyles and values. Tenants were often perceived by owners as

being the cause of problems such as vandalism, loitering and other forms of anti-social behaviour whether evidence existed to support this or not. (Beekman *et al.*, 2001, p. 87)

Thus, when the general findings here are combined with other research it can at least be reasonably hypothesised that the mixed community may not prove to be a stable one.

The second significant aspect of the neighbourhood was found to be perceived neighbourhood decline. This had the effect of increasing the odds that someone would wish to move home, but decreasing the odds that they would actually do so, thus highlighting an issue of residents feeling 'stuck' in declining communities. The effects of perceived neighbourhood decline upon community attachment could be quite significant in the future, since recent national survey evidence shows that whilst most people in the UK consider that their neighbourhood is unchanged in recent years, a large proportion (29 per cent) think that their neighbourhood has got worse, and this proportion is twice the size of the group which thinks their neighbourhood has got better (Burrows, 2002). Furthermore, a significant number of people (25 per cent) are pessimists and think their neighbourhood will get worse over the next two years, again more than think it will get better. Many people expect neighbourhood change to adversely affect them in the future, indeed, more people than live in so-called poor or deprived areas, and this will in turn impact upon the potential to achieve the government's aims of neighbourhood renewal and community cohesion as people begin to think about residing elsewhere but become frustrated in the process.

The above problem is illustrated by the finding that where neighbourhoods are perceived to be in decline, and taking movement intentions into account, local authority tenants are significantly more likely to actually move home than owner occupiers. This reflects growing residential instability in the council sector (Pawson, 1998) and problems for owner occupiers of sustaining an effective housing market in declining areas. It should be noted that in the US, owner occupiers have been seen as bolstering the physical and social fabric of poor neighbourhoods (DiPasquale & Glaeser, 1999; Rohe & Stewart, 1996; Temkin & Rohe, 1998). Interestingly, although owner occupation has been thought to offer some protection against crime, White's (2001) study of US city neighbourhoods suggests that in general crime reduces the level of owner occupation, rather than the effect running the other way. The exception was in low income areas, where owners found it difficult to sell up.

There will be costs to owners trapped in unpopular neighbourhoods, and the analysis here suggests that poor home condition and declining neighbourhood quality in the UK context can both make it relatively difficult for owners to escape to a better area. There will also be costs to the community and neighbourhood: Beekman *et al.* (2001) reported from their research in mixed tenure neighbourhoods that "Where we found tensions to be greatest, the lack of a well functioning housing market appeared to be at the root of the problem" (p. 88). The research supports the need for those measures which have been suggested to help sustain the owner occupied sector in unpopular neighbourhoods, such as a strengthened system of grants to improve the private housing stock in low demand areas; the reduction in housing transaction taxes (stamp duty) in deprived areas; and more streamlined clearance measures (DETR, 2000b). Indeed, the notion that regeneration and improvement of the housing stock ought to apply to private as well as social rented housing in unpopular neighbourhoods deserves greater consideration.

Finally, no evidence was found to support the notion of a distinctive housing culture in deprived areas. In none of the statistical models did interaction terms between neighbourhood perceptions and residing in a poor area have any significant effect upon movement intentions or actually mobility. It would appear that neighbourhood means no more nor less to residents in poor areas as to the general population: residents in poor areas were neither more immune or accustomed to poor neighbourhood conditions (which would have lowered their probability of wanting to move or actually moving compared to what would otherwise be the case); nor were they more sensitive to conditions, or to put it another way, more fickle or unstable (which would have meant them having higher probabilities of wanting to move or actually moving, given certain conditions). In relation to the use of terms such as 'a culture of poverty' or 'the underclass', as applied to residential behaviour in poor neighbourhoods, we might reflect upon George Orwell's comment that "The great enemy of clear language is insincerity". Residents in poor areas respond to negative residential conditions in the same way as the rest of the population; they just experience those conditions more often than others. We do not need special terms to describe this.

Correspondence

Ade J. Kearns, Department of Urban Studies, University of Glasgow, 25 Bute Gardens, Glasgow G12 8RS, UK. Email: a.j.kearns@socsci.gla.ac.uk

References

Atkinson, R. & Kintrea, K. (2001) Disentangling area effects: evidence from deprived and non-deprived neighbourhoods, *Urban Studies*, 38, pp. 2277–2298.

Bate, R., Best, R. & Holmans, A. (Eds) (2000) *On the Move: The Housing Consequences of Migration* (York, YPS for the Joseph Rowntree Foundation).

Beekman, T., Lyons, F. & Scott, J. (2001) *Improving the Understanding of the Influence of Owner Occupiers in Mixed Tenure Neighbourhoods*. Report 89 (Edinburgh, Scottish Homes).

Bramley, G. & Pawson, H. (2002) Low demand for housing: incidence, causes and UK national policy implications, *Urban Studies*, 39, pp. 393–422.

Bramley, G., Pawson, H. & Third, H. (2000) *Low Demand Housing and Unpopular Neighbourhoods* (London, DETR).

Burrows, R. (1999) Residential mobility and residualisation in social housing in England, *Journal of Social Policy*, 28, pp. 27–52.

Burrows, R. (2002) *Can Things Only Get Better? An Analysis of Public Perceptions of Neighbourhood Change* (York, Centre for Housing Policy, University of York).

Butler, E. W., Sabagh, G. & Van Arsdol, M. D. (1964) Demographic and social psychological factors in residential mobility, *Sociology and Social Research*, 48, pp. 139–154.

Centre for Comparative Housing Research (2002) *'How to Choose Choice'. Lessons from the First Year of the ODPM's CBLs Pilot Schemes. A Guide for Social Landlords* (London, Office of the Deputy Prime Minister).

Chan, S. (2001) Spatial lock-in: do falling house prices constrain residential mobility? *Journal of Urban Economics*, 49, pp. 567–586.

Clark, W. A. V. & Cadwallader, M. (1973) Locational stress and residential mobility, *Environment and Behaviour*, 5, pp. 29–41.

Cole, I., Gidley, G., Ritchie, C., Simpson, D. & Wishart, B. (1997) *Creating Communities or Welfare Housing? A Study of New Housing Association Developments in Yorkshire/Humberside* (Coventry, Chartered Institute of Housing).

Commission for Architecture and the Built Environment (2002) *Paving the Way: How we Achieve Clean, Safe and Attractive Streets* (London, CABE).

Cope, H. (2000) *Flexible Allocations Policies and Local Lettings Schemes* (London, National Housing Federation).

Cox, K. R. (1983) Residential mobility, neighborhood activism and neighborhood problems, *Political Geography Quarterly*, 2, pp. 99–117.

De Souza Briggs, X. (1998) Brown kids in white suburbs: housing mobility and the many faces of social capital, *Housing Policy Debate*, 9, pp. 177–221.

Deane, G. D. (1990) Mobility and adjustments: paths to the resolution of residential stress, *Demography*, 27, pp. 65–79.

DoE (1993) *English House Condition Survey: 1991* (London, HMSO).

DETR (1996) *English House Condition Survey. A Summary* (London, DETR).

DETR (1999) *Report by the Unpopular Housing Action Team* (London, DETR).

DETR (2000a) *Quality and Choice: A Decent Home for All. Summary Report* (London, DETR).

DETR (2000b) *Responding to Low Demand Housing and Unpopular Neighbourhoods: A Guide to Good Practice* (London, DETR).

DTLR (2001) *Decent Home Guidance. A Decent Home—The Definition and Guidance for Measurement* (London, DTLR).

DiPasquale, D. & Glaeser, E. (1999) Incentives and social capital: are homeowners better citizens? *Journal of Urban Economics*, 45, pp. 354–384.

Duncan, G. J. & Newman, S. J. (1976) Expected and actual residential mobility, *Journal of the American Institute of Planners*, April, pp. 174–186.

Ellen, I. & Turner, M. (1997) Does neighbourhood matter? Assessing recent evidence, *Housing Policy Debate*, 8, pp. 833–866.

Ford, T. & Pawson, H. (2001) *Low Demand for Housing Association Housing. Measuring Demand: The National Picture*. Housing Corporation Sector Study 7 (London, The Housing Corporation).

Friedrichs, J. (1997) Context effects of poverty neighbourhoods on residents, in: H. Wester-Gaard (Ed.) *Housing in Europe* (Horsholm, Danish Building Research Institute).

Griffiths, M., Park, J., Smith, R., Stirlling, T. & Trott, T. (1996) *Community Lettings: Local Allocations Policies in Practice* (York, York Publishing Services).

Haffner, M. E. & Dol, C. P. (2000) *Housing Statistics in the European Union* (Delft, OTB Research Institute).

Hall, S. & Hickman, P. (2002) Neighbourhood renewal and urban policy: a comparison of new approaches in England and France, *Regional Studies*, 36, pp. 691–696.

Holmans, A. & Simpson, M. (1999) *Low Demand: Separating Fact from Fiction* (York, Joseph Rowntree Foundation/Chartered Institute of Housing).

Kan, K. (1999) Expected and unexpected residential mobility, *Journal of Urban Economics*, 45, pp. 72–96.

Katz, L. F., Kling, J. R. & Liebman, J. B. (2001) Moving to opportunity in Boston: early results of a randomized mobility experiment, *Quarterly Journal of Economics*, 116, pp. 607–654.

Kearns, A. & Parkes, A. (2003) Housing, neighbourhoods and communities, in: J. Curtice & K. Hinds (Eds) *Devolution—Scottish Answers to Scottish Questions* (Edinburgh, Edinburgh University Press).

Keenan, P. (1998) Residential mobility and low demand, a case history from Newcastle, in: S. Lowe, S. Spencer, P. Keenan (Eds) *Housing Abandonment in Britain: Studies in the Causes and Effects of Low Demand Housing* (York, Centre for Housing Policy, University of York).

Landale, N. S. & Guest, A. M. (1985) Constraints, satisfaction and residential mobility: Speare's model reconsidered, *Demography*, 22, pp. 199–222.

Lee, B. A., Oropesa, R. S. & Kanan, J. W. (1994) Neighborhood context and residential mobility, *Demography*, 31, pp. 249–270.

Morenoff, J. D. & Sampson, R. J. (1997) Violent crime and the spatial dynamics of neighborhood transition: Chicago, 1970–1990, *Social Forces*, 76, pp. 31–64.

Murray, C. (1996) The emerging British underclass, in: R. Lister (Ed.) *Charles Murray and the Underclass: the Developing Debate* (London, Institute for Economic Affairs).

Nevin, B., Lee, P., Goodson, L., Murie, A. & Phillimore, J. (2001) *Changing Housing Markets and Urban Regeneration in the M62 Corridor* (Birmingham, Centre for Urban and Regional Studies, University of Birmingham).

Newman, S. J. & Duncan, G. J. (1979) Residential problems, dissatisfaction and mobility, *Journal of the American Planning Association*, 45, pp. 154–162.

Orbell, J. M. & Uno, T. (1972) A theory of neighborhood problem solving: political action vs. residential mobility, *American Political Science Review*, 66, pp. 471–489.

Parker, S. (2001) Streets of shame, *The Guardian 'Society'*, 21 November, p. 4.

Parkes, A., Kearns, A. & Atkinson, R. (2002) What makes people dissatisfied with their neighbour-hoods? *Urban Studies*, 39, p. 2413–2438.

Pawson, H. (1998) The growth of residential instability and tenancy turnover, in: S. Lowe, S. Spencer & P. Keenan (Eds) *Housing Abandonment in Britain: Studies in the Causes and Effects of Low Demand for Housing* (York, Centre for Housing Policy).

Pawson, H. & Bramley, G. (2000) Understanding recent trends in residential mobility in council housing in England, *Urban Studies* 37, pp. 1231–1259.

Richardson, K. & Corbishley, P. (1999) *Frequent Moving: Looking for Love?* (York, Joseph Rowntree Foundation).

Ricketts, E. R. & Sawhill, I. V. (1988) Defining and measuring the underclass, *Journal of Policy Analysis and Measurement*, pp. 316–22.

Rohe, W. M. & Stewart, L. S. (1996) Homeownership and neighbourhood stability, *Housing Policy Debate*, 7, pp. 37–81.

Rosenbaum, E. & Harris, L. E. (2001) Residential mobility and opportunities: early impacts of the moving to opportunity demonstration program in Chicago, *Housing Policy Debate*, 12, pp. 321–346.

Ross, C. E., Reynolds, J. R. & Geis, K. J. (2000) The contingent meaning of neighborhood stability for residents' psychological well-being, *American Sociological Review*, 65, pp. 581–597.

Sampson, R. J. & Wooldredge, J. D. (1986) Evidence that high crime rates encourage migration away from central cities, *Sociology and Social Research*, 70, pp. 310–314.

Social Exclusion Unit (1998) *Bringing Britain Together: A National Strategy for Neighbourhood Renewal.* Cmd 4045 (London, HMSO).

Social Exclusion Unit (2001) *A New Commitment to Neighbourhood Renewal—National Strategy Action Plan* (London, Cabinet Office).

South, S. J. & Crowder, K. D. (1997a) Escaping distressed neighborhoods: individual, community, and metropolitan influences, *American Journal of Sociology*, 102, pp. 1040–1084.

South, S. J. & Crowder, K. D. (1997b) Residential mobility between cities and suburbs: race, suburbanization, and back-to-the-city moves, *Demography*, 34, pp. 525–538.

South, S. J. & Crowder, K. D. (1998) Housing discrimination and residential mobility: impacts for blacks and whites, *Population Research and Policy Review*, 17, pp. 369–387.

Speare, A. (1974) Residential satisfaction as an intervening variable in residential mobility, *Demography*, 11, pp. 173–188.

Stokols, D. & Shumaker, S. A. (1982) The psychological context of residential mobility and well-being, *Journal of Social Issues*, 38, pp. 149–171.

Teitz, M. B. & Chapple, K. (1998) The causes of inner-city poverty: eight hypotheses in search of reality, *Cityscape*, 3, pp. 33–70.

Temkin, K. & Rohe, W. M. (1998) Social capital and neighborhood stability: an empirical investigation, *Housing Policy Debate*, 9, pp. 61–88.

Tiesdell, S. & Allmendinger, P. (2001) Neighbourhood regeneration and New Labour's third way, *Environment and Planning C: Government and Policy*, pp. 903–926.

Urban Task Force (1999) *Towards an Urban Renaissance* (London, E. & F. N. Spon).

Varady, D. P. (1983) Determinants of residential mobility decisions: the role of government services in relation to other factors, *Journal of the American Planning Association*, 49, pp. 184–99.

White, G. E. (2001) Homeownership. Crime and the tipping and trapping processes, *Environment and Behavior*, 33, pp. 325–342.

Wilson, W. (1987) *The Truly Disadvantaged. The Inner City, the Underclass and Public Policy* (Chicago, IL, University of Chicago Press).

Wilson, W. (1996) *When Work Disappears: The World of the New Urban Poor* (New York, Knopf).

Wintour, P. (2002) How mean streets blight lives, *The Guardian*, 29 July, p. 10.

Social Effects of Urban Restructuring: A Case Study in Amsterdam and Utrecht, the Netherlands

ELLEN VAN BECKHOVEN & RONALD VAN KEMPEN

Urban and Regional research centre Utrecht, Faculty of Geographical Sciences, Utrecht University, Utrecht, The Netherlands

[Paper first received 2 December 2002; in final form 6 May 2003]

ABSTRACT   *In the Netherlands, urban restructuring has been a major policy since 1997. Its principal aim is to improve neighbourhoods by demolishing or upgrading low-rent social dwellings and building more expensive rental or owner occupied units. A fundamental idea underlying this policy is to break up the physical and social monotony of urban areas and to achieve a mixed population in terms of income. The consequence of this new mix should be that people interact better and fully enjoy all kinds of facilities in the restructured area. This paper addresses the question of whether this new policy has indeed had these effects. The focus point is the role of the neighbourhood, featuring changes for traditional inhabitants while accommodating the newcomers. Do they use the area? Are their social contacts made there? Or can the restructured area be seen as a dormitory, where the residents have no contact with other people in the immediate environment? The paper is based on a fieldwork study undertaken in the cities of Amsterdam and Utrecht. Lessons for future policies of urban restructuring are formulated.*

KEY WORDS: urban restructuring, social contacts, neighbourhood life

Introduction

Recent literature on Dutch housing policy stresses the importance of urban restructuring. This policy was initiated in 1997, when the Dutch government decided that steps had to be taken to counteract the monotony in terms of population structure in urban pre-Second World War and, notably, early post-Second World War housing areas. As a consequence of earlier building strategies, these neighbourhoods became concentrations of affordable social-rental dwellings. Allocation processes and to some extent the housing policy of the first half of the 1990s have led to increasing numbers of low-income households in these areas.

This increasing concentration caused the Dutch government some disquiet. A new housing policy was put forward in 1997, with the principal aim of diversifying the housing stock in the areas concerned. A change in the housing stock in the targeted areas was expected to result in a social mix and a decrease in the concentration of low-income households. The underlying assumption was that a wider social mix would lead to an intensification of social contacts between the old and the new inhabitants, and the prosperous and the impoverished. There has also been a lively expectation that the new inhabitants would give a new impetus to the targeted neighbourhood, for example by patronising cafes and restaurants and shopping locally. The ultimate result was expected to be the replacement of a monoculture of low-income households by a thriving neighbourhood, characterised by lively social contacts between different groups and fresh opportunities for local amenities such as shops and schools.

This paper reports the extent to which the proposed results can be considered to have been achieved. This assessment is based on an empirical research study of two neighbourhoods, one in Utrecht and the other in Amsterdam. The aim of the study was to identify the effects the process of urban restructuring has had on the social contacts and the activities of both old and new inhabitants of the targeted areas.

The paper contributes to the more general discussion of the possible effects of neighbourhoods on the lives of individuals. Therefore, some consideration has been given to the literature on this topic in the next section. This is followed by a brief description of the aims of the Dutch policy of urban restructuring in the third section. The next section describes the research methods and the neighbourhoods investigated. The empirical results of the research are then given. The final section gives conclusions and a critical evaluation of the policy of urban restructuring.

The Neighbourhood and the Individual: Some Theoretical Comments

In the previous section of this paper, it was stated that the Dutch government perceives problems in the homogeneous social structure of neighbourhoods. The spatial concentration of low-income groups is considered a problem. The idea that spatial concentrations of poor people represent a situation which generates negative developments is not new. The assertion that a neighbourhood can exert a negative influence on its residents appears most frequently in the literature describing life in the American ghettos.

Wilson, for example, declared that the combination of unemployment, the departure of the middle class, the influx of low-income population groups, the relative increase in the share of (poor) elderly residents, and the impoverishment of the remaining population (particularly through increasing unemployment) puts the social organisation of such districts under pressure (Wilson, 1996; see also 1987). Residents of ghettos are restricted not only in their choices as individuals; they also find themselves living in a climate formed by the norms and values prevailing in their immediate environment (the neighbourhood) which may differ from those in mainstream society and may exert a particular negative influence on them. Social isolation and alienation go hand in hand with increased (enforced) neighbourhood orientation. More precisely, Wilson asserts that isolation is a consequence of an activity space restricted to the neighbourhood and, at the same time, of a social network restricted to (a limited number of) neighbourhood residents. Because daily life is dominated by the neighbourhood, it exerts a strong influence on the behaviour and attitudes of its residents (see also Friedrichs, 1997, Wacquant, 1993).

According to Wilson, escape is very difficult for the residents of such districts; they do not have the financial means to move elsewhere. Besides, discrimination also plays a major part in the housing market. The research of such people as Wilson and Wacquant has been confined to the USA context. Nevertheless, the Dutch Social Cultural Plan Bureau (Tesser *et al.*, 1995) has also outlined such a scenario for cities in the Netherlands. They state that areas with a concentration of ethnic minorities do not have a good name among the general public. Many inhabitants of these areas have the feeling that the quality of life in these areas has declined and that the influx of 'foreigners' is the main cause of this (Tesser *et al.*, 1995, p. 15). Tesser *et al.* (p. 429) distinguish between two theoretical perspectives: either migrants live temporarily in these concentration areas (in this case concentration areas are just a pre-phase of sprawl and societal integration), or migrants live there more or less forever. In the latter case concentration areas develop into the direction of ghettos of poverty. The authors do not come to a definitive conclusion for the Netherlands, but it should also be said that they at least forget one other possibility: migrants might see their present housing situation as a very desirable one. In this perspective the area might develop into a kind of ethnic enclave.

From other European studies it has become clear that the trend of mixing neighbourhoods (with respect to income) is absolutely no guarantee for social contacts between different groups. The process of demolishing inexpensive rented dwellings and putting new owner occupied dwellings in their place, does definitely not automatically and frequently lead to social contacts, let alone to the improvement of the socio-economic position of a poor or unemployed individual (Atkinson & Kintrea, 1998; Blokland-Potters, 1998). When people are too different from each other, they are not interested in each other. Their willingness to make contact with each other is not very big, as Atkinson & Kintrea (2002) indicate on the basis of their research in Glasgow and Edinburgh. Moreover, in general people have a variety of networks and only a limited number of these networks are based in the neighbourhood (Healy, 1997; Kearns *et al.*, 2000).

Some authors do emphasise the clear positive functions of a neighbourhood. In a more general sense, Forrest & Kearns (2001) point to the fact that individuals might attach more importance to a neighbourhood and its inhabitants in times of an increasing influence of all kinds of macro-developments, such as globalisation. The neighbourhood becomes a kind of safe haven. Other authors refer, for example, to the importance of social solidarity between neighbours and neighbourhood residents. People can learn from each other and provide mutual support through their local networks (Portes & Sensenbrenner, 1993). The preference for homogeneous neighbourhoods in terms, for example, of ethnicity or lifestyle can be observed in people of all kinds. Having good social contacts can be considered a basic need. It is therefore logical to assume that people prefer to live in neighbourhoods or districts with people 'of their own sort' (see, for example, Hortulanus, 1995). Frequently, the neighbourhood then involuntarily becomes the key place defining the social world of its residents. The quality of these areas and the associated contacts enhance the capability of people to participate adequately in society (Healy, 1998).

It is clear from the literature that social networks and social relations are not in itself good or bad. All kinds of social relations can develop in cities and in neighbourhoods, some more based on strong ties (bonding capital), some more on weak ties (bridging capital) (Granovetter, 1973). Kearns & Forrest (2000) warn us:

> A city can consist of socially cohesive but increasingly divided neigh-
> bourhoods. The stronger the ties which bind local communities, the
> greater may be the social, racial or religious conflict between them. The
> point is that social cohesion at neighbourhood level is by no means
> unambiguously a good thing. (p. 1013)

Especially for those with low incomes, a neighbourhood generally functions
more as a source of bonding capital than as a platform for bridging capital
(Burns *et al.*, 2001). While strong ties within a neighbourhood can be favourable
from the viewpoint of the individual, it can lead to a weakening of ties with the
rest of the society (Healy, 1997).

The possibility must also be considered, however, that the neighbourhood is
not important at all, that it exerts absolutely no influence whatever on the life of
its residents. The idea that the neighbourhood has an important function in
serving as an integration framework has frequently been disputed. In the 1950s,
Van Doorn (1955) asserted that the modern neighbourhood was characterised by
heterogeneity, role segmentation, and a clear need for privacy and anonymity.
Webber (1963) described 'Communities without propinquity' and Stein (1964) an
'Eclipse of community'. Some time later, Anderiessen & Reijndorp (1989)
claimed that the increased variety of cultures had made integration within a
neighbourhood an illusion. In the 1990s, the concept of 'separate worlds' was
much more likely than integration and cohesion to be considered the epitome of
life in a neighbourhood. Everybody has their own contacts, and these only occur
now and again within the neighbourhood. That is the case not only for the
prosperous cosmopolitan, but also for the poor resident of the older city districts.

Activities such as shopping, going to school or work, and recreational activities follow a similar pattern. Public transport, infrastructure and personal
preferences have led to a decline in the need to undertake these activities close
to home. For many, the neighbourhood is merely the place where home happens
to be, serving as the base for an activities space stretching far beyond the
neighbourhood boundaries (see also Friedrichs, 1997; Wellman, 1996).

While it is as yet unclear whether, when, under what circumstances, and to
what extent neighbourhood characteristics influence the lives of individuals, the
literature reveals that the use people make of a neighbourhood varies according
to the following factors: household composition, ideas about how long to stay in
the present area, age, socio-economic variables (education, labour market position, income), ethnicity, former living area, and the process of urban restructuring itself. These factors are elaborated briefly below.

'Household composition' can be important. The presence of children increases
the parents' chances of making contacts, for example in school or after-school
activities. One or two person households, such as students or couples who have
just embarked on living together, are less tightly bound to the neighbourhood
and maintained their activities outside the residential area (see also Van Engelsdorp-Gastelaars & Vijgen, 1991). This is probably also associated with the fact
that this category of residents is frequently characterised by a relatively short
sojourn in the neighbourhood. Thus, not only does the composition of a
household play a part in the development of activities within the neighbourhood; ideas about how long to stay in the present area is also of importance.
When a household stands at the beginning of its housing career and the current
housing situation is probably not perceived as the final station, household

members are probably also less likely to be involved in the life of the neighbour-hood (Campbell & Lee, 1992).

Household composition is usually associated with age. In general terms, the geographic range of activities and contacts in a person's life first increases and later declines. Young children are very strongly oriented to their neighbourhood, while teenagers are not, and neither are people between the ages of 20 and 40 living in one or two person households. As people grow older and perhaps acquire some physical handicap, the neighbourhood again plays a greater part (Flap, 1999). Kleinhans and colleagues (2000) have also come to this conclusion. They assume that neighbourhood orientation is often partial and selective; people are only oriented towards their neighbourhood in certain life phases and for a few social contacts and activities.

The 'socio-economic background' of a household can also play a part in neighbourhood orientation. A low income can prevent a household from partic-ipating in activities that cost money (Musterd & Ostendorf, 1998). As a conse-quence, people with a lower income can be expected to have a smaller action radius, because transport usually costs money (Fischer, 1982; Wilson, 1987; see also Botman & Van Kempen, 2001; Ellen & Turner, 1997; Guest & Wierzbicki, 1999; Henning & Lieberg, 1996). The level of the income is associated among other things with the labour market situation and an individual's educational level. Highly educated people with a consequently high income usually have a wide network of activities. As a result, they often make little use of neighbour-hood facilities; rather, they orientate themselves to the whole city (Blokland-Pot-ters, 1998). The attraction of high-income groups to give the neighbourhood concerned a new impulse would therefore seem to be a high risk strategy; the chance is high that these newcomers are hardly ever to be found in the neighbourhood and so make no use of, for example, local shopping facilities.

'Ethnicity' could be expected to exert an influence, because it is also often associated with low incomes. This association would then mean that people belonging to ethnic minorities might have fewer opportunities to enjoy activities outside the neighbourhood. Additionally, individuals belonging to ethnic groups might find support from people of the same group living in the same neighbourhood (Van Kempen, 2001). However, it might very well be the case that these ideas are based on prejudice. From the literature it becomes at least clear that especially recent immigrants who cannot speak the language of the guest country and immigrants with a low education have the propensity to focus themselves on neighbourhoods where already many of their fellow-countrymen live. They expect to find social, economical and emotional support in that place (Dahya, 1974, Enchautegui, 1997, Fong & Gulia, 1999). From a recent study in the Netherlands it has become clear that, in particular, many older people belonging to the former category of guest workers (specifically Turks and Moroccans) still do not talk Dutch to each other and do not often meet Dutch people at home (Dagevos, 2001). Turks in particular have many contacts with their fellow-coun-trymen in the neighbourhood (Sociaal en Cultureel Planbureau, 2002). They are thus dependent on people from their own group and when these people live in the same neighbourhood, there seems no real reason to leave the neighbourhood for social contacts.

The 'previous residential location' of the new residents may also be put forward as a possible influential factor. When people come from adjoining residential areas, specific neighbourhood aspects may have influenced their decision to move and they will probably (continue to) carry out certain activities in the old neighbourhood. When new residents come from elsewhere, the chance is high that other factors, such as a newly-built dwelling or the location with respect to work, were decisive. In this case, the bond with the neighbourhood is probably less strong.

Finally, the process of 'urban restructuring' itself may have an influence on the orientation of the inhabitants of a neighbourhood. The process of urban restructuring brings with it many changes in the form of the nuisance of building activities, a change in the structure of the amenities, and a changing population structure. The activities of the people involved may also change. This alteration may be associated with the fact that at the time of restructuring some amenities are inaccessible (streets may be temporarily closed), or with the fact that the provision of shops has changed. In addition, there is the chance that close friends and neighbours may have moved to other areas and new people are entering the neighbourhood. All these factors may influence the orientation and neighbourhood bonding of the sitting inhabitants.

The main conclusion to be drawn from this brief overview is that neighbourhood orientation will differ between people and types of areas. Policy aimed at generating neighbourhood orientation, increasing social contacts between groups, and creating a better feeling among the inhabitants about their neighbourhood (neighbourhood bond) will therefore be more successful in some cases than in others. This empirical research sought to find out which of the above mentioned variables could be considered influential in the urban restructuring areas that were selected. Before the findings are reported, first there is a look at the process of urban restructuring itself.

Urban Restructuring in the Netherlands

In the 1990s, the Dutch government came to realise that increasingly fewer households were able to pursue their housing careers within their own neighbourhoods. This was particularly noticeable in residential areas with an over-representation of cheap (social) rental dwellings, notably the areas that were originally built in the second half of the nineteenth century, the first half of the twentieth century and the areas built in the early post-Second World War period (1945–60). The share of owner occupied dwellings in these areas was small (although some exceptions exist) and the quality of the whole stock often left much to be desired. This homogeneity and poor quality of the housing stock accelerated the departure of the well-to-do households. In many cases their place was taken over by low-income households, so that the socio-economic profile of the residents in these areas became increasingly homogeneous in the course of time. In addition to general impoverishment, social tensions were exacerbated in some neighbourhoods.

The increasing concentration of low-income households in these older areas was not unexpected. In fact, the basic philosophy of urban renewal in the 1970s and early 1980s was described as 'building for the neighbourhood'. The principal idea behind this approach was that inhabitants of demolished dwellings had the right to be re-housed in the same neighbourhood. Of course, this policy had the tendency to stabilise the social structure of the targeted neighbourhoods. New dwellings were generally inexpensive, so low-income households in particular were inclined to stay after reconstruction (e.g. see Beaumont et al., 2003).

In 1997, the Memorandum on Urban Renewal [*Nota Stedelijke Vernieuwing*] was brought out to help bring an end to these undesirable developments. In contrast with the urban renewal of the 1970s and early 1980s, the objective was now to achieve a mixed population (Musterd, 1998). In addition, the government wished to bring to an end the increasing problems surrounding the exploitation of dwellings, facilities and companies. The letting of dwellings or shop premises had become so difficult in certain areas that premises standing empty began to set the tone of the urban landscape (Ministerie VROM, 1997). The new urban policy is aimed at creating vital cities: the social and economic vitality of the city should be increased by reducing unemployment, increasing the liveability, the public safety and entrepreneurship in the worst neighbourhoods of the cities. Within this so-called Big Cities Policy, the policy of urban restructuring was specifically aimed at restructuring of the physical environment.

The main aim of the policy of urban restructuring could be seen as extending the choice opportunities of the city's population and make all residential environments accessible for potential residents. The break-up of the monotonous housing stock in the neighbourhoods that was characterised by an over-representation of inexpensive rented dwellings (most of them belong to the social rented housing stock) was considered an important means. Replacing a share of the old housing stock by new buildings of a higher price class would attract and retain the city well-to-do residents, counteract spatial segregation (in terms of income, not in terms of ethnicity), and enhance the quality of living in residential areas. This is interesting, because at the same time the idea of active de-concentration of ethnic minorities still holds sway by some political parties (notably the left-wing Socialist Party) and in different Ministries. A discussion about forced de-concentration took place in the 1970s, following the decision of the city of Rotterdam to allow only a certain percentage of ethnic minorities in neighbourhoods. Probably the Ministry of Housing, Spatial Planning and the Environment did not want to take the risk of starting this discussion all over again and focused its policy on the mix of incomes instead of ethnicity. The improvement, merging, and/or sale of rental dwellings also formed part of the intervention. Supporting measures are also necessary for the benefit of the residents and the residential environment (Ministerie VROM, 1997).

An important idea behind restructuring is the assumption that districts differentiated according to income are particularly viable. Thus, the policy makers assume that intervention in the housing stock will bring about societal effects; the measures will not only improve the spatial quality of the neighbourhood concerned, but also ensure a more diverse population distribution in socio-economic terms. This differentiation of income groups and so forth should contribute positively to the social quality of the neighbourhood concerned; it could mean a fall in the incomes segregation and an enhancement of the quality of living. In this context it is assumed that restructuring will create more chances for societal deprived residents. An increase in social integration is then also anticipated. This ought to be associated with the positive role models which the deprived residents of the areas thereby acquire (see also Kleinhans *et al.*, 2000; Van Kempen & Van Weesep, 1996). The stigmatisation which has marred many areas could become a thing of the past (Musterd *et al.*, 1999; Reijndorp, 1996; Van Kempen *et al.*, 2000).

Finally, efforts are being made to achieve a better competitive position for the neighbourhood on the urban housing market. In the Memorandum on Urban

Renewal it is assumed that differentiation facilitates a housing career within the neighbourhood and creates opportunities for people with a high income coming from elsewhere (see also Musterd *et al.*, 1999). When extra purchasing power is attracted in this manner, it brings with it more support for the local services and facilities. Restructuring can therefore produce an economic advantage for an area (Priemus & Van Kempen, 1998).

The introduction of other, more expensive dwellings and the associated arrival of higher-income households, the attractiveness, the image, and economic support must therefore receive a positive impulse. Buys (1997) adds here that the measures taken must ensure that the various types of residents acquire a bond with the neighbourhood, so that a feeling of unity is created. This is only possible when the housing situation is based on freedom of choice. The memorandum on housing in the twenty-first century [*Mensen, wensen, wonen. Wonen in de 21ᵉ eeuw*] (Ministerie VROM, 2000) also emphasises that all people, regardless of income or origin, must be capable of obtaining the dwelling they desire.

In summary, policy makers in the Netherlands now generally prefer neighbourhoods with a mixed housing stock to homogeneous neighbourhoods. The underlying assumption is that housing differentiation automatically leads to social differentiation and that this is better then a socially homogeneous area. Social differentiation will lead to more contacts between different groups, it is assumed, and to a better use of the neighbourhood of population groups.

Research Method and Research Neighbourhoods

Research Method

To discover whether the process of restructuring has an influence on the neighbourhood bond and the activities pattern of a household, an empirical research study was carried out in two pre-war residential areas in the Netherlands where restructuring interventions have taken place in the last few years. To avoid the results found being too specific for the location concerned, two research areas were chosen. In addition, the interventions had been completed a number of years previously, so that the effects could be readily measured.

The residential areas where the research was carried out are situated in Amsterdam and Utrecht and can be regarded as traditional and relatively impoverished. In the course of the 1990s, problems with respect to both the social and the built-up environment led the local authorities concerned to the decision to intervene. In addition to the intervention in the existing housing stock, the neighbourhoods concerned have been involved in extensions in terms of new construction. In both cases, a previous industrial area acquired a residential function. The new stock consists partly of social-rental dwellings, but also includes a considerable number of owner occupied dwellings in the more expensive price class. A striking difference between the two areas is that on the Amsterdam new construction area, in contrast with that in Utrecht, no facilities have been developed.

On the two new construction areas, between 21 January and 8 February 2002, in total 711 questionnaires were distributed: 405 among households of the new construction project in Amsterdam and 306 in Utrecht. Two groups were identified: those inhabitants in the project who already lived in the neighbourhood (old inhabitants) and those who came from another area (new inhabitants). On the basis of the questionnaire, investigations were made into what part the neighbourhood played in the daily life of the residents. To raise the response level, a personal approach to the respondents was chosen; the questionnaires were distributed and collected in person. This approach yielded a final overall response of 52.3 per cent: 59.3 per cent in Amsterdam and 43.1 per cent in Utrecht (a total of 372 respondents). The different response rates are not easy to explain. The fact that in the Utrecht research population elderly are rather over-represented may explain at least some of this difference: elderly people are less eager to open their doors for an unknown person.

In addition to the questionnaires the effects of the spatial intervention were also investigated on the basis of interviews with key figures. These people are all involved directly or indirectly with the consequences of the intervention. Local authority and police officials, school directors and a number of shopkeepers were included.

It should be emphasised that people who had left the neighbourhood after the restructuring process were not interviewed. Of course, these neighbourhood leavers are often difficult to find. However, within the Netherlands, at least one study has focused on this category (Kleinhans & Kruythoff, 2002). Because of time and budget constraints, those who did not move in the area at all were also not interviewed.

Brief Description of the Neighbourhoods

Staatslieden neighbourhood. This characteristic neighbourhood lies directly to the northwest of the Amsterdam inner city and belongs with three other residential areas to the district of Westerpark. Traditionally, it was a working-class residential area, built between 1881 and 1920. The greatest share of the housing stock consists of small units that are often managed by private landlords; the share of owner occupied dwellings is small (61 per cent and 9 per cent respectively). In the 1970s and 1980s many dwellings were poorly maintained and needed updating. These matters gave the high-income households reasons enough to leave the neighbourhood; they saw too few opportunities for continuing their housing careers there and so chose to move elsewhere. This choice was associated in many cases with the lack of playground facilities and green areas. In many cases, households moved to neighbourhoods which had been renovated in the context of urban renewal and their place was taken over by lower-income groups.

In this manner, the Staatslieden neighbourhood changed slowly but surely into a truly deprived neighbourhood, where the quality of living visibly declined; in the course of time, dilapidated dwellings, deserted industrial premises and litter set the scene in the streets. In addition, the increasing housing need among young people and the large number of properties standing empty attracted squatters. These spatial problems went hand in hand with socio-economic deprivation; in 1995 as many as 56 per cent of the households were on low incomes and at 40 per cent the share of unemployed lay far above the average for the city (Amsterdam: 44 per cent and 32 cent respectively). In addition, drugs misuse led to nuisance and the police increasingly avoided the area (Adriaenssen, 1996; www.cbs.nl).

GWL area. To make the Staatslieden neighbourhood attractive, for among others high-income households, towards the end of the 1980s the Amsterdam local authority started to search for a suitable new construction location within the area. Consequently, the previous industrial area of the Municipal Waterworks [*Gemeente Waterleidingen*] acquired a zoning reallocation for residential purposes.

The development of the area currently referred to as the GWL area took place between 1995 and 1998. The new construction was, in the first instance, intended for residents from the district; households who had lived for five years or more in Westerpark were given priority in the allocation of the dwellings. To give the population composition in the GWL area an heterogeneous character, both high and low-income groups had to be eligible for newly-built dwellings. Consequently, plans were made to develop an equivalent number of rental and owner occupied dwellings.

In the event, 273 social-rental dwellings and 318 owner-occupied dwellings were built on the GWL area (shares of 46.2 per cent and 53.8 per cent respectively). These units were built in the form of multi-family dwellings and formed part of a complex of 16 blocks comprising owner occupied or rental dwellings. In addition to the 591 residential units, they provide accommodation for five communes, each incorporating studio flats, five dwellings for the handicapped, and a housing project for multiple-handicapped children.

The newly-built dwellings have been constructed and are occupied in an environmentally friendly manner. This is expressed among other things in the form of the green and car-free inner areas and the attention has been given to water conservation, economical energy use and waste recycling and disposal. Another striking feature of the area consists of the fact that hardly any facilities have been developed. The district authorities wanted to concentrate the shops in the heart of the old Staatslieden neighbourhood (www.gwl-terrein.nl). As a consequence, the residents are oriented for many activities on the adjacent neighbourhoods (Stadsdeel Westerpark, 2000).

Ondiep. This residential area in Utrecht lies next to the heart of the city, as does the Amsterdam Staatslieden neighbourhood. Ondiep can also be traditionally described as a typical working-class neighbourhood. There are many small pre-war single-family dwellings (53 per cent) built in high density and along narrow streets. Most of them are managed by housing associations (54 per cent) and usually have a low rent (Gemeente Utrecht, 2001). (Data from *Bestuursinformatie gemeente Utrecht 1999/2001* [Local government information for the Utrecht Local Authority 1999/2001] refer to the sub-district Ondiep/2nd Daalse neighbourhood. This area covers a larger area than the main neighbourhood Ondiep, to which the other sources refer.) Although there was previously a mixed housing-work function, the current emphasis is primarily on housing.

An important feature of the neighbourhood is the Amsterdamsestraatweg. This is a busy traffic artery which cuts through the whole northwest district. Many different kinds of facilities can be found there, from Turkish coffee houses to traditional local pubs frequented by the indigenous community, and businesses ranging from small independent enterprises to large supermarket chains. This Amsterdamsestraatweg can then also be appropriately referred to as the mainstay of the area.

Several years previously the area surrounding this mainstay was involved in radical changes. The immediate reason for these changes was the various problems which had been encountered in Ondiep for some time. The quality of both the dwellings and the residential environment had fallen far below acceptable levels. In addition to boarded-up premises and poorly maintained houses, the streets were filled with parked cars and there was a large shortage of green spaces and playground facilities. At the beginning of the 1990s the neighbour-hood also gave an impoverished impression (Wijkbureau Noordwest, 1999).

The problems were not limited to the built-up environment. The neighbour-hood also scored extremely poorly in socio-economic respects; in 1995 as many as 52 per cent of the households had a low income and 42 per cent of the residents were unemployed (Utrecht: 43 and 25 per cent respectively) (www.cbs.nl). The greatest deprivation was in education. In total, 23 per cent of the schoolchildren in Ondiep had been placed in special education. This pro-portion was twice that of the city average (Gemeente Utrecht, 1999).

Plantage. As was the case in Amsterdam, a location in Ondiep was identified where new construction could take place. On this occasion it was the old abattoir area, currently known as 'The Plantage', which underwent a radical change in function. The abattoir area, dating from 1897, covered about 3.5 hectares; an area of such dimensions in a densely built-up residential neighbourhood like Ondiep only becomes available very rarely.

Between 1994 and 1996, the area was built up with a total of 306 dwellings. As in Amsterdam, the new construction consists exclusively of multi-family dwellings. These were built in four blocks around a central square. The complex for the elderly forms a special element. This complex is incorporated in a block where, in addition to 19 social owner occupied dwellings, there are also 58 rental dwellings for residents aged 55 years or more and 40 apartments with care facilities have been developed. These facilities are located in the services centre on the ground floor. The remaining blocks, just as in the Amsterdam situation, consist almost completely of owner occupied or social-rental dwellings. Here too, the owner-occupied/rental distribution is more or less equal (43 per cent owner occupied dwellings and 57 per cent rental dwellings). One block with 72 subsidised (*premie*) owner occupied dwellings, one block with 74 social rental apartments, one with 40 social owner occupied housing and 2 with social rental dwellings.

The public space in the Plantage features a central square. In addition to the many facilities, such as the care centre for the elderly, shops, offices and a library, opportunities have to be provided for the organisation of all kinds of activities. In the summer various festivities take place here.

Empirical Results

Introduction

Have the interventions indeed brought an end to the homogeneity with respect to both the social and the spatial environment? Is there any evidence of interaction between the various resident groups? Do the residents make proper use of the available facilities? These questions are answered by referring to the results of the empirical research. The activities pattern and the neighbourhood bonding of both the old as the new residents are then revealed. Further, reference is made to the households who took up housing within the neighbour-hood after the improvements as the old residents and those who previously lived elsewhere as the new residents. The main question addressed here is to what extent the new residents have made any difference.

Table 1. Comparison of old and new residents per research area (%)

	Amsterdam GWL terrain		Utrecht Plantage		Total	
	Old	New	Old	New	Old	New
Low income	17.9	5.8	35.5	22.0	22.6	11.8
Middle income	53.5	32.6	45.1	50.0	51.3	39.1
High income	28.6	61.6	19.4	28.0	26.1	49.1
Low educational level	22.1	17.8	73.5	45.8	36.7	28.6
Average educational level	9.3	5.9	11.8	14.6	10.0	9.3
High educational level	68.6	76.3	14.7	39.6	53.3	62.1
Job seekers/Disabled	5.8	1.3	5.9	3.1	5.8	2.0
Working	81.4	90.1	35.3	57.3	68.3	77.4
Other	12.8	8.6	58.8	60.4	25.9	20.6
Tenant	55.2	25.0	58.8	51.6	56.2	35.2
Owner-occupier	44.8	75.0	41.2	48.4	43.8	64.8
Households with children	52.9	54.6	27.3	11.5	45.8	37.9
One/two person households	47.1	45.4	72.7	88.5	54.2	62.1
< 56 years	95.4	92.8	52.9	56.2	83.5	78.6
> 56 years	4.6	7.2	47.1	43.8	16.5	21.4
Dutch	87.2	94.7	88.2	91.7	87.5	93.5
Non-Dutch	12.8	5.3	11.8	8.3	12.5	6.5
Total (abs)	87	152	34	96	121	248

Source: own survey (2002).
Notes: Low income: < 1125 Euro net per month; Low level of education: secondary school or lower
High income: > 2250 Euro net per month; Higher level of education: HBO or university.

Inhabitants

A majority of the respondents in the research study belong to the group of new residents; at least two-thirds of the households surveyed lived elsewhere before the intervention work. According to the aims of the restructuring policy these newcomers should bring about societal effects and achieve the important objective of creating a more heterogeneous population (Kleinhans, 2001). Table 1 shows that the new inhabitants can indeed be considered to be different from the old inhabitants. In contrast with the old residents, a majority of this group has a high income, a high level of education, a job and are owner occupiers. The two groups differ significantly from each other with respect to income and tenure; the strength of the relationship, as indicated by Cramèr's V, amounts in both cases to 0.2. The areas differ from each other significantly in terms of income, educational level, household composition, age, and tenure ($V = 0.3; 0.4; 0.4; 0.5$ and 0.2).

There are, however, significant differences between the two research areas. In the Amsterdam study area the income differences between the old and the new inhabitants are much larger than in the Utrecht area. In addition, the Amsterdam area has acquired relatively far more new inhabitants with a higher education, a higher income, more people with a job and more households with children. Ondiep specifically attracted a large number of elderly people.

To some extent the reasons for the differences can be derived from the underlying ideas in the intervention in the respective neighbourhoods. The new construction in the Utrecht restructuring area was partly intended for the elderly, so that almost half the residents surveyed were older than 55 years. They differ from the residents of the new construction area in Amsterdam, where only 6 per cent of the respondents belong to this age category. This difference in age distribution has clear consequences for the socio-economic situation. In both areas, the elderly frequently only have a low educational level and are usually no longer active on the labour market. In this group, high incomes are the exception rather than the rule. In addition, the elderly usually no longer have children living at home.

Whether the developments described have led to the desired integration is discussed in the following section. The results of the research reveal that in the event the high-income residents carry out most of their activities outside the neighbourhood, so that a situation may well have arisen where the old and new residents live alongside rather than together with each other.

Activities of Old and New Inhabitants

Table 2 reveals that a majority of both the old and the new residents, regardless of their socio-economic background, tend to remain within their own neighbourhoods for trips to the supermarket, the bank or the post office. We have distinguished three kinds of areas: the restructured area itself, the neighbourhood of which it forms a part and areas elsewhere. On the other hand, in most cases the activities which lie in the more personal sphere, such as recreation and visits to friends or family, are undertaken elsewhere. Most of the residents are therefore *not* oriented towards their own neighbourhood for a large share of their activities.

The differences between the two research areas are quite considerable. The research areas differ significantly in terms of use of bank and post office, use of shops for daily shopping, and primary education (V = 0.5; 0.8; 0.1). A majority of all the residents (old and new) in the Amsterdam new construction area do their daily shopping in the adjoining neighbourhood; the absence of shops in the new construction area more or less obliges them to be so oriented. In Utrecht on the other hand, where a complete shopping centre has been developed around the new construction, the residents depend for their daily shopping to a much smaller extent on the adjoining neighbourhood. A large majority of the respondents also reported that they did not leave their own area for daily shopping and made hardly any use of facilities in the adjoining residential area.

Visits to cafes, clubs and societies and social contacts are, for both the old and the new residents, chiefly located outside the residential area. For these activities residents in Amsterdam are nevertheless oriented to their own neighbourhood to a greater extent than are the residents of the new construction area in Utrecht. Table 2 shows, for example, that 11.5 per cent of the new inhabitants in the Amsterdam research area have social contacts within the Staatslieden neighbourhood: a considerably different situation from that in Utrecht, where only 2.9 per cent of the new households have social contacts with residents in Ondiep. Of course, both percentages are not particularly large. Expecting that suddenly old and new residents will start to interact with each other is probably not very realistic when both groups are so heavily oriented on areas outside their own neighbourhood.

Previously in this paper, it was stated that certain environmental, household and personal characteristics are capable of playing a decisive part in the location

Table 2. Locations where old and new residents carry out their activities, per research area (%)

	Amsterdam			Utrecht		
Old inhabitants (*n* = 121)	GWL area	Staatslieden-neighbourhood	Elsewhere	Plantage	Ondiep	Elsewhere
Trips to bank/post office	-	68.8	31.2	29.0	58.1	12.9
Trips to café/restaurant	5.4	35.1	59.5	12.5	43.8	43.7
Visits to friends/family	11.0	24.7	64.3	9.1	45.5	45.4
Trips to shops for daily shopping	-	85.5	14.5	79.4	11.8	8.8
Recreation	9.9	53.5	36.6	6.3	56.3	37.4
Clubs and societies	-	39.4	60.6	-	63.2	36.8
Primary education	-	61.1	38.9	-	100	-

	Amsterdam			Utrecht		
New inhabitants (*n* = 248)	GWL area	Staatslieden-neighbourhood	Elsewhere	Plantage	Ondiep	Elsewhere
Trips to bank/post office	-	74.3	25.7	30.2	40.7	29.1
Trips to café/restaurant	8.3	31.6	60.2	5.4	7.1	87.5
Visits to friends/family	12.3	11.5	76.2	10.0	2.9	87.1
Trips to shops for daily shopping	-	79.1	20.9	78.0	6.6	15.4
Recreation	7.8	38.3	53.9	4.8	12.9	82.3
Clubs and societies	-	45.9	54.1	-	33.3	66.7
Primary education	-	64.0	36.0	-	66.7	33.3

Source: own survey (2002).

where activities are undertaken. This indeed transpires to be the case in a number of respects. Thus, in addition to household composition, the availability of services and facilities is of importance: families with children undertake more activities within the neighbourhood than one and two person households, and the availability of shopping outlets determines to some extent the behaviour of both old and new residents (see the Table in the Appendix). There are also some important differences between old and new residents: a majority of the old residents with no job, on a low income, and having a low educational level undertake most of their activities within the neighbourhood, while this is hardly ever the case for the newcomers. Visits to cafés or restaurants are influenced by household composition ($V = 0.1$). The maintenance of social contacts (visits to friends or families) within or outside the neighbourhood is influenced by the educational level, the household composition, and tenure ($V = 0.3$; 0.3; 0.2). The recreation behaviour is influenced by the household composition and tenure ($V = 0.2$). The patronage of clubs and societies is influenced by income, educational level, the labour market situation, age, and tenure ($V = 0.4$; 0.5; 0.5; 0.3; 0.4). Finally, the location of primary education is influenced by educational level and nationality ($V = 0.4$). The use of shops for daily shopping, social contacts and the recreation behaviour is influenced by household composition ($V = 0.1$; 0.3; 0.3).

A possible explanation for this difference is provided by the fact that the dwelling choice of the newcomers is often determined by the prospect of a newly-built dwelling located coincidentally in one of the research areas. In such cases a household has not chosen the neighbourhood specifically. In this way the chance arises that many daily activities are not undertaken within the new residential area, but in the old residential area, for example, or somewhere completely different. For many activities there is no necessity to carry them out in the new neighbourhood. For the old residents who have built up contacts over the years there may often be reasons for remaining within the neighbourhood. These residents have merely maintained their locally oriented activities pattern.

In addition to the differences in the provision of services and facilities, the population composition in the two areas provides an explanation for the differences found. For example, the fact that a large share of the respondents in Utrecht consists of the elderly influences the activities pattern; more than half this group has no contact with residents from the adjacent neighbourhood. They simply see no reason for visiting the adjacent neighbourhood. On the other hand, the presence of the large share of children around the new construction in Amsterdam in many cases provides a reason for contacts between parents to take place there; a majority of the children follow primary education within the residential area.

Finally, there is a specific look at the differences between Dutch and non-Dutch respondents. In many cases the non-Dutch respondents on average seem to do more activities in the neighbourhood than the Dutch. This holds for the old, as well as for the new inhabitants. It is striking that all non-Dutch belonging to the category of old inhabitants send their children to a school within the neighbourhood, while the corresponding figure for the new inhabitants is only 20 per cent. Probably, however, this has not much to do with preferences of the parents themselves: when the new inhabitants came to live in the neighbourhood, the schools there accepted no more pupils because they had reached their maximum capacity. Therefore, the newest inhabitants were forced to look for a school somewhere else.

Neighbourhood Bonding

In addition to the activities pattern, the neighbourhood bond determines the part played by the neighbourhood in the life of the residents. When asking questions about neighbourhood bonding the whole neighbourhood has been referred to, not just the newly constructed part. In contrast with expectations, it appears that this has hardly any relation with socio-economic background or household composition. Households with a weak socio-economic position, in particular the elderly, are more closely oriented to the neighbourhood than one or two person households with a high income (Table 3). It is striking, however, that a large proportion of the households attach hardly any value to the residential area; respondents indicate that they could live anywhere, or have nothing to do to with the neighbourhood, which therefore only serves as a place of residence. These results are in conformance with the assertions of Wellman (1996) and Friedrichs (1997), among others. Households identify less with one territory or another so that the part played by the neighbourhood has lost its importance; it can no longer be taken for granted that one's neighbours share the world in which one lives.

Table 3. Comparison of residents' characteristics and neighbourhood bonding per research area (%)

| | Old inhabitants (*n* = 121) | | | | New inhabitants (*n* = 248) | | | |
| | GWL terrain | | Plantage | | GWL terrain | | Plantage | |
	Strong	Weak	Strong	Weak	Strong	Weak	Strong	Weak
Low income	20.0	-	45.5	-	12.5	25.0	11.1	22.2
High income	75.0	-	50.0	-	28.2	22.4	13.0	47.8
Low educational level	36.8	5.3	52.0	8.0	11.1	29.6	11.4	18.2
High educational level	62.7	1.7	20.0	20.0	29.3	21.6	10.5	57.9
Job seekers/ Disabled	20.0	-	50.0	-	-	50.0	-	66.7
Working	64.3	1.4	25.0	33.3	27.0	23.4	12.7	23.7
Tenant	50.0	2.1	45.0	15.0	18.4	28.9	10.2	32.7
Owner-occupier	64.1	2.6	42.9	14.2	28.9	21.1	10.9	43.5
Households with children	64.4	-	44.4	22.2	33.7	16.9	9.1	45.5
One/two pers. Households	47.5	5.0	45.8	8.3	17.4	60.4	10.6	36.5
> 56 years	25.0	25.0	50.0	6.2	9.1	18.2	7.1	26.2
Non-Dutch	27.3	-	50.0	50.0	12.5	25.0	12.5	37.5
Total (abs)	49	2	15	5	40	35	10	36

Source: own survey (2002).
Notes: Low income: <1125 Euro net per month; Low educational level: secondary school or lower
High income: >2250 Euro net per month; High educational level: HBO of University.
The neighbourhood bond is measured on the basis of a questionnaire item which asks about the strength of the bond; answer categories run from 'very strong bond' to 'very weak bond'. 'Moderate bond' has been omitted from the table.

The old and the new residents also differ from each other (Table 3). While a majority of the old residents feel a strong bond with the residential area, in general the newcomers have a weak or moderate bond. This quite often appears to be associated with a short sojourn, or the fact that respondents have maintained their social contacts elsewhere.

Comparison of the research areas revealed several more differences. The bonding of respondents in Amsterdam to their residential area appears to be much stronger than for the respondents in Utrecht. The research areas differ significantly with respect to neighbourhood bonding (V = 0.2). In both areas, the divergent population composition provides a possible explanation: the large share of households with children in Amsterdam is more strongly tied to the neighbourhood than the many one and two person households in the Utrecht new construction area (Table 2). In addition, many respondents in Amsterdam only feel tied to the new construction area: they attach more value to this area than to the rest of the neighbourhood (despite the fact that they have to leave the area for almost all facilities, see earlier in this paper).

Influence of Urban Restructuring

From the above it emerges that restructuring measures via the spatial environ-

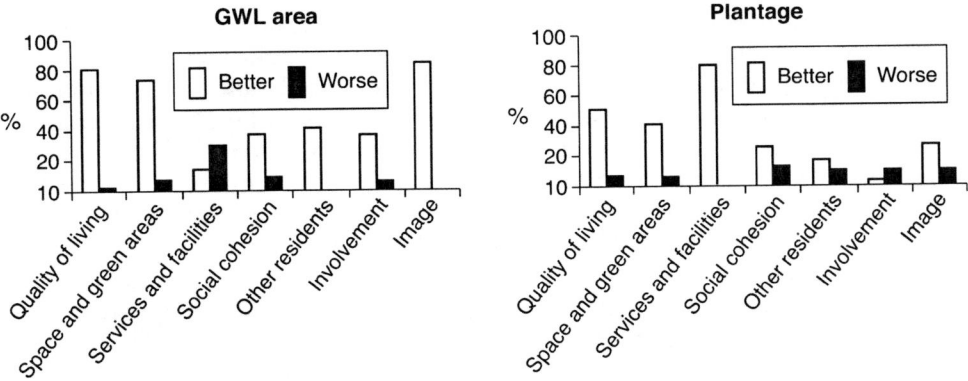

Figure 1. Opinions of old residents about the changes after the intervention with respect to certain neighbourhood aspects, per research area (%).
Source: own survey (2002).
Note: The answer category 'the same' has been omitted from the Figure.

ment have an influence on the social environment; the new construction has indeed attracted higher-income households to the neighbourhoods and so a heterogeneous population has been brought about. That is not to say that the old residents of the areas concerned are happy with the results. What do they think, for example, about the arrival of the new residents? Has involvement with the neighbourhood changed since the intervention?

Before discussing the influence of the restructuring, the investigation into why residents moved after the intervention within the same neighbourhood is first reported. It appears from the questionnaire that the new construction played a large part in both areas: for more than half the respondents the prospect of a newly-built (and affordable) dwelling within the same neighbourhood was the most important reason for staying on. In addition, they were in many cases referred to the favourable location near the centre of the city. The social environment also appears to exert an influence: a large proportion of the old residents has remained within the residential area because of the contacts they had built up. What is also striking is the fact that respondents in Amsterdam are very positive about the ideology behind the new construction project; as many as one-third of the old residents moved from the Staatslieden neighbourhood to the GWL area on account of the environmentally friendly design of the project.

Figure 1 shows that residents are satisfied with aspects of the restructuring other than the new construction and the ideas underlying the intervention. Respondents are particularly positive about the changes that have taken place in the quality of living, the increased space, the green areas and the image of the neighbourhood.

Although in both areas the intervention was evaluated as good, the opinions of the old residents with respect to certain matters were highly divergent (Figure 1). The research areas differ significantly from each other in their opinions about the developments, the green area, the facilities, and their involvement with the neighbourhood (V = 0.3; 0.6; 0.3). The only aspect on which the Utrecht research area scored better was the provision of services and facilities. In relation to what has previously been reported, the residents there are very satisfied with the available provision, while in Amsterdam opinions are quite different.

With respect to the social cohesion and the population composition the developments were evaluated more positively in Amsterdam than in Utrecht. What is also striking is the difference in terms of involvement in the neighbourhood; in contrast with the Plantage, where after the intervention a small decline was observed, residents of the GWL area felt a greater involvement; old residents of the Staatslieden neighbourhood apparently attach more importance to the composition of the neighbourhood population than do the old residents in Ondiep. The fact that there are differences in this respect is also apparent from the developments concerning the social contacts of old residents. Almost two-thirds of the respondents on the Amsterdam new construction area had more contact with their next-door neighbours than in the previous housing situation; a difference with Utrecht of 30 percentage points. Here, in the opinion of many people the car-free and child-friendly character of the project in Amsterdam plays an important part (31 per cent). In addition, a quarter of the respondents referred to the lifestyle of the new neighbours. This conforms with their own lifestyle and so facilitates social contacts. In Utrecht the opposite is the case. The different lifestyle of the new neighbours there is responsible for a decline in social contacts. Hortulanus' assumption (1995) is confirmed here: every individual prefers a residential area with residents whose lifestyle conforms as far as possible with one's own.

If the contacts with residents from the adjacent neighbourhood are then examined, it appears that the figures for the two areas differ again. Almost a quarter of the old residents on the GWL area have more contacts within the Staatslieden neighbourhood. Again, the presence of children appears to play a important part. In Utrecht on the other hand, more than three-quarters of the respondents reported that the intervention had not had any influence on their contacts with residents from the adjacent neighbourhood.

In general terms, the old residents are thus satisfied with the interventions which have taken place within the research areas. However, these matters have not had any automatic influence on the pattern of activities. As mentioned above, it appears that households turn elsewhere for many activities; the neighbourhood is merely used for trips to the supermarket or the primary school (Table 2). The fact that, after the intervention, neighbourhood involvement has increased for a share of the respondents is not to say that they automatically carry out more activities in the neighbourhood. This is also apparent from the questionnaire: more than three-quarters of the respondents did not agree, or had no opinion about the statement that since the intervention they had undertaken more activities within the neighbourhood.

Conclusions and Evaluation

On the basis of the findings reported in this paper, it appears that in general the neighbourhood plays a limited part in the life of the residents; a majority of all residents, both the old and the new, undertake most of their activities outside their own neighbourhood. This includes, for example, shopping trips and visits to recreational facilities, but also visits to friends and relatives. The idea that urban restructuring is a positive influence for the neighbourhood in terms of more expenditure in local outlets, must therefore be treated with caution (although spending on daily shopping in the Staatslieden neighbourhood did indeed rise after the intervention). A positive influence in terms of increasing and intensive social contacts between the old and new inhabitants of the neighbourhoods also did not happen: people in the neighbourhoods seem to live alongside each other, not together. On the basis of the literature cited earlier in this paper, this outcome was not so very surprising: people like to live together with those who are 'like them' and if this is not the case, the interest in each other is not very easily generated, let alone sustained.

This is not to say that the restructuring interventions were pointless. They brought about the renovation of the neighbourhoods and changed the composition of the population. These changes have their repercussions on the atmosphere within a residential area.

In addition to the provision of facilities and services, restructuring can also influence social integration by directing measures to a certain target group. When, for example, a large share of the new housing stock is intended for the elderly, the social contacts of these households seem to become particularly limited to the new construction area; there is hardly any sign of interaction with the rest of the neighbourhood. In a residents' group which consists to a large extent of young families with children, mutual contacts are indeed observed; parents meet each other on the street or the school playground. The assumption that residents with the same background get on more easily with each other than households who have nothing in common is thus again confirmed.

Although the neighbourhood plays a limited part in the life of most residents, urban restructuring can positively influence the impression a neighbourhood gives and the involvement in a residential area. Moreover, it should always be kept in mind that restructuring serves some other functions. It can be of utmost importance to improve the structure of the housing stock in cases where the dwellings have a low to very absolute quality. Moreover, in some areas some dwellings may not be wanted anymore with a high vacancy rate as a consequence. Finally, urban restructuring can lead to new opportunities for making a housing career within the city or even within the neighbourhood. The ultimate goal of urban restructuring is not social cohesion, but, as has been stated earlier in this paper, to restructure the physical environment in order to contribute to social and economic vitality of the city as a whole.

Acknowledgements

This paper is based on a research study (see Van Beckhoven & Van Kempen, 2002) carried out for the Dutch Ministry of Housing (Directorate-General of Housing) and the Netherlands Graduate School of Housing and Urban Research (Nethur).

Correspondence

Ronald Van Kempen, Urban and Regional research centre Utrecht, Faculty of Geographical Sciences, Utrecht University, Heidelberglaan 2, PO Box 80115, 3508 TC Utrecht, the Netherlands. E-mail: R.vanKempen@geog.uu.nl

References

Adriaenssen, L. (1996) *Een dwarse buurt: het herscheppingsverhaal van de Staatsliedenbuurt en Frederik Hendrik buurt 1971–1996* (Amsterdam, Wijkcentrum Staatslieden-Hugo de Grootbuurt).

Anderiesen, G. & Reijndorp, A. (1989) *Gescheiden werelden: sociale segmentering in 19ᵉ eeuwse stadswijken* (Amsterdam, Stedelijke Netwerken).

Atkinson, R. & Kintrea, K. (1998) *Reconnecting Excluded Communities: The Neighbourhood Impacts of Owner Occupation* (Edinburgh, Scottish Homes).

Atkinson, R. & Kintrea, K. (2002) *'Opportunities and Despair, It's All in There', or, 'Every Area Has Its Problems': Everyday Experiences of Area Effects* (Glasgow, Department of Urban Studies, University of Glasgow).

Beaumont, J., Burgers, J., Dekker, K., Dukes, T., Musterd, S., Staring, R. & Van Kempen, R. (2003) Urban policy in the Netherlands, in: J. Vranken, J. Beaumont & I. Van Nieuwenhuyze (Eds) *On the Origins of Urban Development Programmes in Nine European Countries*, pp. 119–137 (Antwerpen, Garant).

Blokland-Potters, T. (1998) *Wat stadsbewoners bindt; sociale relaties in een achterstandswijk* (Kampen, Kok Agora).

Botman, S. & Van Kempen, R. (2001) *Spatial Dimensions of Urban Social Exclusion and Integration: The Case of Rotterdam, The Netherlands* (Amsterdam, Amsterdam study centre for the Metropolitan Environment).

Burns, D., Forrest, R., Flint, J. & Kearns, A. (2001) *Empowering Communities: The Impact of Registered Social Landlords on Social Capital* (Edinburgh, Scottish Homes).

Buys, A. (1997) *De ideale mix? Een verkenning van visies, feiten en verwachtingen ten aanzien van de bevolkingssamenstelling van buurten en wijken* (Amsterdam, RIGO Research en Advies BV).

Campbell, K. E. & Lee, B. A. (1992) Sources of personal neighbor networks: social integration, need, or time? *Social Forces*, 70, pp. 1077–1100.

Dagevos, J. (2001) *Perspectief op integratie: over de sociaal-culturele en structurele integratie van etnische minderheden in Nederland* (Den Haag, Wetenschappelijke Raad voor het Regeringsbeleid).

Dahya, B. (1974) The nature of Pakistani ethnicity in industrial cities in Britain, in: A. Cohen (Ed.) *Urban Ethnicity*, pp. 77–118 (London, Tavistock).

Ellen, I. G. & Turner, M. A. (1997) Does neighborhood matter? Assessing recent evidence, *Housing Policy Debate*, 8, pp. 833–866.

Enchautegui, M. E. (1997) Latino neighborhoods and Latino neighborhood poverty, *Journal of Urban Affairs*, 19, pp. 445–467.

Fischer, C. S (1982) *To Dwell Among Friends* (Chicago, University of Chicago Press).

Flap, H. (1999) Buurt of gemeenschap: 'meeting' of 'mating', in: B. Völker & R. Verhoeff (Eds) *Buren en Buurten*, pp. 11–34 (Amsterdam, SISWO).

Fong, E. & Gulia, M. (1999) Differences in neighborhood qualities among racial and ethnic groups in Canada, in: *Sociological Inquiry*, 69, pp. 575–598.

Forrest, R. & Kearns, A. (2001) Social cohesion, social capital and the neighbourhood, *Urban Studies*, 38, pp. 2125–2143.

Friedrichs, J. (1997) Context effects of poverty neighbourhoods on residents, in: H. Vestergaard (Ed.) *Housing in Europe*, pp. 141–160 (Horsholm, Danish Building Research Institute).

Gemeente Utrecht (1999) *Utrecht Monitor* (Utrecht, Bestuursinformatie Gemeente Utrecht).

Gemeente Utrecht (2001) *Utrecht Monitor* (Utrecht, Bestuursinformatie Gemeente Utrecht).

Granovetter, M. S. (1973) The strength of weak ties, *American Journal of Sociology*, 78, pp. 1360–1380.

Guest, A. M. & Wierzbicki, S. K. (1999) Social ties at the neighborhood level: two decades of GSS evidence, *Urban Affairs Review*, 35, pp. 92–111.

Healy, P. (1997) Social exclusion, neighbourhood life and governance capacity, in: H. Vestergaard (Ed.) *Housing in Europe*, pp. 88–110 (Horsholm, Danish Building Research Institute).

Healy, P. (1998) Institutionalist theory, social exclusion and governance, in: A. Madanipour, Cars, G. & Allen, J. (Eds) *Social Exclusion in European Cities; Processes, Experiences and Responses*, pp. 53–73 (London, Jessica Kingsley Publishers).

Henning, C. & Lieberg, M. (1996) Strong ties or weak ties? Neighbourhood networks in a new perspective, *Scandinavian Housing and Planning Research*, 13, pp. 3–26.

Hortulanus, R. P. (1995) *Stadsbuurten; Bewoners en beheerders in buurten met uiteenlopende reputaties* (Utrecht, VUGA).

Kearns, A. & Forrest, R. (2000) Social cohesion and multilevel urban governance, *Urban Studies*, 37, pp. 995–1017.

Kearns, A., Atkinson, R. & Parkes, A. (2000) *A Geography of Misery or an Epidemic of Contentment? Understanding Neighbourhood (Dis)Satisfaction in Britain* (Glasgow, Department of Urban Studies, University of Glasgow).

Kleinhans, R., Veldboer, L. & Duyvendak, J.W. (2000) *Integratie door differentiatie? Een onderzoek naar de sociale effecten van gemengd bouwen* (Rotterdam, Erasmusuniversiteit).

Kleinhans, R. (2001) *De sociale impact van herstructurering; onderzoeksopzet: versie September 2001* (Delft, Onderzoeksinstituut OTB).

Kleinhans, R. & Kruythoff, H. (2002) *Herstructurering: in het spoor van de vertrekkers* (Den Haag, DGVH/Nethur).

Ministerie van Volkshuisvesting, Ruimtelijke Ordening en Milieubeheer (1997) *Nota Stedelijke Vernieuwing* (Den Haag, Ministerie VROM).

Ministerie van Volkshuisvesting, Ruimtelijke Ordening en Milieubeheer (2000) *Nota Mensen-Wensen-Wonen* (Den Haag, Ministerie VROM).

Musterd, S. (1998) Sleutelpositie wijk bij herstructurering? *Geografie*, March, pp. 13–14.

Musterd, S. & Ostendorf, W. (1998) Segregation and social participation in a welfare state: the case of Amsterdam. In: S. Musterd & W. Ostendorf (eds.), *Urban Segregation and the Welfare State: Inequality and Exclusion in Western Cities*, pp. 191–205 (London, Routledge).

Musterd, S., Priemus, H. & Van Kempen, R. (1999) Towards undivided cities: the potential of economic revitalisation and housing redifferentiation, *Housing Studies*, 14, pp. 573–584.

Portes, A. & Sensenbrenner, J. (1993) Embeddedness and immigration: notes on the social determinants of economic action, *American Journal of Sociology*, 98, pp. 1320–1350.

Priemus, H. & Van Kempen, R. (1998) Herstructurering stadswijken verdient kans, *Geografie*, 7, pp. 4–8.

Reijndorp, A. (1996) Bevordert herpositionering de leefbaarheid? *Nieuw Tijdschrift voor de Volkshuisvesting*, 7, pp. 6–10.

Sociaal en Cultureel Planbureau (2002) *Zekere banden: sociale cohesie, leefbaarheid en veiligheid* (Den Haag, Sociaal en Cultureel Planbureau).

Stadsdeel Westerpark (2000) *Eigentijdse ecologie: Gemeentewaterleidingterrein; een autoluwe woonwijk in Amsterdam Westerpark* (Amsterdam, Stadsdeel Westerpark).

Stein, M. (1964) *The Eclipse of Community* (New York, Glencoe).

Tesser, P. T. M., Van Praag, C. S., Van Dugteren, F. A., Herweijer, L. J. & Van der Wouden, H. C. (1995) *Rapportage minderheden 1995: concentratie en segregatie* (Rijswijk, Sociaal en Cultureel Planbureau).

Van Beckhoven, E. & Van Kempen, R. (2002) *Het belang van de buurt: de invloed van herstructurering op activiteiten van blijvers en nieuwkomers in een Amsterdamse en Utrechtse buurt* (Utrecht, DGVH/NETHUR).

Van Doorn, J. A. A. (1955) Wijk en stad: reële integratiekaders? In: S. J. Groenman & H. de Jager (Eds) *Staalkaart der Nederlandse Sociologie*, pp. 231–253 (Assen, Van Gorcum).

Van Engelsdorp-Gastelaars, R. & Vijgen, J. (1991) Stadsbuurten en woonkernen in de jaren negentig; hun veranderende betekenis als lokaal woonmilieu, in: R. Van Kempen, S. Musterd & W. Ostendorf (Eds) *Maatschappelijke veranderingen en stedelijke dynamiek*, pp. 107–119 (Delft, Delftse Universitaire Pers).

Van Kempen, R. (2001) Social exclusion: the importance of context. In: H. T. Andersen & R. van Kempen (eds.), *Governing European Cities. Social Fragmentation, Social Exlcusion and Urban Governance*, pp. 41–70 (Aldershot: Ashgate).

Van Kempen, R. & Van Weesep, J. (1996) Segregatie: een probleem? Perspectieven op bewoningspatronen en sociale segmentatie, in: H. B. G. Ganzeboom & W. C. Ultee (Eds) *De sociale segmentatie van Nederland in 2015*, pp. 119–171 (Den Haag, Sdu Uitgevers).

Van Kempen, R., Hooimeijer, P., Bolt, G., Burgers, J., Musterd, S., Ostendorf, W. & Snel, E. (2000) *Segregatie en concentratie in Nederlandse steden: mogelijke effecten en mogelijk beleid* (Assen, Van Gorcum).

Wacquant, L. J. D. (1993) Urban outcasts: stigma and division in the black American ghetto and the French urban periphery, *International Journal of Urban and Regional Research*, 17, pp. 366–383.

Webber, M. (1963) Order in diversity: communities without propinquity, in: L. Wingo Jr. (Ed.) *Cities and Space*, pp. 23–54 (Baltimore, John Hopkins University Press).

Wellman, B. (1996) Are personal communities local? A Dumparian reconsideration, *Social Networks*, 18, pp. 347–354.

Wijkbureau Noordwest (1999) *Utrecht Noordwest, een wijk in beweging: 10 jaar stadsvernieuwing in Utrecht Noordwest* (Nieuwegein, Hollandsch Glorie bv).

Wilson, W. J. (1987) *The Truly Disadvantaged; The Inner City, The Underclass and Public Policy* (Chicago, the University of Chicago Press).

Wilson, W. J. (1996) *When Work Disappears* (Boston, Harvard University Press).

Other Sources

www.cbs.nl
www.research-and-statistiek.amsterdam.nl
www.gwl-terrein.nl

Appendix

Residents' characteristics and the activities which residents undertake within the Staatslieden neighbourhood and Ondiep respectively (percentage per category).

Table Appendix

Old inhabitants (*n* = 121)	Visit to				Other		
	Bank/ post office	Cafe/ Restaurant	Friends/ family	Shops (daily)	Recreation	Clubs and societies	Primary education
Low income	76.1	50.0	60.0	100	68.8	76.9	66.7
High income	76.8	48.1	34.5	86.2	48.1	22.2	58.8
Low educational level	73.0	52.2	57.1	90.5	70.9	72.0	92.9
High educational level	72.1	40.0	28.1	84.2	59.3	29.2	33.3
Job seekers/Disabled	71.4	75.0	40.0	71.4	80.0	50.0	*
Working	70.3	38.0	33.3	84.0	60.9	31.3	47.7
Tenant	73.8	52.2	51.0	92.2	73.3	66.7	48.4
Owner-occupier	74.5	34.1	28.3	81.1	52.4	28.0	60.9
Households with children	70.8	48.8	55.6	92.3	74.4	55.6	53.7
One/two persons households	75.9	37.0	27.1	82.5	51.2	43.8	*
<56 years	70.8	41.0	38.6	85.6	63.6	40.0	*
>56 years	89.5	71.4	50.0	95.6	60.0	75.0	*
Dutch	72.4	43.0	38.8	87.4	59.7	45.8	43.2
Non-Dutch	90.0	45.5	50.0	85.7	90.0	75.0	100.0
Total (abs)	80	39	38	102	55	54	38

New inhabitants (*n* = 248)	Visit to				Other		
	Bank/ post office	Cafe/ Restaurant	Friends/ family	Shops (daily)	Recreation	Clubs and societies	Primary education
Low income	81.8	50.0	31.3	91.7	33.3	60.0	42.9
High income	76.9	35.6	19.4	83.3	44.8	35.6	37.7
Low educational level	78.3	37.9	19.0	76.9	35.7	45.2	21.4
High educational level	70.1	31.7	19.1	83.6	38.6	39.4	41.7
Job seekers/Disabled	60.0	25.0	*	80.0	*	*	*
Working	71.7	31.4	20.6	81.0	38.5	36.7	37.9
Tenant	79.5	32.6	27.3	83.8	33.3	42.9	40.0
Owner-occupier	69.7	31.5	17.2	79.7	38.1	38.0	39.2
Households with children	80.0	39.3	29.2	88.0	52.4	48.6	39.4
One/two person Households	68.4	25.7	12.6	76.9	24.5	35.7	*
<56 years	72.0	32.6	19.9	82.2	36.8	37.0	39.8
>56 years	77.3	21.4	20.7	77.1	37.0	50.0	*
Dutch	72.2	32.2	19.3	80.4	36.9	40.0	41.7
Non-Dutch	85.7	22.2	30.8	93.3	36.4	42.9	20.0
Total (abs)	165	60	40	194	70	43	37

Source: own survey (2002)

Notes:
Low income: < 1125 Euro net per month
Low educational level:
secondary school or lower
High income: > 2250 Euro net per month
High educational level:
HBO of University
To avoid the table becoming too large and unnecessarily complicated, the two areas have been examined together.
* no data or not relevant

Neighbourhood Effects and Social Mobility: A Longitudinal Analysis

SAKO MUSTERD, WIM OSTENDORF & SJOERD DE VOS

Department of Geography and Planning, University of Amsterdam, Amsterdam, the Netherlands

[Paper first received 19 November 2002; in final form 7 April 2003]

ABSTRACT   What impact do neighbourhoods have on social mobility? For years, this question has received widespread international attention in scholarly debates and within society at large. This paper seeks to contribute to this discussion by presenting the results of an investigation into the relationship between household social mobility and the composition of the residential environment. The analyses are based on an extensive empirical longitudinal study conducted in the Netherlands. The most remarkable conclusion is that, in the Dutch context, the environment has only a modest influence on the social mobility of households with a weak economic position. It was found that the chance of a household living purely on welfare benefits at the beginning of the study period to escape the 'welfare trap' was barely dependent on the number of similarly challenged households in the immediate vicinity. Interestingly, the environment proved to have a more powerful effect on the social mobility of households with a stronger economic position. The probability that households with at least one paid job at the beginning of the research would still have a job at the end clearly decreases as the share of benefit-dependent households in the neighbourhood rises. A possible explanation for this is that for the first category (weak starting position) the negative effect of their own welfare situation is far more determinative for their future prospects than the composition of their environment. Because these negative individualistic conditions are absent for the second category (stronger starting position), environmental factors may play a relatively larger role. Another interpretation is that area-based policies are not just targeting the areas with bigger problems more intensively, but especially the long-term unemployed in these areas, and not so much the short-term unemployed (those who had a job at the start of the research period and lost the job afterwards).

KEY WORDS: neighbourhood effects, social mobility, longitudinal, the Netherlands

Neighbourhoods and Social Mobility

Neighbourhood composition is receiving increasing attention in urban research and in discussions on housing and urban planning. It appears that in the Netherlands, but also elsewhere in Europe and the US, questions regarding the influence of neighbourhood composition are currently topical and have been for some time. In Dutch policy discussions, this has translated itself into calls for promoting the stimulation of mixed neighbourhoods and, more generally, staving off polarisation (see e.g. Musterd et al., 1999). Although other concepts are employed in the international literature on urban issues, the essence is the same: a concern for segregation and the negative effects living in 'ghettos' may have (see e.g. Galster, 2002). Not so much the concentrations *per se*, but the negative effects of these concentrations would have for individuals living there, neighbourhood effects, are the cause of such concern.

Evidence can be found in the literature for the idea that neighbourhoods with a high concentration of poverty are stigmatised, and that this exogenous factor creates obstacles for upward social mobility, integration and participation for residents. Such environments are also assumed to negatively affect the endogenous, socialisation process of those growing up there, with decreased chances for social mobility and integration as a result. Moreover, as neighbourhoods with great concentrations of poor residents are generally typified by substandard facilities, this can further inhibit the developmental potential of their inhabitants. The logical conclusion continues to be that mixing the population at the district and neighbourhood level could prevent such unwanted developments from occurring.

A wide base of support exists for these kinds of reactions in political and policy circles. Such arguments also appear quite sympathetic towards the plight of residents, and advocates obviously have the best in mind for these individuals. Still, there are grounds for critically examining the situation. The assumptions that lie at the foundation of the espoused visions and policy recommendations should be based on analyses that answer a number of questions on segregation and social mobility. However, such studies are not readily available. This was pointed out by Galster & Zobel (1998) for the US. These authors are not alone. Atkinson & Kintrea (2001), for example, in their review of the Anglo-Saxon literature, quote both researchers that defend the neighbourhood-effects hypothesis and researchers that cast great doubt on its validity. The differences between the two camps can largely be explained by the fact that neighbourhood effects are hard to measure. Moreover, because the demands placed on the datasets are so high, they are often impossible to meet. A common result, particularly in European research, is that only a few areas are compared, only limited samples are used and only cross-sectional data employed. Additionally, Atkinson & Kintrea did not avoid these limitations in their own research. Especially the use of statistical cross-sectional data instead of large-scale dynamical longitudinal data is a great handicap in the study of social processes. In the US data facilities seem to be much better and also longitudinal research projects can be found more often (cf. Sampson et al., 2002).

This contribution seeks to address a number of these deficiencies by presenting the results of a study with a very large sample size (almost a third of the Dutch population) that distinguishes between a large number of areas and which uses longitudinal data. The contribution does not consider all possible environmental effects (e.g. schools and test scores, or the workplace and social participation), but focuses on just the relationship between the social composition of the residential environment and (changes in) employment status. This was done by posing the question of the degree to which a relationship exists between the spatial concentration of poor people and individual social mobility. The research question was formulated as follows:

Do households living in areas where a large proportion of households have a weak economic position have less favourable economic prospects than households with the same economic position living in areas where a large proportion of households have a stronger economic position, after controlling for other attributes?

This contribution provides an answer to this question. Before presenting this, however, the next section will elaborate on the social and scientific debate on the influence of the environment on social mobility as it has manifested itself in the Netherlands, Europe and the US. The third section will then take a closer look at the main concepts and data used for the study. The empirical findings will be presented in the following section, and the final section will draw some conclusions from these results.

The Social Policy and the Scientific Debate

The notion that neighbourhoods have an impact on social development potential has a long history in the Netherlands. Post-war politics were heavily influenced by Social Democratic and Christian Democratic beliefs regarding redistribution and egalitarianism. This had the effect that, after the restoration of the housing stock that had been seriously damaged during the Second World War, a continual call was made for 'balanced' residential environments, which, it was assumed, could help to prevent social unrest. Until very recently, this belief has underpinned Dutch housing and urban development policy. Until the mid-1990s, there was a strong call for urban renewal projects that would create socially heterogeneous residential environments; this position is articulated in key policy documents such as *De Gedifferentieerde Stad* [The differentiated city] (1996) and the *Nota Stedelijke Vernieuwing* [Report on urban renewal] (1997). It was obviously felt that this provided the correct framework for dealing with issues of social and cultural integration and participation. Consequently, 'income neighbourhoods', a euphemism for urban areas with a relatively homogeneous population in terms of income, were to be avoided at all costs as they would inhibit integration and contribute to 'ghetto formation' (Duivesteijn, 1996).

A similar standpoint was taken by academics. Van Kempen *et al.* (1991), for example, argued that:

> ... spatial segregation according to income is, in our opinion, a serious problem ... If one wishes to avoid this using a market-oriented policy, then action must be taken to ensure that a large degree of differentiation of the housing stock (in terms of price of the stock) is produced at the neighbourhood/district level. This can mean that in neighbourhoods where cheap housing stock has traditionally been concentrated, more attention should be given to the construction of more upscale housing alternatives in the near future. (p. 188)

Criticisms of this viewpoint were more prevalent in the scientific community than in government (Buit, 1977; Musterd & Ostendorf, 1995). In fact, policies that take as a point of departure rapidly growing ghettos and their negative impacts on social mobility have come under increasing fire (see e.g. Musterd, 2002; Ostendorf & Musterd, 1997; Ostendorf *et al.*, 2001; VROM-raad advies, 1999). These studies found that, among other things, the Dutch welfare state has mitigated social disparities in the Netherlands, and this has kept levels of segregation relatively modest. Because of this, the authors expect few negative effects for the developmental potential of residents. Next to this, mixing of economic categories appears not to result in more social interactions between these categories. This insight seems to have led to a recent decision by the Ministry of Housing, Spatial Planning and the Environment (VROM) to give more room for the residential demand (see the reports *Mensen, Wensen, Wonen* [people, desires, living], *Wonen in de 21ᵉ eeuw* [living in the twenty-first century] (2000, p. 176). However, the desire among political parties to promote population mixes by mixing housing types is still present.

However, at the local (municipal) level, objectives regarding social mixing are still clearly present. Interestingly, reference is still usually made to national policy. Examples include the policy of Amsterdam (*Amsterdam complete stad*, 1999) and the countless other projects being carried out in urban neighbourhoods throughout the Netherlands. In an overview provided by Buys (1997), it appears that in districts with a large proportion of uniform inexpensive (often social) housing, attempts are being made to increase variation via demolition, unit merging, changes in ownership, renovation, and the like. Demolition and rebuilding implies the construction of more expensive homes to help change the social composition of the neighbourhood.

Views on the negative effects produced by concentrations of poor people are not confined to the Netherlands; mixed-housing policy is an important policy area and research topic in other countries as well. For decades, this has been the policy spearhead of the American Department of Housing and Urban Development (HUD). It is also the cornerstone of much social scientific research. This attention has led once again to the view that the spatial concentration of poor people leads to the perpetuation of their disadvantaged situation, and, conversely, that mixing the population will lead to a 'positive-sum game'. Opinions vary, however, on the underlying causes of sustained poverty. Generally speaking, there are two explanations. The first states that early on in the socialisation process, 'cultures of poverty' develop and persist through a process of social inheritance originating from the immediate environment, and even within households, from which there is no escape (Lewis, 1966). Wilson (1987) pointed to the absence of sufficient role models in neighbourhoods abandoned by middle-class residents. The second explanation can be called the 'neighbourhood matters' model (Galster & Killen, 1995). Using terms such as the 'geography of opportunity', authors in this tradition argue that the residential environment and the neighbourhood can produce a significant contribution to the development of individuals, and that the neighbourhood can offer greater social opportunities if more 'good examples' are present. Values, aspirations and preferences are all seen as influenced by the neighbourhood.

In the US, such beliefs regarding 'mixed neighbourhoods' have been part of government policy since the 1970s. One of the most well-known policy is the Gautreaux programme set up in the latter half of the 1970s to offer residents of Chicago public housing more opportunities to get ahead in life. Under this programme, black residents of inner-city housing projects could, under certain conditions, receive vouchers that would provide them access to white middle-class suburban areas. Allocation took place randomly: some were relocated to the suburbs, and others went to different inner-city neighbourhoods. This method was attractive to researchers because it provided a clear experiment group and a clear control group. The Gautreaux programme enjoyed relatively positive evaluations. Rosenbaum (1995), for example, found that the children of households moving to mixed dwellings in the suburbs scored better on indicators of high-school completion and college entry, went to better colleges, were less likely to be unemployed, and obtained more prestigious and better-paid jobs compared to city-movers. However, these results can be questioned. The conditions under which the vouchers were issued implied an important pre-selection of candidates: one had to be debt-free, have less than four children, no arrears in rent payment, no history of vandalism, and show no signs of 'unacceptable housekeeping'. Added to this were the effects of self-selection: participation in the programme was on a voluntary basis. Because of this, doubts persist regarding the effect of the programme, even though significant differences could be established between those who moved to the suburbs and those who remained in the cities. Galster & Zobel (1998) reviewed the literature to determine whether the US housing policy targeted at diffusion did indeed lead to a reduction of social problems and found, as stated earlier, little evidence to support this claim—most conclusions found no non-linear effects (see also Johnson *et al.*, 2002).

A more recent programme, and a follow-up of Gautreaux, is the Moving to Opportunity (MTO) programme, a demonstration programme undertaken in five cities. This also offered residents the opportunity to move to a stronger economic environment. Here too, a number of laudatory evaluations were produced (once again, positive effects were found), and, like its predecessor, critics pointed to the high probability of self-selection for households moving to the mixed suburban environments (see e.g. Johnson *et al.*, 2002).

Although European countries vary in welfare-state type and the level of intervention in social processes, various European countries outside of the Netherlands are conducting similar policies directed at population-mixing and 'social balance'. These policies are often part of a wider programme such as the 'area-based initiatives' in the UK (see Kearns, 2002) or the '*politique de la ville*' with its '*contracts de ville*' in France (see Jacquier, 2001). Here too, the realisation of mixed environments or the prevention of 'problem concentrations' play an important role, and here too there is only limited research to support it.

Data

In the analyses, figures were employed that were derived from income tax files by the Dutch Central Bureau of Statistics (CBS). The data, which are from administrative records, were available for 1994 and for 1989. This study had a sample size of approximately 2 million 'key persons' (those who filled in the tax forms), and the other members of their household. The database of 1994 therefore includes data for over 5 million people, about a third of the entire country. After weighting the data, the database could provide a representative picture of the Dutch population. The available data include place of residence (six-digit postcode), income, demographics (age, sex, marital status), background (country of birth, and parents' country of birth) and social status (paid job, pension, unemployed, on disability or welfare benefits or other categories such as housewives/househusbands or children). The people in the database have been followed over time.

It should be underlined that the 1989 data were obtained by using the 1994 sample as a basis, and then looking back to the situation of the key persons in 1989 (comparable data was collected for both years, and data was collected for the other household members in 1989 as well). This made it possible to follow the development of this group of people over the period 1989–94. In addition, this creates an image of the residential situation in 1989, allowing investigation of whether the 1989 environment influenced developments in the 1989–94 period. Of course, this procedure did not produce a representative sample for 1989. But because such a representative sample was not readily available for 1989, it was decided to assume that this method did produce a reasonable picture of the situation in 1989. Because of this, there was no recourse but to use the same weights as in 1994. This has a disadvantage, however: the 1989 key persons were five years older in 1994, as were the others in their household (if the same). The sample generated for 1989 will therefore be almost certainly too young. The consequences of this will be returned to later.

Economic Position of Households

An important decision in the research concerned the size of the units to study. Should the development of individuals or households be looked at? Because the household situation is the most important for people since it is within households that individuals tend to support each other most, it was decided to conduct research at this household level, but relevant characteristics of members of the household were also taken into account.

It was decided to focus attention on the economic position (i.e. employment situation) of a household. The question then becomes whether households that live in an area where many households have a weak economic position run a greater risk of remaining in or falling into a similar state.

In order to answer this question, the data were aggregated to the household level. Three categories were used to describe household economic position. The first category, benefits only, is made up of households that live entirely on benefits: no members have a paid job or retirement pension; all receive unemployment, disability or welfare benefits, or (for housewives/househusbands and children) live with others that do. Households falling into this 'benefits only' category are identified as those with 'a weak economic position' as stated in the research question. The second category, at least pension, comprises households in which nobody has a paid job, but at least one member enjoys an income from a private and/or state pension (AOW) or early retirement (VUT). Households falling into the third category, at least a paid job, have at least one gainfully employed member. This household classification system was used for both 1989 and 1994 data.

Table 1 displays an overview of the economic position of the households for the two years. As with all computations in this study, the weights of the different households were taken into account when calculating the percentages in order to obtain the most accurate picture possible; the absolute numbers of households use non-weighted values. In 1994, about one in eight households lived exclusively on benefits. About a quarter fell into the second (at least pension) category. The great majority of households had at least one paid job.

At first glance, a comparison between the 1989 and 1994 data would seem to indicate a worsening of economic positions in the Netherlands. However,

Table 1. The economic position of households in
1989 and 1994 (%)

	1989	1994
Benefits only	9.4	13.2
At least pension	19.1	23.9
At least a paid job	71.5	62.9
Total	100.0	100.0
Number of households	1 749 387	1 867 958

Source: CBS, Regional Income Survey (RIO) 1994 and 1989;
own computation.

as stated earlier, the 1989 data is probably based on a too-young population. Clearly, the share of households with a pension would be less in this younger sample. The lower percentage of households surviving on benefits in 1989 is also probably a result of the same distortion (younger households are less likely to live only on benefits than older households).

Figure 1 depicts the spatial distribution of 'weak' household concentration in 1994 at the level of three-position postal code areas (presenting a more detailed picture is, due to reasons of privacy, prohibited). Households that live only on benefits are evenly distributed throughout the country; only a small proportion of areas greatly exceed the national average of 9.5 per cent with values of 18 per cent or higher. These areas are also quite varied: some are urban, some rural. The other extreme, in which the percentage of 'benefits only' households is lower than 5.5 per cent (and thus well below the 9.5 per cent national average) is also quite diffuse. These areas exist in both the heavily urbanised West as well as in other parts of the country, and are less pronounced in cities and more in suburban areas.

Social Environment

In this study, the social environment was defined in terms of the households living within a given distance from a single household. To measure this, a circle was drawn around each household, and the economic position of all households within this circle were analysed. Because the interpretation of the results did not markedly differ for different radii (experiments were carried out with 250, 500, 750, 1000, 1500, 2000 and 5000 m.); only the results for areas with a 250-metre radius will be presented (Musterd *et al.*, 2001, p. 33). For social interactions in the residential areas in the Netherlands, this radius fits best.

In order to classify the household environment in 1989, the percentage of all benefits-only households in the area around the household were looked at. To do this, the 1989 sample derived from the 1994 data had to be used, and the same weights for both years were used. As already mentioned, this method produces a somewhat overly optimistic picture for the year 1989 because it is based on a younger population sample. Consequently, the areas surrounding the households also reflected this optimism. However, this did not lead to a systematic distortion, and the possible effect of this is rather small compared to the differences found between the composition of the environments of the

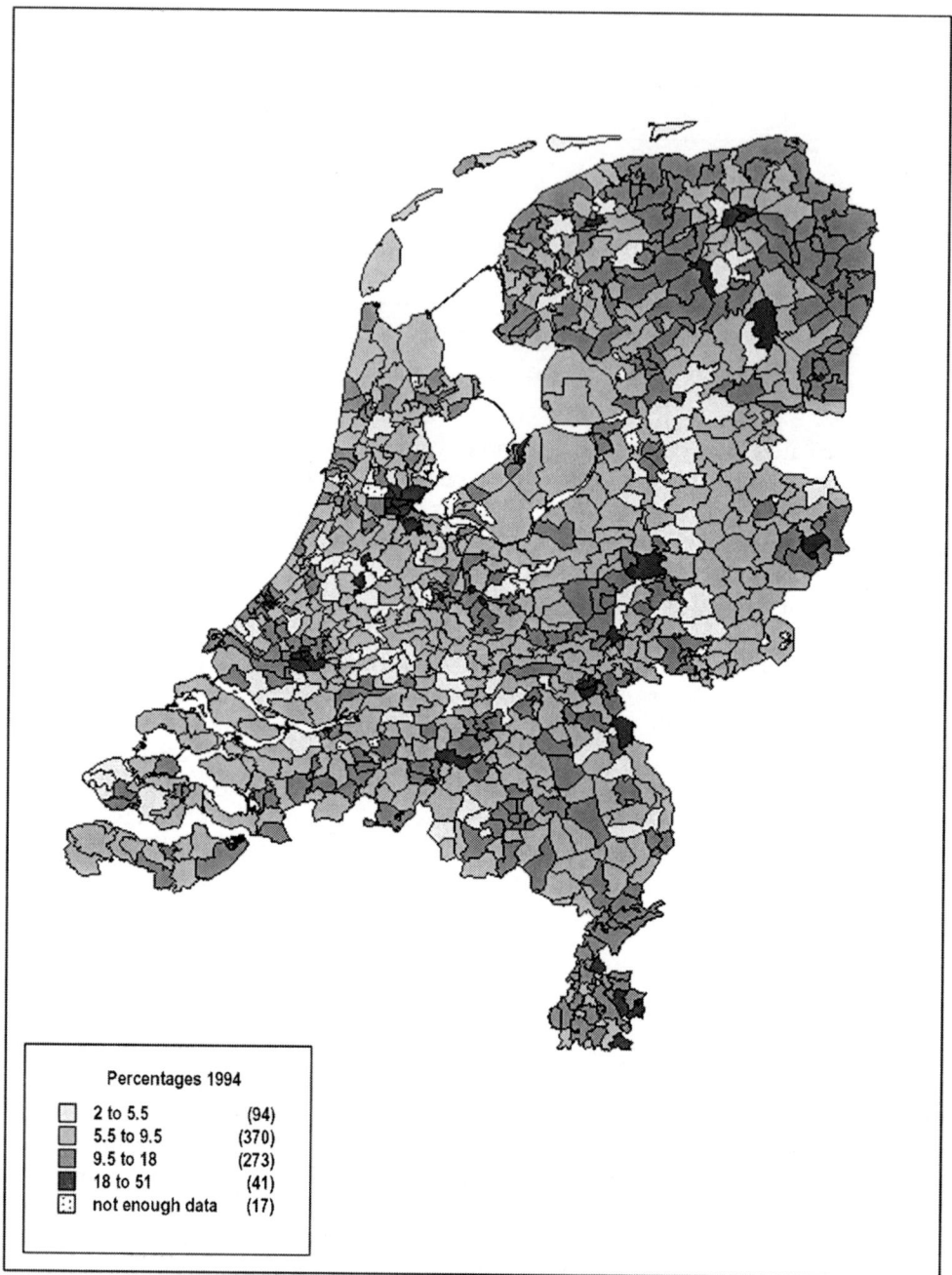

Figure 1. Percentage of households living on benefits in 1994; three-position postal code areas.

various households. It can therefore be assumed that this problem did not significantly impair the comparability of the household environments in 1989.

The goal of the research is to discover whether the residential environment of a household has a bearing on developments the household undergoes.

Table 2. Relationship between economic positions in 1989 and 1994 (%)

1989	1994				
	Benefits only	At least pension	At least a paid job	Relative total	Absolute total
Benefits only	53.3	16.0	30.6	100.0	134 993
At least pension	2.1	94.3	3.6	100.0	247 026
At least a paid job	9.1	8.1	82.7	100.0	1 247 684
Relative total	12.0	25.8	62.1	100.0	
Absolute total	156 661	337 620	1 135 422		1 629 703

Source: CBS, Regional Income Survey (RIO) 1994 and 1989; own computation.

Specifically, the research wanted to find out whether the economic position of a household in 1994 had been influenced by households with a weak economic position living in the vicinity in 1989. There is, however, another thorny issue in using the composition of the environment as an explanatory variable: the environment itself may have changed during the period 1989–94. Naturally, this may occur if the household in question moved house (we will return to this point later). Even if the household did not move, the residential environment may still have changed due to others moving and/or changes in their economic position. Unfortunately, this changing composition of the environment could not be taken into account as an explanatory factor in the analyses. Obviously, data for the composition of the environment in 1994 (the only other available data) could not be used because these figures are partly the result of the influence which the environment in 1989 has had.

Only a limited number of households could be included in the analyses. In order to make the environmental factor reliable enough to use, a sufficient number of other households from the sample had to live within the same area. A standard was established, for the 1989 sample, that at least 100 households must live in the residential environment. Because of this, over one-third of all households could not be included in the analyses.

Results

How did the households fare over the period 1989–94? The answer to this question is given in Table 2. This Table includes all households for which a sound link could be made between the 1989 and 1994 data.

The Table above generates some interesting insights. The continuity is, as may be expected, the greatest in the 'at least pension' category: almost all households remained in the same category over the period 1989–94. This contrasts starkly with benefit-dependent households. Slightly over half of these households remained in this unenviable position. Of those who did manage to escape, some did so by reaching pension age. The share of those who escaped from their benefit situation by finding a paid job is clearly smaller than that continuing to be dependent on benefits. The vast majority of households that had at least a paid job in 1989 also had a job in 1994. Few entered the 'only benefits' category, and even fewer the 'at least pension' category. This movement was much smaller than households entirely dependent on benefits in 1989 because, as mentioned before, members of such households are generally older than those with paid jobs.

Table 3. Benefit-dependent households in 1989 versus their situation in 1994, and the composition of the environment in 1989 within a 250-metre radius

% of 'weak'(benefit dependent) households in the area in 1989	Number of benefit dependent households	1994 situation for all households			1994 situation for all households not in 'at least pension' category
		Only benefits	At least pension	At least paid job	Only benefits
0–2	760	34.7	27.3	38.0	47.7
2–4	3603	42.6	25.5	31.9	57.2
4–6	6751	45.8	22.6	31.6	59.2
6–8	8485	46.8	22.0	31.2	60.0
8–10	9139	48.9	19.3	31.8	60.6
10–12	9212	49.9	18.3	31.8	61.1
12–14	8940	51.1	16.9	32.0	61.5
14–16	8638	51.8	14.7	33.5	60.7
16–20	13 366	53.5	13.4	33.1	61.8
20–30	21 777	57.0	8.8	34.2	62.5
30–40	7 654	60.4	6.0	33.6	64.3
40–50	667	67.4	4.5	28.1	70.6
50–75	380	90.0	7.9	2.0	97.8
75–100	464	96.8	2.9	0.4	99.6
Total	99 836	52.9	14.7	32.4	62.0

Source: CBS, Regional Income Survey (RIO) (1994) and 1989 supplement; own calculation.

How do these economic developments relate to the composition of the neighbourhood? To answer this, various analyses were carried out using data for 'only benefits' households in 1989 and households with at least a paid job in 1989. The other 'at least pension' category was much less interesting.

Benefit-dependent Households

How did life treat households that lived entirely on benefits in 1989? Was their situation in 1994 affected by the composition of their environment in 1989? Table 3 displays the results of the research. This Table only includes households in sufficiently dense environments (i.e. where at least 100 households lived within a 250-metre radius).

For the purposes here, the last column is the most relevant. As stated, escaping benefit dependency simply by reaching pension age can hardly be considered a great achievement. Movement towards this category only obscures things, and has therefore been omitted from the last column. For households subsisting purely from benefits in 1989, the following applies. If they lived in an area in which they comprised only 2 per cent of the population, then 47.7 per cent remained in this situation, while 52.3 per cent had found employment. On the other hand, benefit-dependent households living in an area where at least half of the population faced in a similar situation had very little chance of finding a paid job. In the 50–75 per cent range, almost 98 per cent remained without a job in 1994. Finally, an existence based on benefits appears virtually inescapable above the 75 per cent mark.

It is clear that the chance of finding a paid job is highest in the first row (less than 2 per cent 'weak' households), and lowest in the last two rows (at least 50 per cent). There seem to be two thresholds. The first one, after 2 per cent 'weak' households in the environment, requires further investigation, which is beyond the scope of this paper. The second threshold, after 40–50 per cent weak households in the environment must at least partly be ascribed to the presence of special residential services for the disabled, in these areas. In the most populated ranges, it can be observed that the chance of escaping from benefits does fall as the share of 'weak' households in the area rises, but the difference is much less acute. Moreover, the order is not always consistent. The conclusion can be drawn that the chance of escape is dependent on the environment, but only to a minor extent.

As an aside, it is interesting to note that the movement to the pension category is closely tied to the environment. The greater the proportion of 'weak' households in the area, the fewer households on benefits move to the pension category. Obviously, this cannot be attributed to the environment, because pensions are acquired purely on the basis of age. A possible explanation could be that 'benefits only' households living in areas with many others like themselves tend to be younger than those living in more affluent neighbourhoods. After checking the data, it appears that this is indeed the case: the average age of the 'key persons' gradually decreases as the share of benefit-only households in the area increases; there is approximately a 10-year age difference between the two extremes (0–2 per cent and over 75 per cent).

This finding immediately calls into question the previously drawn conclusion that, for the benefit-dependent households, the environment plays only a minor role in their chances for escape. Here, it can be seen that benefit-only households in more affluent areas are much older than their compatriots in poorer areas. Because it is known that older people, once in a welfare situation, are much less likely to escape, this 'age effect' could be working against a possible environmental effect. If an attempt were made to correct for this, then it would probably show that the environmental effect would become more pronounced.

Households with a Paid Job

Were households with at least one paid job in 1989 affected by their environment? Were they hindered by the existence of less-fortunate households in their immediate area? Table 4 displays the research findings to these questions. It appears as if the relationship between household and environment is surprisingly strong in the transition from the paid-job to the benefits-only category. The larger the share of households with a weak economic position in the area, the greater the probability that the paid job status is lost. The trend is also clearly evident for neighbourhoods in the 4–30 per cent range. There is a slight drop in the 50–75 per cent range, but this was based on a small sample size. There seems to be a threshold at the level of environments where at least 20 per cent of the population is benefit dependent. The chance to experience downward social mobility increases significantly after the 20 per cent barrier.

From this data it appears that 'at least a paid job' households in 1989 living in 'bad neighbourhoods' ran a much greater risk of losing their job and becoming dependent on benefits than those in 'good neighbourhoods'. This finding might have something to do with the number of household members

Table 4. Households with a paid job in 1989 versus their situation in 1994, and the composition of the environment in 1989 within a 250-metre radius

% of 'weak' households in the area in 1989	Number of households	1994 situation for all households			1994 situation for all households not in 'at least pension' category
		Only benefits	At least pension	At least paid job	Only benefits
0–2	61603	5.6	7.1	87.4	6.0
2–4	112 071	6.4	7.8	85.8	7.0
4–6	121 544	7.2	7.9	84.9	7.9
6–8	107 966	8.2	8.1	83.8	8.9
8–10	86 573	9.4	8.1	82.5	10.2
10–12	69 301	10.4	8.2	81.4	11.3
12–14	53 045	11.4	7.9	80.7	12.4
14–16	41 713	12.4	8.1	79.5	13.5
16–20	53 510	13.6	7.7	78.7	14.7
20–30	57 997	17.8	6.1	76.1	19.0
30–40	13 583	23.5	4.7	71.8	24.7
40–50	762	23.3	4.7	72.0	24.5
50–75	217	19.6	11.3	69.0	22.1
75–100	90	35.5	0.0	64.5	35.5
Total	779 975	9.9	7.7	82.4	10.8

Source: CBS, Regional Income Survey (RIO) (1994) and 1989 supplement; own calculations.

that had a paid job—the larger the household, the greater the chance that at least one might keep a job. The data bear this out: the average number of employed household members falls steadily from 1.86 in environments with less than 2 per cent 'weak' households, to 1.48 in 75 per cent-and-over areas. Similarly, the percentage of single person households increases for the households under investigation from 4 per cent to 39 per cent. If these factors are taken into account, then the environmental effects become somewhat weaker.

Other Influences on Social Mobility

The findings seem to point to the existence of environmental effects. On the other hand, these effects could possibly be either caused or inhibited by other household attributes. In the discussion of Table 3, the importance of age was indicated; if this is corrected for, the environmental effect is enhanced somewhat. In the discussion of Table 4, the role that the number of household members with a job can play was mentioned, and the special case of single person households; if this is corrected for, the environmental effect is actually lessened.

There are other factors that could influence the results, such as level of education. People in poor neighbourhoods may be less educated, and therefore more prone to losing a job and becoming dependent on benefits. Density may also play a role. Assumptions are often made regarding levels of density and

Table 5. Various households in 1989 versus their situation in 1994

Household type in 1989	Number of households	1994 situation for all households			1994 situation for all households not in 'at least pension' category
		Benefits only	At least pension	At least paid job	Benefits only
Benefits only:					
All	134 993	53.3	16.0	30.6	63.5
Urban	32 645	56.0	11.5	32.4	63.3
Single person	34 967	68.9	16.0	15.1	82.0
Non-movers	86 850	56.6	19.6	23.9	70.3
At least a paid job:					
All	1 247 684	9.1	8.1	82.7	9.9
Urban	119 670	15.2	8.2	76.6	16.6
Single person	54 823	14.7	9.4	75.9	16.2
Non-movers	802 068	7.5	10.6	81.9	8.4

Source: CBS, Regional Income Survey (RIO) (1994) and 1989 supplement; own calculations.

disadvantaged persons. In a multicultural nation like the Netherlands, this may also relate to the specific ethnicities of households. It would also be interesting to observe whether a household had moved because those remaining would have been exposed to the environment for the entire period 1989–94.

In order to explore some of these issues, Table 5 traces the development of the groups just mentioned for the period 1989–94.

First, there will be a look at the households that found themselves dependent on benefits in 1989. If the movement to the pension category is disregarded, then it appears that single person households have an especially difficult time escaping from benefits: over 80 per cent remain on benefits. This is understandable since only one person in such households could solve the problem. Households that did not move also scored less favourably than those who did. This is also not surprising. Moving house is sometimes the result of finding a job elsewhere, and also may indicate initiative. In other words, spatial mobility (moving) and social mobility (being hired) are often linked. Finally, urban households (that is, households residing in one of the three largest Dutch cities: Amsterdam, Rotterdam and The Hague) have a 'normal' chance of escaping benefits. This is noteworthy considering that cities contain relatively high numbers of single person households. Because of this, it would be expected that big-city residents would be more likely to remain in a benefit-only situation. This finding is also interesting since discussions about disadvantage and environmental effects are generally directed at the situation in cities, as epitomised by the Dutch Big Cities Policy. A lower chance of escape would be expected for urban residents. On the other hand, cities also contain many young and dynamic households, and these may have served to restore the balance.

If households that had at least a paid job in 1989 are examined, then it is principally the urban and single person households that ran a high risk of losing this position. This is quite logical for single person households—the chance of losing all the jobs in the household increases as the number of members decreases. The households that did not move seem, in this case, to fare slightly better than households that did.

In order to determine whether the environmental effects found can be 'explained' by these other factors, several additional analyses were performed. Some of this concerns the analyses for the urban, single person households and non-moving groups. For households that lived entirely on benefits in 1989, the environmental effect becomes somewhat weaker if the urban and single person households are looked at (there is no change in environmental effect for non-moving households, and combinations of groups do not yield any new insights). For households with a job in 1989, the environmental effect is clearly perceptible for urban and non-moving households, and somewhat weaker for single person households.

Separate analyses, somewhat hampered by missing data, for the most important ethnic minority groups in the Netherlands (Surinamese and Antillean on the one hand, and Turk and Moroccan on the other) gave no evidence that environmental effects for these groups are any different than for others in the Netherlands. The role of education cannot be directly established because this piece of information is not collected in the same data. Still, cross-checking this at the aggregate level with data from the national housing-demand study (WBO) gives the impression that education offers only a marginal alternative explanation to the environmental effects found.

There are some final statements to be made about the role of age. It has already been noted that the environmental effect for benefit-dependent households in 1989 is somewhat more pronounced if a correction is made for age. This notwithstanding, the relationship is stronger for households with at least a paid job, even when a correction is made for age. This is true for all households together, but especially if only urban households are looked at. It is most powerful for single person urban households.

Conclusions

This study made a distinction between households that lived entirely on benefits in 1989 and households that had at least one paid job in this same year. The latter group experienced the most significant environmental effect. For these households, the chance of falling into a situation where they must depend on benefits for their livelihood rises in proportion to the share of economically disadvantaged households in their immediate area. For the first group, households subsisting entirely on benefits in 1989, the environmental effect was manifest as well, but less outspoken. When categories like urban dwellers and especially single person households are examined, the results for 1989 benefits-only households point to a weak environmental effect; the effect was much stronger for household types with a paid job in 1989.

These findings are remarkable. The literature that addresses the link between environment and social mobility is generally more oriented towards people who already find themselves in a disadvantaged position (i.e. are unemployed or on disability or welfare benefits) than those who are gainfully employed. Those with paid jobs surely experience positive stimulation by operating within a working milieu and profit from being on a working-day schedule and socialising with other employed people. Those caught in the benefit system do not have these advantages and moreover have more time to become exposed to the negative inputs emanating from their environment. Unemployment itself can be seen as a negative factor—some argue that joblessness is the biggest cause of unemployment, and that it is imperative that these people find work as quickly as possible. Employed people, in contrast, do not experience these negative effects of being unemployed. This could translate itself into a heightened environmental effect, because they are less desensitised to the negative inputs from their surroundings. Another plausible explanation gives credit to state intervention. Dutch poverty-aimed policies are fairly universal, but also more selective so-called area-based policies are applied. It may be hypothesised that, as an outcome of these policies, poor people in poor neighbourhoods who are regarded to be in need of support, especially the long-term unemployed, will receive more attention from the welfare state than less poor people, such as those who have had a job, but have recently become unemployed. That would imply that a neighbourhood effect would exist both for the clearly poor (long-term unemployed) and for the less poor (formerly employed, but recently unemployed), but that this effect is neutralised for the clearly poor by welfare state interventions, whereas this effect is not neutralised for the less poor. The latter have to take care of their own until they actually get into serious trouble.

When the environmental effects in the Dutch context are discussed (e.g. the Big Cities Policy), attention is much more focused on those with a weak economic profile than people for whom this does not (yet) apply. The same applies to the idea of promoting mixed neighbourhoods. It seems that people think that environmental effects only concern the disadvantaged. The results of this study, however, suggest that both groups can be influenced by their environment, and, more surprisingly, that the environment effect is actually stronger for those who do not (yet) find themselves in the most disadvantaged position. If that were true, there would be huge policy implications. From an efficiency point of view, mixed neighbourhood policies should be stopped.

Acknowledgements

The authors are grateful to George Galster for his stimulating support and to three anonymous referees for their comments on earlier versions of this paper.

Correspondence

Sako Musterd, Department of Geography and Planning, University of Amsterdam, Nieuwe Prinsengracht 130, 1018 VZ Amsterdam, the Netherlands. Email: s.musterd@frw.uva.nl

References

Amsterdam complete stad (1999) Stadsvisie tot 2010. Stadsvisie en Meerjarenontwikkelingsprogramma's Grotestedenbeleid (Amsterdam, Bureau Grotestedenbeleid).

Atkinson, R. & Kintrea, K. (2001) Disentangling area effects: evidence from deprived and non-deprived neighbourhoods, *Urban Studies*, 38, pp. 2277–2298.

Buit, J. (1977) Over ruimtelijke ongelijkheid en stadsvernieuwing; enkele kanttekeningen, *Stedebouw & Volkshuisvesting*, pp. 611–618.

Buys, A. (1997) *De ideale mix?* Een verkenning van visies, feiten en verwachtingen ten aanzien van de bevolkingssamenstelling van buurten en wijken (assisted by M. de Groot & D. Hoogewoud) (Amsterdam, RIGO).

De gedifferentieerde stad (1996) Gezamenlijke rapportage van de vier grote steden en het Rijk (Zoetermeer, Ministerie VROM).

Duivesteijn, A. (1996) De stad als spiegel van de samenleving, *Woningraad Magazine*, 3, pp. 33–40.

Galster, G. (2002) Trans-Atlantic perspectives on opportunity, deprivation and the housing nexus, *Housing Studies*, 17, pp. 5–12.

Galster, G. & Killen, S. (1995) The geography of metropolitan opportunity: a reconnaissance and conceptual framework, *Housing Policy Debate*, 6, pp. 7–44.

Galster, G. & Zobel, A. (1998) Will dispersed housing programmes reduce social problems in the US? *Housing Studies*, 13, pp. 605–622.

Jacquier, C. (2001) Urban fragmentation and revitalization policies in France: a new urban governance in the making, in: H. T. Andersen & R. Van Kempen (Eds) *Governing European Cities. Social Fragmentation, Social Exclusion and Urban Governance* (Aldershot, Ashgate).

Johnson, M. P., Ladd, H. F. & Ludwig, J. (2002) The benefits and costs of residential mobility programs for the poor, *Housing Studies*, 17, pp. 125–138.

Kearns, A. (2002) Response: from residential disadvantage to opportunity? Reflections on British and European policy and research, *Housing Studies*, 17, pp. 145–150.

Lewis, O. (1986) The culture of poverty, in: R. T. LeGates & F. Stout (Eds) *The City Reader* (London/New York, Routledge).

Musterd, S. (2002) Response: mixed housing policy: a European (Dutch) perspective, *Housing Studies*, 17, pp. 139–143.

Musterd, S. & Ostendorf, W. (1995) *Grote steden: maatschappelijke dynamiek en ruimtelijke segregatie; een beknopt literatuuroverzicht* (Amsterdam, AME-Universiteit van Amsterdam).

Musterd, S., Priemus, H. & Van Kempen, R. (1999) Towards undivided cities: the potential of economic revitalisation and housing redifferentiation, *Housing Studies*, 14, pp. 573–584.

Musterd, S., Ostendorf, W. & de Vos, S. (2001) *Armoedeconcentraties en sociale effecten in dynamisch perspectief* (Amsterdam, Universiteit van Amsterdam, AME).

Mensen, Wensen, Wonen; Wonen in de 21ᵉ eeuw (2000) Nota Wonen (Den Haag, Ministerie van Volkshuisvesting, Ruimtelijke Ordening en Milieubeheer).

Nota Stedelijke Vernieuwing [Report on Urban Renewal] (1997) (Den Haag, VROM/Projectgroep Herijking BELSTATO).

Ostendorf, W. & Musterd, S. (1997) *Maatschappelijke bezorgdheid over sociale segregatie RMO-advies Kwaliteit van de buurt* (Den Haag, Sdu uitgevers).

Ostendorf, W., Musterd, S. & Vos, S de (2001) Social mix and the neighbourhood effect. Policy ambitions and empirical evidence, *Housing Studies*, 16, pp. 371–380.

Rosenbaum, J. E. (1995) Housing mobility strategies for changing the geography of opportunity, *Housing Policy Debate*, 6, pp. 231–270.

Sampson, R. J., Morenoff, J. D. & Gannon-Rowley, T. (2002) Assessing 'neighbourhood effects': social processes and new directions in research, *Annual Review of Sociology*, 28, pp. 443–478.

Van Kempen, R., Teule, R. B. J. & Van Weesep, J. (1991) Volkshuisvestingsbeleid in de jaren negentig: perspectieven voor lage inkomens, in: R. Van Kempen, S. Musterd & W. Ostendorf (Eds) *Maatschappelijke verandering en stedelijke dynamiek* (Delft, Delftse Univeritaire Pers).

VROMraad (1999) *Stad en Wijk: verschillen maken kwaliteit*, Advies 013 (Den Haag).

Wilson, W. J. (1987) *The Truly Disadvantaged, The Inner City, The Underclass and Public Policy* (Chicago, University of Chicago Press).

Investigating Behavioural Impacts of Poor Neighbourhoods: Towards New Data and Analytic Strategies

GEORGE GALSTER

Wayne State University, Detroit, USA

[Paper first received 10 December 2002; in final form 1 April 2003]

ABSTRACT *Three challenges confront statistical researchers of neighbourhood impacts on individual behaviours: (1) operationalising 'neighbourhood processes'; (2) potentially non-linear relationships between neighbourhood characteristics and outcomes; and (3) the selection bias problem. To better comprehend these challenges and overcome them, the paper proposes an overarching conceptual framework wherein outcomes of interest are affected by neighbourhood interacting in a mutually causal fashion with housing tenure, housing wealth, household socio-economic status, and mobility behaviour. It advances a five-equation, simultaneous system for home ownership, mobility expectations, housing wealth, household socio-economic status and neighbourhood character. Although current US census data do not provide perfect proxies for neighbourhood processes, there is evidence that a battery of them could represent reasonable operationalisations. Tests for non-linearity could be conducted in this framework. This model could use a sufficiently robust set of instrumental variables to overcome the issue of neighbourhood selection bias, and thereby produce considerably more precise estimates of neighbourhood impacts on individual outcomes of interest. Implications for qualitative research approaches also are drawn.*

KEY WORDS: neighbourhoods, behavioural impacts, non-linearities, thresholds, selection

Introduction

The empirical investigation of the behavioural and psychological impacts of poor or otherwise disadvantaged neighbourhoods on their residents has assumed many methodological guises, aptly represented by papers from European scholars appearing above in this Special Issue of *Housing Studies*. Each approach offers its own strengths and weaknesses (in particular, see Duncan *et al.*, 1997, Duncan & Raudenbush, 1999; Haveman & Wolfe, 1995; Manski, 1993, 1995, 2000; Sampson *et al.*, 2002). Instead of critiquing these individually, this paper offers an overarching set of suggestions for how this field of inquiry may be advanced on both sides of the Atlantic through multivariate statistical modelling based on longitudinal databases containing observations of individuals or households.

There are three central challenges confronting statistical researchers of neighbourhood impacts on individual behaviours: (1) operationalising 'neighbourhood processes'; (2) non-linear relationships between neighbourhood characteristics and behavioural outcomes; and (3) the selection bias problem. To comprehend better these challenges and overcome them, a general conceptual framework is proposed in this paper. The framework suggests that the impact of neighbourhood cannot be seen independently from that of household tenure and mobility decisions. After this framework, an econometric model for quantifying neighbourhood impacts that overcomes these three challenges is presented. Although the discussion will focus on measuring the behavioural impacts of poor neighbourhoods on children and adolescents, much of the analysis may also be applied to adults.

Throughout the paper an attempt is made to bring to bear methodological discussions emanating from a variety of disciplines. There is also a move beyond the traditional realm of housing researchers to tap insights produced by the 'social interactions' literature, much of which is never framed in a spatial, let alone housing, context. Although this material is presented in the most accessible fashion that is feasible, it is a fact that much of this material is technically challenging. It is hoped that the readership of *Housing Studies* may find a 'user-friendly' introduction here, which serves as a motivator for deeper explorations of the literature cited.

A Framework for Comprehending the Impacts of Poor Neighbourhoods

The thesis in this paper is straightforward: to advance the investigation of the impact of local neighbourhood on a variety of human outcomes, one must comprehend in as holistic a fashion as possible all the factors that contribute significantly to the outcome in question, and the causal interrelationships among these various factors. Unfortunately, extant literature has fallen short in this arena (cf. recent reviews by Earls & Carlson, 2001; Leventhal & Brooks-Gunn, 2000; Robert, 1999; Sampson *et al.*, 2002).

A Holistic Framework

Figure 1 portrays a structural model. Outcomes of interest are determined by three sets of exogenous or predetermined variables: characteristics of individuals (e.g. gender, race), observed parental characteristics (e.g. education, age), and unobserved parental characteristics (e.g. ambition, morality). They are also influenced by a set of parental characteristics that may more properly be modelled as endogenous to the residential context (e.g. parental work history, marital status). The key contribution of this model is the specification of neighbourhood/tenure/mobility expectations/housing wealth/household socio-economic status as *simultaneously* determined. The rationale follows in brief.

- Tenure and neighbourhood selections are *simultaneously* determined: if economic status constrains a household to a set of 'affordable' neighbourhoods, but in all these there is much social instability/problems and concomitant expectations of property value deflation, there will be little motivation to buy; if a household would like to buy, certain neighbourhoods may not be selected if they hold little prospect for property appreciation. Admittedly, this scenario is

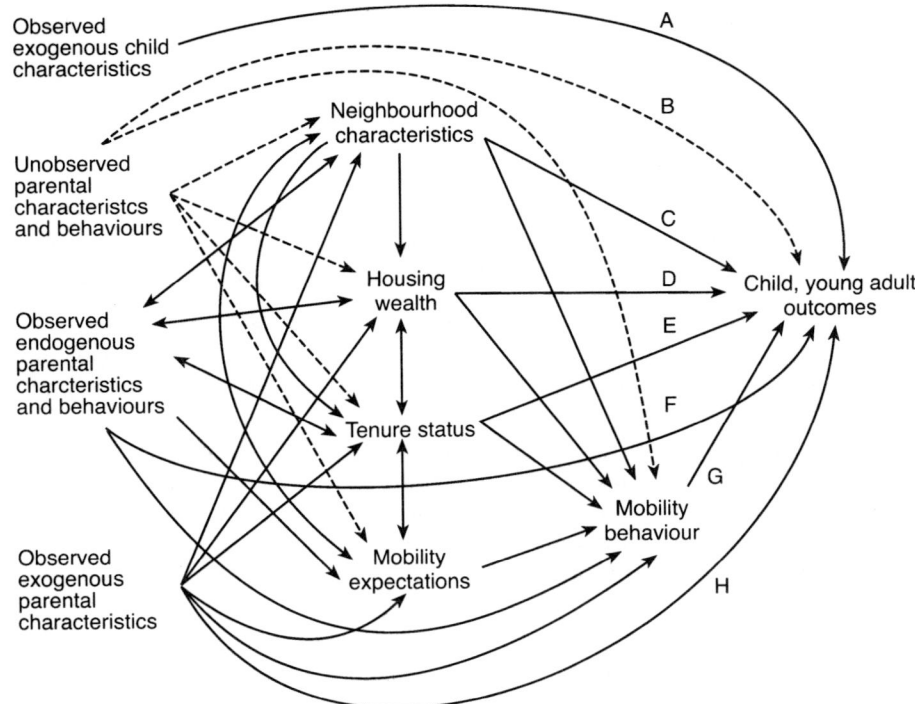

Figure 1. A structural model of neighbourhood and child and young adult outcomes.

formulated with a market-dominated housing context in mind. Sako Musterd has noted that in European contexts of stricter market regulations, 'emergency buyers' may exist who have low socio-economic status yet are virtually compelled to purchase low-quality units in undesirable neighbourhoods. This can occur when strong housing demands and limited vacancies in the social rented stock produce a shortage of affordable private rental units (Kesteloot, 1998).

- Tenure and neighbourhood *and* mobility expectations (expected duration of stay) are also *simultaneously* determined: if you expect to remain long in a home/city, given your employment and life-cycle stage situation, you may be more likely to bear the high transactions costs of buying; *and* you will try harder to avoid weak/declining neighbourhoods; in turn, if you can purchase a home, and succeed in doing so in a good neighbourhood, you will probably expect to move less in the future.

- Parental wealth is another endogenous variable: non-housing wealth will affect the down-payment constraint and thus affect the ability to become a first-time home owner; once a home owner the combination of housing and non-housing wealth will affect one's ability to remain so; neighbourhood characteristics may affect inter-temporal changes in housing wealth of home owners through externality effects and the identification of submarkets wherein intra-metropolitan home appreciation rates will differ

It is recognised that the addition of housing tenure and mobility behaviour as key determinants of behavioural outcomes is somewhat unconventional, so further evidence is provided below.

Housing Tenure, Residential Stability and Child Outcomes

The literature suggests several causal mechanisms, direct and indirect, through which parental tenure may affect a variety of outcomes for children living in the home. Some are posited to have direct affects on children's residential environments that could affect, in turn, a variety of outcomes (path D in Figure 1):

- Housing maintenance and repairs: evidence has shown that home owners maintain their dwellings to higher standards than otherwise identical households who are renting (Galster, 1983, 1987; Mayer, 1981), which may affect differentially the health of resident children.
- Home owners may acquire a distinctive set of skills, such as those related to do-it-yourself home repairs, negotiating with contractors, plumbers, etc., seeking refinancing. Insofar as these may be transferable to children, the latter will benefit (Boehm & Schlottmann, 1999; Green & White, 1997).
- Home owners may have more financial stake in the occupied residence, and thus more motivation to monitor and control activities of children (both their own as well as neighbour's) that might threaten the neighbourhood's property value (Haurin *et al.*, 2002b, c)

Although it is not possible to distinguish among the above hypotheses, Haurin *et al.* (2002b, c) provide empirical support to the net relationship. They find that home ownership is positively related to both indices of the cognitive/stimulative and emotional/supportive dimensions of the home environment, in a well-controlled, treatment-effects model. These two indices, in turn, prove strongly predictive of children's maths and reading test scores and an index of children's behavioural problems. Moreover, home ownership still proves significant in predicting test scores (although not behaviours) when these home environment indices (and other parental and neighbourhood characteristics) are controlled. Most effects on children cited in the literature, however, putatively transpire indirectly through tenure's affect on residential stability (path E in Figure 1) and wealth (path C).

The argument regarding stability proceeds as follows. Due to the high transactions costs of home sale and purchase (Haurin *et al.*, 1988), owners typically reside in any given unit longer than renters (Lee *et al.*, 1994; Rohe & Stewart, 1996). In turn, this enhanced stability can have two impacts on children. First, home owners will be more willing to invest in building positive relationships and helping networks (i.e. 'social capital') among neighbours. This claim is supported by a series of empirical observations: home owners are more likely than renters to participate in local political activities (Rossi & Weber, 1996), informal social participation (Hunter, 1975; Jeffers & Dobos, 1984), and commitment to neighbourhood (Austin & Baba, 1990). Such greater social capital among home owners may assist them in raising their children in a variety of ways, from material support in time of emergency to informal monitoring and control of their children's activities by neighbours (Coleman, 1988, 1990). Second, as children remain longer in a neighbourhood they are likely to become better known to other adults in the neighbourhood, thus rendering them more subject to behavioural limitations through neighbours' 'collective efficacy' (Sampson *et al.*, 1999). There is consistent empirical support for the claim that a large part of the observed positive impacts of home ownership on children transpires indirectly through its effect on residential stability (Aaronson, 2000; Harkness & Newman, 2002)

As for wealth, the conventional argument is that home owners will increase their equity position through the appreciation of their housing asset, a financial option unavailable to renters. Were this true, home owners would then be able to invest more in the educational and nurturing aspects of the children's environment, thereby improving various outcome measures. Of course, the presumption of this argument is that, by purchasing a home, a household makes a superior financial investment choice. This presumption clearly is violated in certain neighbourhoods and in certain metropolitan areas during particular periods, and it may be questioned for the nation as a whole for an extended period (Nesslein, 2000). Unfortunately, Green & White (1997), Boehm & Schlottmann (1999), and Harkness & Newman (2002) did not control for wealth. Interestingly, Haurin *et al.* (2002b, c) find that wealth was unrelated to either cognitive or emotional dimensions of the home environment, children's maths and reading test scores or an index of children's behavioural problems, controlling for tenure and other parental characteristics.

Challenge 1: Operationalising 'Neighbourhood Processes'

The first issue is what to measure regarding neighbourhood processes that is posited have behavioural impacts. The question may be put, how is it that neighbourhood effects transpire and how can these processes be adequately measured (Raudenbush & Sampson 1999)? A reading of the literature suggests that: (1) both the 'bad' and the 'good' aspects of the neighbourhood need to be included in predicting most outcomes, and (2) different aspects predict different outcomes. On the first point, the 1997 Russell Sage neighbourhood-effects book edited by Brooks-Gunn *et al.* seem particularly compelling. They argue that some measure of the presence of 'high risk' neighbours is important, where 'risk' is typically operationalised as poverty, single-parent households, idleness among adults, welfare receipt. So, too, are measures of a conceptually distinct effect: the absence or presence of more affluent, middle-class neighbours who may serve as role models and provide financial and social stability to the neighbourhood, operationalised as adults with college degrees or adults in 'middle-class' occupations. On the second point, the evidence suggests some provocative correlations between different socio-economic-demographic characteristics of census tracts (homogeneous areas of roughly 4000 inhabitants, available from the US decennial census) and a variety of outcomes of interest (Gephart, 1997; Sampson *et al.*, 2002).

But, presumably, these tract-level indicators are serving as proxies for underlying processes associated with the neighbourhood. Is there any evidence that this is the case? Two distinct sorts of processes, intra-neighbourhood and extra-neighbourhood, may be usefully identified (Sako Musterd noted this observation). The first relates to social processes occurring amongst residents of the neighbourhood (Friedrichs, 1998; Raudenbush & Sampson, 1999). The second relates to the (perhaps erroneous) perceptions and attitudes that key actors located outside the neighbourhood have about conditions within it.

Potential Proxies for Intra-neighbourhood Social Processes

There are several studies that find strong evidence that US census tract-level socio-economic and demographic indicators (often collapsed into factor indices) are strongly related to various intra-neighbourhood social processes, networks, and subjective impressions held by neighbours, as measured by surveys of residents. Put differently, the neighbourhood is not necessarily the dominant arena for social interaction for all groups; the ecological correlations discussed below are consistent with this observation. However, the studies are not perfectly consistent, and suggest that tract-level socio-economic-demographic indicators are, at best, imperfect proxies (Sampson *et al.*, 2002).

Sampson *et al.* (1997) interviewed residents in 343 Chicago 'neighbourhood clusters' composed of about 8000 people each. They developed multi-item scales of 'informal social control' and 'social cohesion and trust', which they found so highly correlated that they could be combined into a single index of 'collective efficacy'. The collective efficacy index was, in turn, regressed on three composite factor-score indexes based on aggregate, census data for the neighbourhoods: 'concentrated disadvantage', 'immigrant concentration' and 'residential stability'. The authors find that all were highly statistically significant predictors of collective efficacy (stability was positively correlated). All three aggregate level indicators also proved strongly correlated with residents' perceptions of neighbourhood violence, and in Sampson (1997) the level of youth delinquency.

A companion study related these same three neighbourhood factors to three different aspects of social organisation within the neighbourhood, using a sample of 238 British communities (Sampson & Groves, 1989). They found that: neighbourhood residential stability was directly related to local friendship networks, neighbourhood socio-economic status was inversely related to unsupervised peer groups and directly related to organisational participation, and neighbourhood ethnic heterogeneity was directly related to unsupervised peer groups.

In related work, Sampson *et al.* (1999) statistically relate three dimensions of social capital for children's well-being to 1990 census tract information:

- 'intergenerational closure' (degree to which adults and children in community are linked)
- 'reciprocated exchange' (intensity of inter-family and -adult interaction with respect to child rearing)
- 'expectations for informal social control of children' (whether adults expect each other to intervene on behalf of children)

Both the first two were strongly related to neighbourhood stability and concentrated affluence, not concentrated poverty; the last was negatively related to concentrated poverty.

Cook *et al.* (1997) conducted interviews with parents in 137 census tracts in Prince George's County, MD, and their 11–15 year-old children in their local middle schools. A comprehensive array of subjective multi-item scales related to 'social process' were developed from these surveys, ranging from social control and cohesion, to neighbourhood resources, satisfaction and participation rates; they were aggregated to the tract level. These scales were then analysed in light of 10 census tract variables. They found that they were able to use tract demographic variables to predict "very high percentages of the neighbourhood-level variation in social process" (pp. 109–110). Correlations among the neighbourhood social process variables and the tract demographics averaged 0.37. The combination of percentage white (or black), median income, and percentage in professional–technical occupations alone produced a multiple R of 0.77 when predicting variation in a global neighbourhood social process measure. Their principal components analysis resulted in one dominant factor, wherein virtually all the social process and tract demographic variables loaded heavily. They conclude that they "do not find clear demarcation into process and demographic factors" (p. 113).

Elliott *et al.* (1996) gathered statistical and interview information from neighbourhoods in Chicago and Denver. From aggregating parents' responses about their neighbourhoods they created three measures of neighbourhood organisation: informal control, social integration and informal networks. Interviews with youths in these areas produced three constructs related to their outcomes: 'pro-social competence' (personal efficacy, educational performance, activities and expectations, commitment to conventionality); 'conventional friends' (proportions of friends who are pro-social, and proportion who are delinquents); 'problem behaviours' (variety of criminal behaviours and drug usage types). They found that tract-level factor-score 'neighbourhood disadvantage' reduced informal control in both sites, reduced social integration in Denver, but was unrelated to informal social networks in either site. The impact of neighbourhood disadvantage on all three youth outcomes was largely mediated by informal control in both sites, but there was a significant direct path nevertheless.

Coulton *et al.* (1999) interviewed parents in 20 different block groups in Cleveland and derived neighbourhood-level subjective measures of neighbourhood quality, facilities, disorder and control over children. These were then correlated with three factor-analyzed objective indices of neighbourhood structure: impoverishment, child care burden and residential instability. Only two pairs of measures (out of a possible 12) proved statistically significantly related: perceived quality and neighbourhood impoverishment score and perceived disorder and neighbourhood impoverishment score.

Kohen (forthcoming) examined a national sample of Canadian youth and their neighbourhoods during the 1990s. They found that the neighbourhood statistical variables: percent poor, percent affluent and percent female heads all correlated to a significant degree (rho in absolute value between 0.24–0.30) with respondents' subjective assessments of social disorder. The neighbourhood percent poor was correlated with the subjective assessment of social cohesion at 0.21.

Potential Proxies for Extra-neighbourhood Processes

Individuals' behaviours may not only be affected by social processes in which they engage within the neighbourhood, but also by the constraints imposed by key actors who do not reside in the given neighbourhood but may, nevertheless, form strong perceptions and attitudes regarding the place and those who reside there. These key actors include potential employers, financial institutions and other groups controlling access to markets and other resources.

Were, for example, potential employers to stigmatise residents of a particular neighbourhood (perhaps due to their perceptions of unproductive social norms or poor-quality local schools), these residents might well come to believe that their options for good-paying jobs were extremely limited. They may choose, as a result, different 'career paths' involving welfare dependency, criminal activities or substance abuse. This relationship between behaviours and perceptions of spatially variant opportunities arising both from within and outside the neighbourhood is at the heart of the 'metropolitan opportunity structure' theory developed by Galster & Killen (1995).

Unfortunately, in contrast to intra-neighbourhood social processes, there is little to suggest appropriate measures of such extra-neighbourhood processes. As far as is known, no study has attempted to statistically relate perceptions of key actors about neighbourhoods to socio-economic or demographic indicators measured in those places.

Conclusions about Proxies for Neighbourhood Processes

US evidence suggests that readily available, census tract data on socio-economic and demographic composition may serve as reasonable operationalisations of intra-neighbourhood social processes, although a wide range of such variables should be used, and the set varies depending on the outcome in question being modelled. However, these indicators are imperfect measures, so there remains a crucial need for future research efforts to measure such social process variables directly (Friedrichs, 1998; Gephart, 1997; Raudenbush & Sampson, 1999; Sampson *et al.*, 2002). Besides those noted above, measures of institutional resources, organisational participation, collective supervision of youth, clarity and consensus regarding group norms, intra- and extra-neighbourhood social networks for adults and children, are especially salient. In addition, much more needs to be done to measure perceptions held by external actors that may affect opportunities of neighbourhood residents and, thereby, their behaviours.

Challenge 2: Non-linear Neighbourhood Impacts

A second challenge confronting neighbourhood impact research is ascertaining whether the effects of any particular facet of the residential environment are linear across the range of variation in that facet. There are ample theoretical reasons to believe that it is not. This section first discusses the theoretical bases for non-linear neighbourhood effects, then addresses the central statistical and policy issues that make this question more than of academic interest.

Theoretical Bases for Non-linear Neighbourhood Effects

There are three distinct, not mutually exclusive, behavioural mechanisms suggested by extant theory through which a non-linear, threshold-like relationship between neighbourhood characteristics and individual outcomes measured as continuous variables may be produced: collective socialisation, contagion and gaming. The first two rely upon collective actions and social intercourse to create thresholds; the other involves more atomistic attitudes and behaviours. There is also another source of non-linearity that inherently arises when considering individual outcomes that are measured in discrete, dichotomous terms. Consider each.

Collective socialisation theories focus on the role that social groups exert on shaping an individual's attitudes, values and behaviours (e.g. Simmel, 1971,

Weber, 1978). Such an effect can occur to the degree that: (1) the individual comes in social contact with the group, and (2) the group can exert more powerful threats or inducement to conform to its positions than competing groups. These two preconditions may involve the existence of a threshold. Given the importance of interpersonal contact in enforcing conformity, if the individuals constituting the group in question were scattered innocuously over urban space, they would be less likely to be able either to convey their positions effectively to others with whom they might come in contact or to exert much pressure to conform. It is only when a group reaches some critical mass of density or power over a predefined area that it is likely to become effective in shaping the behaviours of others. Past this threshold, as more members are recruited, the group's power to sanction non-conformists probably grows non-linearly. This is especially likely when the position of the group becomes so dominant as to become normative in the area. More modern sociological treatises closely related to collective socialisation also suggest thresholds, such as Wilson's (1987) contention that as a critical mass of middle class families leave the inner-city, low-income blacks left behind become isolated from the positive role models that the erstwhile dominant class offered. Economists also have developed several mathematical treatises involving collective socialisation effects in which thresholds often emerge as solutions to complex decision problems under certain assumptions (Akerlof, 1980; Galster, 1987, ch. 3; Brock & Durlauf, 2001).

The basic tenet of contagion models is that if decision makers live in a community where some of their neighbours exhibit non-normative behaviours, they will be more likely to adopt these behaviours themselves. In this way, social problems are believed to be contagious, spread through peer influence. Crane (1991) proposes a formal contagion model to explain the incidence and spread of social problems. He contends that the key implication of the contagion model is that there may be critical levels of incidence of social problems in neighbourhoods. He states that if "the incidence of problems stays below a critical point, the frequency or prevalence of the problem tends to gravitate toward some relatively low-level equilibrium. But if the incidence surpasses a critical point, the process will spread explosively. In other words, an epidemic may occur, raising the incidence to an equilibrium at a much higher level" (p. 1227).

Gaming models assume that, in many decision situations involving neighbourhoods, the personal costs and benefits of alternative courses of action are uncertain, depending on how many other actors choose various alternatives. The individual's expected payoff of an alternative varies, however, depending on the number or proportion of others who make a decision before the given actor does. Thus, the concept of a threshold amount of observed prior action is central in this type of model. The well-known prisoners' dilemma is the simplest form of gaming model (Schelling, 1978), but more sophisticated variants have been developed and applied to a variety processes occurring in neighbourhoods (Granovetter, 1978; Granovetter & Soong, 1986).

Finally, non-linearities can arise out of the very nature of the dichotomous choice process being investigated. For example, individual choices to move, switch housing tenures, or participate in the labour market are conventionally modelled with a logit or probit functional relationship. This fact will have important methodological implications, as explained below.

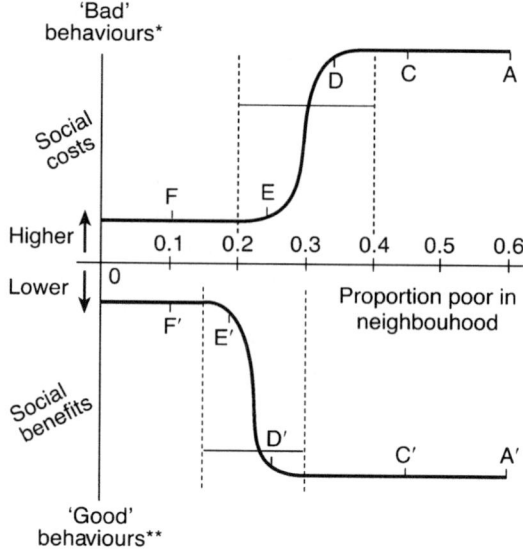

Figure 2. Summary of observed relationships between neighbourhood poverty
rates and individual behavioural outcomes in the US.
Notes: *crime, school leaving, duration of poverty as young adult; **hours of work,
income, wages.

Evidence on Non-linear Neighbourhood Effects

Unfortunately, few extant empirical studies explicitly test for non-linear relationships between neighbourhood conditions and various individual outcomes
(Quercia & Galster, 2000). The review here suggests that the evidence from the
US may be summarily (if tentatively) portrayed as in Figure 2 (Galster, 2002; cf.
Johnson *et al.*, 2002). The independent impacts of neighbourhood poverty rates
in encouraging negative outcomes for individuals such as crime, school leaving
and duration of periods of poverty appear to be nil unless the neighbourhood
exceeds about 20 per cent poverty, whereupon the effects grow rapidly until the
neighbourhood reaches approximately 40 per cent poverty; subsequent increases
in poverty appear to have no marginal effect. Analogously, the independent
impacts of neighbourhood poverty rates in discouraging positive behaviours like
working appear to be nil unless the neighbourhood exceeds about 15 per cent
poverty, whereupon the effects grow rapidly until the neighbourhood reaches
roughly 30 per cent poverty; subsequent increases in poverty appear to have no
marginal effect. Existing empirical specifications cannot definitively distinguish
between relationships that are characterised by discontinuous step functions or
by a continuous, logit-like relationship, so both are portrayed in Figure 2.
    The European evidence related to potential non-linear neighbourhood effects
is even more limited and inconclusive. Ostendorf *et al.* (2000) compared 'income-
mixed' neighbourhoods in Amsterdam with 'homogeneous' ones, to ascertain
whether this aspect of neighbourhood was related to an individual's chances of
living in poverty. Although their statistical technique permitted non-linearities,
no strong relationship of any kind was observed. Musterd *et al.* (2003, this issue)
relate the proportion of neighbouring households on social benefits to the
chances of individuals' upward and downward mobility in the Netherlands

during the 1990s. Although arguably some non-linearities are evinced at the extreme values of neighbourhood conditions, they have different thresholds and appear less dramatic in impact than the US evidence portrayed in Figure 2.

The Methodological Importance of Non-linear Neighbourhood Effects

Even if Challenge 1 were met and neighbourhood social processes were precisely measured, it still may not be possible to distinguish statistically the source of some observed effect, what Manski (1993, 2000) has called the 'reflection problem'. Following Manski, two distinct sorts of processes can be distinguished within neighbourhoods, endogenous and exogenous. Endogenous processes are those in which one person's behaviour is influenced by the aggregation of the same behaviours by neighbours, as might be generated by contagion or peer group effects. This process is endogenous in the sense that it generates positive feedback effects between individuals and group behaviours. Exogenous processes are those in which one person's behaviour is influenced by an exogenous or pre-determined characteristic of neighbours (ethnicity, class, religion, housing tenure) or the neighbourhood as a place (accessibility, public service level, institutional resources, stigmatisation). Manski (1993, 2000) demonstrates that it is mathematically impossible to distinguish these two processes if both are related in a linear fashion to a continuous variable measuring behaviour outcomes.

There are several potential avenues out of this bind (Manski, 2000). For the purposes here, however, one of the most useful is non-linearity. If the endogenous effect occurs in a non-linear fashion it is possible to identify it empirically. Of course, the prior theoretical and empirical sections suggest strongly that this is precisely the case for a wide range of behaviours of interest. Moreover, Brock & Durlauf (2001) have explored the non-linearity associated with a dichotomous outcome, and have developed a discrete choice model of social interactions wherein the endogenous effect can be clearly identified. In sum, exploring non-linearity in neighbourhood effects is not merely an academic curiosity; it may be considered a fundamental empirical requirement in advancing the field.

The Policy Importance of Non-linear Neighbourhood Effects

Important policy implications follow from serious explorations of non-linear neighbourhood effects (Galster, 2002; Galster & Zobel, 1998; Haurin *et al.*, 2002a; Johnson *et al.*, 2002). As one illustration, relationships as portrayed in Figure 2 imply under very general conditions that social well-being overall will be improved if the fraction of poor households in US neighbourhoods with higher than 20 per cent poverty rates could be reduced and, correspondingly, their fractions in neighbourhoods with less than 5 per cent poverty rates increased. For a more complete and rigorous argument, see Galster (2002).

As another illustration, recall from above that non-linearity permits the unambiguous clarification of whether neighbourhood effects are primarily generated by endogenous or exogenous intra-neighbourhood processes. Such clarification holds important implications for the expected magnitude of policy impact. Endogenous processes imply social multipliers among neighbours. Thus, a policy that positively affects one individual or household may end up yielding a multiplied benefit as the altered behaviour of the direct beneficiary of the policy is spread to neighbours (Haurin *et al.*, 2002a).

Considerably more attention needs to be paid to exploring non-linear neighbourhood effects in future investigations on both sides of the Atlantic. However, it would indeed be surprising were these investigations to reveal cross-national similarities in non-linear neighbourhood effects, given the differences in welfare states, labour markets, race and class segregation and housing policies (Musterd, 2002).

Challenge 3: The Selection Bias Problem

Previous statistical studies based on non-experimental data have taken only a partial view of the patterns embodied in Figure 1. It is now conventional, for example, to recognise that unmeasured parental characteristics must be considered in the analysis, to overcome the problem of neighbourhood selection. The most basic selection issue is that certain types of parents who have certain (unmeasured) motivations and skills related to their children's upbringing will move to certain types of neighbourhoods. Any observed relationship between neighbourhood conditions and child outcomes may therefore be biased because of this systematic spatial selection process, even if all the observable characteristics of parents are controlled (Manski, 1995, 2000; Duncan *et al.*, 1997). Flipped on its head, the problem can be formulated as omitted variables bias. Is the observed statistical relationship between outcomes and neighbourhood indicative of neighbourhood's independent effect, or merely unmeasured (uncontrolled) characteristics of parents that truly affected child outcomes but also (spuriously, in the extreme) led to neighbourhood choices as well? The direction of the bias has been the subject of debate, with Jencks & Mayer (1990) and Tienda (1991) arguing that neighbourhood impacts are biased upwards, and Brooks-Gunn *et al.* (1997) arguing the opposite.

If Figure 1 were adopted as a working premise, the selection process becomes much more complicated than merely the independent selection in neighbourhood, rather embodying the interdependent selections of neighbourhood, tenure and mobility. In the US there have been two approaches in overcoming selection bias: random assignment experiments and econometric modeling based on non-experimental data. Both are considered below.

Experimental Evidence

Data on outcomes that can be produced by an experimental design whereby individuals or households are randomly assigned to different neighbourhoods clearly is the preferred method for avoiding biases from selection. In this regard, the Moving to Opportunity (MTO) demonstration has been touted conventionally as *the* study from which to draw conclusions about the magnitude of neighbourhood effects (e.g. Goering *et al.*, 2002; Katz *et al.*, 2001; Leventhal & Brooks-Gunn, forthcoming; Ludwig *et al.*, 2000, 2001a, 2001b; Rosenbaum, 1995; Rosenbaum & Harris, 2001). Although the research design indeed randomly assigns those public housing residents who volunteer to one of three experimental groups, it does not fully control the assignment of neighbourhood characteristics of the two experimental groups receiving tenant-based rental subsidies, and thus does not fully purge the relationship between neighbourhood characteristics and unmeasured parental characteristics (Sampson *et al.*, 2002). Of course, the group that receives only a rental subsidy with no mobility counselling and no locational restrictions can select from a wide range of neighbourhoods. But even the treatment group receiving intensive mobility counselling and assistance, although constrained to move initially to a neighbourhood with less than 10 per cent poverty rates, nevertheless has the ability to choose neighbourhoods varying on their school quality, home ownership rates, racial composition, local institutional resources, etc. Moreover, subsequent to their initial, constrained location they are free to move to different, higher-poverty neighbourhoods should they choose (as many have; Goering *et al.*, 2002).

Thus, MTO does not fully finesse the selection bias issue. Unless a social experiment is designed wherein the precise neighbourhood conditions are randomly assigned to participants and then these locations fixed for a substantial period, data gathered will need to be analysed using one of the methods described in the next section.

Econometric Models Based on Non-experimental Data

A second type of study has used cross-sectional or longitudinal data collected from surveys of households residing in a variety of neighbourhoods. This approach then uses multiple regression analysis to control for other, non-neighbourhood factors to ascertain the impact of the latter set of variables on a variety of outcomes. A variety of methods have been used to deal with the selection issue.

Sibling Studies. Sibling studies typically use PSID or NLSY or some other longitudinal dataset with large samples of siblings (Aaronson, 1997, 1998; Plotnick & Hoffman, 1999). Assuming that families do not move across neighbourhoods in response to differences in unmeasured characteristics of children, one can use the inter-temporal variations in neighbourhood conditions experienced by the family to assess impacts on siblings. The central logic is that the observed outcome for any given child is partly a function of a parental fixed-effect: an error term associated with unmeasured parental characteristics, the same characteristics that partly drive observed neighbourhood characteristics. Thus, estimating a model of the *differences* in outcomes between siblings allows the researcher to eliminate this fixed effect and discern the impacts of different neighbourhood environments the siblings may have experienced at different ages.

To estimate this fixed effect specification accurately, several concerns must be addressed (Aaronson, 1998). First, if parents' effectiveness in parenting evolves over time, younger children may be exposed to a different unobserved effect than their older siblings. The analysis should therefore control for birth order. Second, outcomes may be affected by *changes* in family circumstances (unemployment, divorce, etc.) that also may affect neighbourhood choice. This implies that the analysis must control to the extent possible for such measured changes, and assume that they are changing consonant with unmeasured characteristic changes. There are several other econometric challenges faced with this fixed effect estimator; see Aaronson (1998). Third, there remains a concern that typically there is limited variation in the characteristics of neighbourhoods that families move among under circumstances *not* associated with major changes in family circumstances (Levine & Painter, 2000), resulting in imprecise estimates (Aaronson, 1998). Fourth is the problem of small samples of siblings typically available even in the largest datasets. Because of these concerns, this approach holds circumscribed promise.

Instrumenting Neighbourhood. A different technique is using instrumental variables. In the first stage of this technique, a regression is estimated wherein the dimension of neighbourhood in question in regressed on one or more explanatory variables that, hopefully, are highly correlated with the neighbourhood characteristic but uncorrelated with unmeasured parental characteristics. The predicted values for the neighbourhood characteristic yielded by this first stage regression, which presumably are purged of spurious correlation with unmeasured parental characteristics, are employed in a second-stage regression explaining outcomes. In a clever and sophisticated variant of the IV approach applied to junior high test scores, Levine & Painter (2000) use average high school test scores as an instrument proxying directly for unmeasured parental characteristics, since it cannot be causing observed junior high achievement. The challenge of this method, of course, is identifying first-stage variables that reasonably meet the aforementioned correlation criteria.

A variety of variables have been employed in this role in previous work on neighbourhood effects. In the seminal example of instrumental variables, Evans *et al.* (1992) used metropolitan-level variables for unemployment rate, median family income, poverty rate, and percentage of adults completing college as identifying variables predicting the 'neighbourhood variable': proportion of students in the local school who are economically disadvantaged. Analogously, Foster & McLanahan (1996) used city-wide labour market conditions as identifying variables predicting neighbourhood high school dropout rates. Interestingly, they found that the use of the IV did not substantially change the neighbourhood impact estimate on drop-out rates for girls, but did for boys.

Two problems remain with these metropolitan- or city-wide instruments. First, not only the neighbourhood context but also the larger, city/metro context may influence outcomes for a given neighbourhood's residents. Put differently, the 'opportunity structure' has several spatial scales of importance (Galster & Killen, 1995). Thus, the neighbourhood variable instrumented in the above fashion will embody an amalgam of both spatial scales; the distinct impacts of the neighbourhood scale cannot be discerned. Second, if families choose their city/metro area on the basis of the average quality of its neighbourhoods (or particular neighbourhoods of intended residence), the instrument will not be purged of unmeasured parental characteristics. Nevertheless, the instrumental variable approach offers the greatest potential for future work, and is critical in the specification proposed next.

A Proposed Econometric Model for Estimating Neighbourhood Impacts on Individual Behaviours

No extant work has attempted to specify the full joint neighbourhood/tenure/ mobility/wealth/behavioural effects structural model embodied in Figure 1. Thus far it has been argued that the desired relationship shown by arrow C in Figure 1 is difficult to estimate accurately because: (1) unmeasured parental characteristics affect the choice of neighbourhood (as well as simultaneously chosen tenure and mobility) thereby creating selection bias, and (2) C is likely a non-linear relationship. This section will propose a procedure for surmounting these difficulties.

The instrumental variable approach outlined above is drawn upon, but extended. The use of a longitudinal database of individuals is assumed (such as the US Panel Study of Income Dynamics or the population register files maintained in several Northern European countries). The proposed method consists of the following steps: (1) specify a structural equation system for all endogenous variables thought to be influenced by unmeasured parental characteristics; (2) estimate for each year in the database an ordinary least squares (OLS) regression for each endogenous variable as a function of all exogenous and predetermined variables in the system; (3) use the parameters in (2) to calculate an instrumental variable estimate of the endogenous variables for each individual, separately for each year; (4) based on the instruments in (3), calculate summary instrumental variable estimates for each of several developmental stages for the individual; and (5) employ the variables in (4) as explanatory variables in OLS regressions predicting various outcomes for children or young adults, permitting non-linear relationships for the variables measuring neighbourhood characteristics.

The structural equation system proposed for home ownership (HO), mobility expectations (ME), neighbourhood type/character (N), housing wealth (W), and household socio-economic status (SES) for the current period is:

HO = f(**ME, N, SES**, race-ethnicity, family life-cycle stage, *non-housing wealth, relative costs of owning and renting in metro, prior period ownership status, prior period ownership status interacted with* **W**)

ME = f(**HO, N, SES**, race-ethnicity, *changes in family size/stages, prior period ownership status, duration since previous move, age of head*)

N = f(**HO, ME, SES**, race-ethnicity, family life-cycle stage, *metro area poverty rate, median income, etc., metro area segregation by race, metro area segregation by class, metro area proportion not moving in last 5 years*)

W = f(**HO, N**, *changes in N in recent past, metro area home price index*)

SES = f(**N, HO, W**, race-ethnicity, family life-cycle stage, *non-housing wealth, metro area proportions in various income and educational categories*)

where **bold** are endogenous variables, *italics* signify exogenous, unique variables forwarded as candidates for identification of one or more equations in this system. Implicit in each function (designated f) is a form permitting the test of non-linear relationships with N.

It could be subsequently estimated (via OLS) how *ex post* observed mobility behaviour **M** (e.g. duration of home ownership during childhood, average duration of stay in residence during childhood) was related to the aforementioned variables, to measure their indirect effect on child outcomes via changing mobility:

M = f(**HO, N, W, ME, SES**, race-ethnicity, *changes in family size/stages, duration since previous move, age of head*)

This system of equations confronts the analyst with another challenge associated with step 2: identifying robust, uniquely identifying instrumental variables. Even if tenure choice, wealth and mobility were not brought into the model, instrumenting neighbourhood itself is complex. As noted above, several neighbourhood dimensions would be desired in a multiple regression as predictor variables for a particular behavioural outcome. But, as each dimension of neighbourhood must be thought of as subject to parental choice, each would need a unique, identifying instrument.

This challenge may not be as daunting as first appears. The corresponding figures for the larger geographic area in which the observed neighbourhood is located, either the city or county are proposed as identifying instruments (as has been done by Evans *et al.*, 1992; Foster & McLanahan, 1996). For instance, an acceptable instrument for the census tract level percentage home ownership should be the rate of home ownership in the city in which the neighbourhood is located. Fortunately, several studies provide guidance about how the other parts of the equation system above may be identified and instrumented.

The modelling of housing tenure choice and mobility as a joint decision has, for example, become quite conventional; see Zorn (1988), and Ioannides & Kan (1996) for seminal work. Similarly, modelling tenure choice jointly with expected future mobility has been undertaken for some time; see Boehm (1981), Ioannides (1987) and Rosenthal (1988).

In the most recent and ambitious work of this genre, Kan (2000) models three simultaneous equations predicting: current year's tenure choice, current year's mobility choice, and expected future mobility behaviour (operationalised through the PSID question: Do you think you might move in the next couple of years?). Through theoretically justifiable exclusions, lagged demographic and tenure status variables, and macro-economic variables, Kan manages to identify the system. He controls for household unobserved heterogeneity by a random effects specification exploiting the panel nature of PSID, and estimates parameters with a maximum simulated likelihood algorithm. Kan investigates tenure choice as an end in itself, not its impact on children.

Haurin *et al.* (2002b, c) provide an application of the two-stage procedure in their study of home ownership impacts on a variety of children's outcomes. They do not specify a structural model, and do not model a joint tenure/neighbourhood/mobility choice process. Rather, they exploit the panel nature of PSID to control for unobserved parental fixed affects that would influence all three decisions. They label their fixed-effects model as a 'treatment effects' approach. They also employ an additional, two-stage estimation procedure in an attempt to estimate the (unbiased) effects of home ownership (duration), their key tenure variable. Their instrument for duration of home-owning is estimated in first stage equation via Tobit, then included in second-stage estimation procedure. Identifying the first stage ownership choice equation (with unique variables excluded from the second stage) was accomplished through substantial investments in data collection re: relative prices of owning vs. renting; downpayment constraints on parents, and permanent income variables.

Harkness & Newman (2002) model a variety of child outcomes using the PSID, with key explanatory variables of interest being tenure, neighbourhood characteristics, parental equity, and household residential stability. They employ no statistical procedures to correct for the selection problem. They recognise that mobility and tenure are jointly determined, so they estimate a model of mobility as a function of instrumented tenure. Surprisingly, they do not use this instrumental variable for tenure in their main child outcomes regressions! They use three variables to create this instrument: (1) ratio of the number of single-family to multifamily units built in the corresponding census region in the year prior to the observation (proxy for relative attractiveness of ownership); (2) per capita value of highway capital stock in corresponding state (ease of auto travel should promote ownership); and (3) ratio of home owner to renter housing payments for corresponding census region (relative tenure costs). For the whole sample of child ages these collectively did a poor job of predicting home ownership.

Only one work has modelled the joint tenure/neighbourhood choice process: Deng *et al.* (2003). They employ a nested multinomial logit specification wherein residential location, the lower level choice, is estimated as a multinomial logit conditional on tenure choice (i.e. the influence of locational attributes on residential choice is based on characteristics of each household and tenure choice of that household). The cross-tenure coefficient differences represent the relative attractiveness of a locational attribute to prospective owners compared to renters there. The results of this first stage estimate are used to calculate an 'inclusive variable' for each household in the sample, representing the value of ownership relative to renting across all location options. The difference between the inclusive values from owning and renting is included as a regressor in the second-stage tenure choice model.

Assuming step 2 can be completed successfully, steps 3 and 4 in the method are trivial. Step 5 also is straightforward. It could involve a variety of experiments with specifications permitting non-linear impacts of neighbourhood variables, including quadratic, multiple categorical dummy variables, and splines.

Conclusions and Implications for Qualitative Research

This paper argued that to advance the investigation of the impact of neighbourhood on a variety of human outcomes, one must comprehend in as holistic a fashion as possible all the factors that contribute to the outcome in question, and the causal interrelationships among these various factors. In this vein, a model was forwarded (Figure 1) wherein outcomes of interest were affected by neighbourhood acting in a mutually causal fashion with housing tenure, housing wealth, household status and mobility behaviour. It was argued that this model could use a sufficiently robust set of instrumental variables to overcome the issue of omitted parental characteristics (i.e. neighbourhood selection bias), and thereby produce unbiased estimates of neighbourhood impacts on individual outcomes of interest. Several neighbourhood-related variables could be inserted into this model as proxies for neighbourhood processes, and equations could be readily tested for non-linear relationships. Such non-linearities could permit the identification of endogenous neighbourhood processes.

The issue of how neighbourhood social processes should be measured remains a complex, unresolved one. There are several studies finding that tract-level socio-economic-demographic indicators are strongly related to various intra-neighbourhood social processes. However, the studies are not perfectly consistent, and suggest that census tract-level socio-economic-demographic indicators are, at best, imperfect proxies. There is a crucial need for future research efforts to measure variables related to institutional resources, organisational participation, collective supervision of youth, clarity and consensus regarding group norms, intra- and extra-neighbourhood social networks for adults and children. The same is true for extra-neighbourhood processes involving, e.g. stigmatising of neighbourhood by key actors.

There are ample theoretical reasons to believe that the magnitude of neighbourhood effects is not linear, but instead is likely characterised by a non-linear, threshold effect. Unfortunately, few extant empirical studies explicitly test for non-linear relationships between neighbourhood conditions and various outcomes for children and youth. Those that do in the US however, support the theoretical position. Considerably more attention needs to be paid to this issue in future investigations, for both statistical and policy reasons.

Beyond measuring more comprehensively the key aspects of neighbourhood, however, there is yet another central data need: parental variables. The central methodological hurdle that studies of neighbourhood impact must surmount relates to unobserved parental characteristics that simultaneously may be guiding both neighbourhood choice and child and youth outcomes. Obviously, if we can measure directly a wider array of such parental characteristics as parenting behaviours, the issue of selection can be dealt with in a straightforward manner with control variables, instead of the more challenging instrumental variables approach proposed here.

Before finishing, it would be remiss not to connect the discussion to the growing amount of high-quality case-study and qualitative scholarship related to neighbourhood impacts. This qualitative work is essentially complementary to the quantitative efforts to measure precisely the magnitude of neighbourhood effects, because it is aimed at uncovering the how and why of any observed impact. Although statistical results can, in principle, distinguish between some of the alternative causal mechanisms, it is thought that much more in-depth, qualitative analyses will be required (see, for example, the recent series of papers by Sampson and his colleagues, and Briggs, 1997). For a review of the theoretical links between neighbourhood processes and individual outcomes, see Atkinson *et al.* (2001); Duncan *et al.* (1997); Friedrichs, 1998; Gephart (1997); Haurin *et al.* (2002a); Jencks & Mayer (1990) and Sampson *et al.* (2002).

A fruitful area upon which to base such investigations is a host of 'natural quasi-experiments': idiosyncratic public policy initiatives in various locales involving subsidised housing that creates variation in neighbourhood environments for tenants. These policies in the US could be inclusionary zoning ordinances, scattered-site public housing schemes, or mixed-income redevelopments of public housing sites (like HOPE VI). These can be considered, at best, quasi-experimental designs insofar as tenants being observed may still have some latitude in choosing neighbourhoods, although their choices typically are limited by the programme design. However, the potential of self-selection to bias conclusions regarding the mechanisms of neighbourhood impact are considerably less serious than in the case of measuring magnitude of effects.

There are several prominent examples of such opportunistic research that have provided valuable insights into mechanism of neighbourhood impact. Rosenbaum *et al.* (2002) recently probed qualitatively how the neighbourhoods of Gautreaux programme movers into Chicago suburbs have enhanced their self-efficacy. Similarly, Briggs (1997, 1998) interviewed poor, minority youth who moved to scattered-site public housing in white, middle-class neighbourhoods under the auspices of the Yonkers desegregation consent decree. Kleit (2001,

2002) conducted insightful social network analysis of low-income residents of mixed-income housing developments in Montgomery County, MD.

More efforts along these lines would prove fruitful. Either classic anthropological case study, control-experimental group, or pre-post longitudinal designs (including retrospective comparisons) could be contemplated. There are ample opportunities emerging in the US public policy arena, including HOPE VI developments, court-ordered public housing authority desegregation consent decrees, and innovative local housing authority initiatives. In the Western European context, several nations are adopting policies for increasing the income and/or tenure diversity of large social housing estates, which may offer additional opportunities for testing neighbourhood impacts in a quasi-experimental context (Kearns, 2002; Musterd, 2002).

Acknowledgements

The author wishes to thank Sako Musterd and anonymous referees for helpful suggestions on an earlier draft, and Jackie Cutsinger and Ron Malega for their research and production assistance.

Correspondence

George Galster, Wayne State University, Detroit, MI 48202 USA. Email: aa3571@wayne.edu

References

Aaronson, D. (1997) Sibling estimates of neighborhood effects, in: J. Brooks-Gunn, G. Duncan & J. Aber (Eds) *Neighborhood Poverty: Vol. II. Policy Implications in Studying Neighborhoods* (New York, Russell Sage Foundation).

Aaronson, D. (1998) Using sibling data to estimate the impact of neighborhoods on children's educational outcomes, *Journal of Human Resources*, 33, pp. 915–946.

Aaronson, D. (2000) A note of the benefits of homeownership, *Journal of Urban Economics*, 47, pp. 356–369.

Akerlof, G. (1980) A theory of social custom, of which unemployment may be one consequence, *Quarterly Journal of Economics*, 94, pp. 749–775.

Atkinson, R. & Kintrea, K. (2001) Area effects: what do they mean for British housing and regeneration policy? *European Journal of Housing Policy*, 2, pp. 147–166.

Atkinson, R., Kintrea, K., Austin, M. & Baba, Y. (2001) Disentangling area effects: the contributions of place to household poverty, *Urban Studies*, 38, pp. 2277–2298.

Austin, M. & Baba, Y. (1990) Social determinants of neighborhood attachments, *Sociological Spectrum*, 10, pp. 59–78.

Boehm, T. (1981) Tenure choice and expected mobility: a synthesis, *Journal of Urban Economics*, 10, pp. 375–389.

Boehm, T. & Schlottman, A. (1999) Does home ownership by parents have an economic impact on their children? *Journal of Housing Economics*, 8, pp. 217–232.

Briggs, X. (1997) Moving up versus moving out: researching and interpreting neighborhood effects in housing mobility programs, *Housing Policy Debate*, 8, pp. 195–234.

Briggs, X. (1998) Brown kids in white suburbs: housing mobility and the many faces of social capital, *Housing Policy Debate*, 9, pp. 177–221.

Brock, W. & Durlauf, S. (2001) Interactions-based models, in: J. Heckman & E. Learner (Eds) *Handbook of Econometrics*, Vol. 5 (Amsterdam, North-Holland).

Brooks-Gunn, J., Duncan, G. & Aber, J. (Eds) (1997) *Neighborhood Poverty: Vol. 1 Context and Consequences for Children* (New York, Russell Sage Foundation).

Coleman, J. (1988) Social capital and the creation of human capital, *American Journal of Sociology*, 94, pp. S95–S120.

Coleman, J. (1990) *Foundations of Social Theory* (Cambridge, MA, Harvard University Press).

Cook, T., Shagle, S., Degirmencioglu, S., Coulton, C., Korbin, J. & Su, M. (1997) Capturing social process for testing mediational models of neighborhood effects, in: J. Brooks-Gunn, G. Duncan & L. Aber (Eds) *Neighborhood Poverty: Vol. II, Policy Implications in Studying Neighborhoods* (New York, Russell Sage Foundation).

Coulton, C., Korbin, J. & Su, M. (1999) Neighborhoods and child maltreatment: a multi-level study, *Child Abuse and Neglect*, 23, pp. 1019–1040.

Crane, J. (1991) The epidemic theory of ghettos and neighborhood effects on dropping out and teenage childbearing, *American Journal of Sociology*, 96, pp. 1226–1259.

Deng, Y., Ross, S. & Wachter, S. (2003) Racial differences in homeownership: the effect of residential location, *Regional Science and Urban Economics*, 33, pp. 517–556.

Duncan, G., Connell, J. & Klebanov, P. (1997) Conceptual and methodological issues in estimating causal effects of neighborhoods and family conditions on individual development, in: J. Brooks-Gunn & G. Duncan & J. Aber (Eds) *Neighborhood Poverty: vol. 1, Context and Consequences for Children* (New York, Russell Sage Foundation).

Duncan, G. & Raudenbush, S. (1999) Assessing the effect of context in studies of child and youth development, *Educational Psychology*, 34, pp. 29–41.

Earls, F. & Carlson, M. (2001) The social ecology of child health and well-being, *Annual Review of Public Health*, 22, pp. 143–166.

Elliott, D., Wilson, W., Huizinga, D., Elliott, A. & Rankin, B. (1996) The effects of neighborhood disadvantage on adolescent development, *Journal of Research in Crime and Delinquency*, 33, pp. 389–426.

Evans, W., Oates, W., & Schwab, R. (1992) Measuring peer group effects: a study of teenage behavior, *Journal of Political Economy*, 100, pp. 966–991.

Foster, E. & McLanahan, S. (1996) An illustration of the use of instrumental variables: do neighborhood conditions affect a young person's chance of finishing high school? *Psychological Methods*, 1, pp. 249–260.

Friedrichs, J. (1998) Do poor neighborhoods make their residents poorer? Context effects of poverty neighborhoods on their residents, in: H. Andress (Ed.) *Empirical Poverty Research in a Comparative Perspective* (Aldershot, Ashgate).

Friedrichs, J. (2002) Response: contrasting US and European findings on poverty neighborhoods, *Housing Studies*, 17, pp. 101–106.

Galster, G. (1983) Empirical evidence on cross-tenure differences in home maintenance and conditions, *Land Economics*, 59, pp. 107–113.

Galster, G. (1987) *Homeowners and Neighborhood Reinvestment* (Durham, NC, Duke University Press).

Galster, G. (2002) An economic efficiency analysis of deconcentrating poverty populations, *Journal of Housing Economics*, 11, pp. 303–329.

Galster, G. & Killen, S. (1995) The geography of metropolitan opportunity: a reconnaissance and conceptual framework, *Housing Policy Debate* 6, pp. 7–43.

Galster, G. & Zobel, A. (1998) Will dispersed housing programmes reduce social problems in the US? *Housing Studies*, 13, pp. 605–622.

Gephart, M. (1997) Neighborhoods and communities as contexts for development, in: J. Brooks-Gunn, G. Duncan & J. Aber (Eds) *Neighborhood Poverty: Vol. I. Context and Consequences for Children* (New York, Russell Sage Foundation).

Goering, J., Feins, J. & Richardson, T. (2002) A cross-site analysis of initial Moving to Opportunity demonstration results, *Journal of Housing Research*, 13, pp. 1–30.

Granovetter, M. (1978) Threshold models of collective behavior, *American Journal of Sociology*, 83, pp. 1420–1443.

Granovetter, M. & Soong, R. (1986) Threshold models of diversity: Chinese restaurants, residential segregation, and the spiral of silence, *The Journal of Sociology*, 18, pp. 69–104.

Green, R. & White, M. (1997) Measuring the benefits of homeowning: effects on children, *Journal of Urban Economics*, 41, pp. 441–461.

Harkness, J. & Newman, S. (2002) Homeownership for the poor in distressed neighborhoods: does it make sense? *Housing Policy Debate*, 13, pp. 597–630.

Haurin, D., Hendershott, P. & Ling, D. (1988) Home ownership rates of married couples: an econometric investigation, *Housing Finance Review*, 7, pp. 85–108.

Haurin, D., Dietz, R. & Weinberg, B. (2002a) *The impact of neighborhood homeownership rates: a review of the theoretical and empirical literature* (Columbus, OH, Department of Economics Working Paper, Ohio State University).

Haurin, D., Parcel, T. & Haurin, R. (2002b) Impact of home ownership on child outcomes, in: E.

Belsky & N. Retsinas (Eds) *Low Income Homeownership: Examining the Unexamined Goal* (Washington, DC, Brookings Institution Press).

Haurin, D., Parcel, T. & Haurin, R. (2002c) Does home ownership affect child outcomes? *Real Estate Economics*, 30, pp. 635–666.

Haveman, R. & Wolfe, B. (1995) The determinants of children's attainments: a review of methods and findings, *Journal of Economic Literature*, 33, pp. 1829–1878.

Hunter, A. (1975) The loss of community: an empirical test through replication, *American Sociological Review*, 40, pp. 537–551.

Ioannides, Y. (1987) Residential mobility and housing tenure choice, *Regional Science and Urban Economics*, 17, pp. 265–287.

Ioannides, Y. & Kan, K. (1996) Structural estimation of residential mobility and housing tenure choice, *Journal of Regional Science*, 36, pp. 335–363.

Jeffers, L. & Dobos, J. (1984) Communication and neighborhood mobilization, *Urban Affairs Quarterly*, 20, pp. 97–112.

Jenks, C. & Mayer, S. (1990) The social consequences of growing up in a poor neighborhood, in: L. Lynn & M. McGeary (Eds) *Inner-city Poverty in the United States* (Washington, DC, National Academy Press).

Johnson, M., Ladd, H. & Ludwig, J. (2002) The benefits and costs of residential mobility programmes for the poor, *Housing Studies*, 17, pp. 125–138.

Kan, K. (2000) Dynamic modeling of housing tenure choice, *Journal of Urban Economics*, 48, pp. 46–69.

Katz, L., Kling, J. & Liebman, J. (2001) A Moving to Opportunity in Boston: early results of a randomized mobility experiment, *Quarterly Journal of Economics*, 116, pp. 607–654.

Kearns, A. (2002) Response: from residential disadvantage to opportunity? Reflections on British and European policy and research, *Housing Studies* 17, pp. 145–150.

Kesteloot, C. (1998) The geography of deprivation in Brussels and local development strategies, in: S. Musterd & W. Ostendorf (Eds) *Urban Segregation and the Welfare State* (London and New York, Routledge).

Kleit, R. (2001) The role of neighborhood social networks in scattered-site public housing residents' search for jobs, *Housing Policy Debate*, 12, pp. 541–573.

Kleit, R. (2002) Job search networks and strategies in scattered-site public housing, *Housing Studies*, 17, pp. 83–100.

Kohen, D., Brooks-Gunn, J., Leventhal, T. & Hertzman, C. (forthcoming) Neighborhood income and physical and social disorder in Canada: associations with young children's competencies, *Child Development*.

Lee, B., Oropesa, R. & Kanan, J. (1994) Neighborhood context and residential mobility, *Demography*, 31, pp. 249–270.

Leventhal, T. & Brooks-Gunn, J. (2000) The neighborhoods they live in, *Psychological Bulletin*, 126, pp. 309–337.

Leventhal, T. & Brooks-Gunn, J. (forthcoming) Moving to Opportunity: an experimental study of neighborhood effects on mental health, *American Journal of Public Health*.

Levine, D. & Painter, G. (2000) How much of school effects is just sorting? Identifying causality in the national education longitudinal survey. Unpublished manuscript, University of Southern California.

Ludwig, J., Duncan, G. & Pinkston, J. (2000) Neighborhood effects on economic self-sufficiency: evidence from a randomized housing-mobility experiment. Working paper, February 2000, no. 159 (Evanston, IL, Northwestern University/University of Chicago Joint Center for Poverty Research).

Ludwig, J., Duncan, G. & Hirschfield, P. (2001a) Urban poverty and juvenile crime: evidence from a randomized housing-mobility experiment, *Quarterly Journal of Economics*, 116, pp. 655–679.

Ludwig, J., Ladd, H. & Duncan, G. (2001b) The effects of urban poverty on educational outcomes: evidence from a randomized experiment, in: W. Gale & J. R. Pack (Eds) *Brookings-Wharton Papers on Urban Affairs* (Washington, DC, Brookings Institution).

Manski, C. (1993) Identification of endogenous social effects: the reflection problem, *Review of Economic Studies*, 60, pp. 531–542.

Manski, C. (1995) *Identification Problems in the Social Sciences* (Cambridge, MA, Harvard University Press).

Manski, C. (2000) Economic analysis of social interactions, *Journal of Economic Perspectives*, 14, pp. 115–136.

Mayer, N. (1981) Rehabilitation decisions in rental housing, *Journal of Urban Economics*, 10, p. 76–94.

Musterd, S. (2002) Response: mixed housing policy: A European (Dutch) perspective, *Housing Studies*, 17, pp. 139–144.

Musterd, S., Ostendorf, W. & de Vos, S. (2003, this issue) neighbourhood effects and social mobility: a longitudinal analysis, *Housing Studies*, 18, pp. 877–892.

Nesslein, T. S. (2000) *Owning versus renting: is the promotion of homeownership for the poor good social policy?* Paper presented at the 22nd Annual Research Conference, Association for Public Policy Analysis and Management, Seattle WA, November.

Ostendorf, W., Musterd, S. & de Vos, S. (2001) Social mix and the neighbourhood effect: policy ambition and empirical support, *Housing Studies*, 16, pp. 371–380.

Plotnick, R. & Hoffman, S. (1999) The effect of neighborhood characteristics on young adult outcomes: alternative estimates, *Social Science Quarterly* 80, pp. 1–18.

Quercia, R. & Galster, G. (2000) Threshold effects and neighborhood change, *Journal of Planning Education and Research*, 20, pp. 146–163.

Raudenbush, S. & Sampson, R. (1999) 'Ecometrics': toward a science of assessing ecological settings, with application to the systematic social observation of neighborhoods, *Sociological Methodology*, 29, pp. 1–41.

Robert, S. (1999) Socioeconomic position and health: the independent contribution of community socioeconomic context, *Annual Review of Sociology*, 25, pp. 489–516.

Rohe, W. & Stewart, L. (1996) Home ownership and neighborhood stability, *Housing Policy Debate*, 7, pp. 37–81.

Rosenbaum, J. (1995) Changing the geography of opportunity by expanding residential choice: lessons from the Gautreaux program, *Housing Policy Debate*, 6, pp. 231–269.

Rosenbaum, J. & Harris, L. (2001) Residential mobility and opportunities: early impacts of the moving to opportunity demonstration program in Chicago, *Housing Policy Debate*, 12, pp. 321–346.

Rosenbaum, J., Reynolds, L. & DeLuca, S. (2002) How do places matter? The geography of opportunity, self-efficacy, and a look inside the black box of residential mobility, *Housing Studies*, 17, pp. 71–82.

Rosenthal, S. (1988) A residence time model of housing markets, *Journal of Public Economics*, 36, pp. 87–109.

Rossi, P. & Weber, E. (1996) The social benefits of homeownership: empirical evidence from national surveys, *Housing Policy Debate*, 7, pp. 1–35.

Sampson, R. (1997) Collective regulation of adolescent misbehavior: validation results for eighty Chicago neighborhoods, *Journal of Adolescent Research*, 12, pp. 227–244.

Sampson, R. & Groves, W. B. (1989) Community structure and crime: testing social disorganization theory, *American Journal of Sociology*, 94, pp. 774–802.

Sampson, R., Raudenbush, S. & Earls, F. (1997) Neighborhoods and violent crime: a multilevel study of collective efficacy, *Science*, 277, pp. 918–924.

Sampson, R., Morenoff, J. & Earls, F. (1999) Beyond social capital: spatial dynamics of collective efficacy for children, *American Sociological Review*, 64, pp. 633–660.

Sampson, R., Morenoff, J., & Gannon-Rowley, T. (2002) Assessing 'neighborhood effects': social processes and new directions in research, *Annual Review of Sociology*, 28, pp. 443–478.

Schelling, T. (1978) *Micromotives and Macrobehavior* (New York, Norton).

Simmel, G. (1971) *Georg Simmel on Individuality and Social Forms* (Chicago, University of Chicago Press).

Tienda, M. (1991) Poor people and poor places: deciphering neighborhood effects of poverty outcomes, in: J. Haber (Ed.) *Macro-Micro Linkages in Sociology* (Newbury Park, Sage).

Weber, M. (1978) *Economy and Society* (Berkeley, University of California Press).

Wilson, W. (1987) *The Truly Disadvantaged* (Chicago, University of Chicago Press).

Zorn, P. (1988) An analysis of household mobility and tenure choice, *Journal of Urban Economics*, 24, pp. 113–128.

Re-shaping the Geography of Opportunity: Place Effects in Global Perspective

XAVIER DE SOUZA BRIGGS

Harvard University, John F. Kennedy School of Government, Cambridge, USA

[Paper first received 1 April 2003; in final form 13 May 2003]

ABSTRACT *Studies of the effects of micro-level contexts on human development and socio-economic 'opportunity' run the risk of excluding important factors, including the dynamism of those contexts and the effects of globalisation on local places. Comparative analyses are particularly demanding, since varied elements of an 'opportunity structure' may operate, some directly and others indirectly, to affect behaviour and outcomes of interest. This paper connects concerns about local place effects on human life to the larger global conversation about increased social inequality and sharper economic competition among localities, in effect, addressing sorting at macro, inter-local, and intra-local levels. The European studies presented in this volume are discussed, and a typology of interventions (actions to re-shape local place effects) is proposed for further debate.*

KEY WORDS: globalisation, human development, neighbourhoods, research methods, public policy

Introduction

This age of information, or better yet, of information overload, demands, from time to time, that those of us who work in the knowledge business think hard about how much we actually contribute to getting big, urgent questions answered. As *The Economist* put it recently, academia is where people "have a habit of crawling along the frontiers of knowledge with a magnifying glass, blind to the wide vistas opening up before them, and often reducing the most engaging subjects to tedious debates about methodology". An impatient newcomer to the domain of research featured in this special issue might rightfully ask, "Why all the fuss about the role of place in human development and problems of poverty?". The quick response would no doubt cite concerns about concentrated poverty and spatial segregation in the US, about social exclusion in Europe, and about neighbourhood or other context effects on individual fortunes (everywhere). A more considered follow-on would note how these concerns have, remarkably, sustained political attention and influenced the direction of public policies (in a number of countries) and not just of academic seminars.

But to play the role of devil's advocate for a moment, perhaps we *are* housing and space-obsessed researchers who write what we know, and to make matters worse, dwell in minutiae, more than what the world needs to know. More generously put, perhaps we should do more, from time to time, to link our concerns to the larger concerns of the day, to show what leverage we offer to larger efforts to act on public problems. That is, beyond detailing the 'what' of our concerns and findings, we are obliged to communicate the 'so what' in ways that contribute significantly to learning and public action.

This paper has three principal aims. The first is to articulate a more compelling case for re-shaping local places in ways that improve human life. Rather than review and extend what we already do to analyse the power of place (as others have in this volume), the paper begins by situating place debates in the larger debates over social inequality and social protection in a changing world. Peripheral vision is healthy in research, and it is crucial in effective policy and practice.

The second aim of this paper is to refine elements of a framework that may enable more fruitful comparative analyses of place effects on human development, inequality, and 'opportunity'. Frameworks that lack genuinely *global* application, i.e. that do not stretch to accommodate every region's patterns and policy frames, let alone every culture's assumptions, can still be immensely valuable, of course. Being less 'portable', such frameworks often generate more specific advice for scholars, practitioners and policy makers. But the signs are that a few cross-cutting questions about place, patterns of segregation and opportunity now concern a great many actors around the globe. Moreover, globalisation, together with rapid population growth in many of the world's city-regions, make it urgent that we get better at having a global conversation, one with both greater analytic reach and more positive impacts on action. Building on the frameworks for comparison, therefore, the third aim of this paper is to outline a typology of strategies that *action* key ideas about place effects and to review the evidence presented by European colleagues (in this issue) on what motivates some of these strategies in particular places, what the strategies entail, and what they may accomplish. (The authors in this volume are not exclusively concerned with poverty, of course, but in all instances, they analyse place effects or place dynamics.) The sections that follow pursue each of these aims in sequence.

Place and Opportunity in Global Perspective

What would it mean to define a more global perspective on the links between local and sub-local conditions, the power of local place, and human well-being and opportunity? Or to render inequalities, both in outcomes and opportunities, in such perspective? Whatever the specifics of such a perspective, 'global' would have at least two meanings. The first relates to level of analysis. As students of social exclusion in Europe and of de-industrialisation in the US have underlined (e.g. Allen *et al.*, 1998), the global view must define some links between sub-local and local conditions on one hand, i.e. city-regions and cities, as well as the neighbourhoods or other small areas embedded in them, and the non-local forces that help shape those conditions. This is part of a larger project of explanation in the social sciences: to link myriad changes from the global to the local, or the very macro to the very micro, and understand effects of those changes on human life.

These levels, and those in between, are not only reflected in market or social dynamics that operate at various geographic scales (to affect production and consumption, to shape cultural and political attitudes and social structures) but at multiple levels of intervention, defined as intentional actions by all three sectors (public, private and non-governmental) to improve human development and conditions of inequality. This includes affecting economic distribution, as well as citizenship, community bonds, and other correlates of human well-being, both individual and collective. These could be social investments (education, training, health), income transfers (social security, income assistance), place subsidies (for area-based upgrading and local economic development), and other policies and practices that might be considered social protection (police, fire, etc.). While all front-line practice may be local, decisions and target areas for these interventions run from the supra-national (e.g. Western Europe, Southern Africa) to the sub-local (my neighbourhood in inner-city Boston, a district in Amsterdam or Rio).

From universities and think tanks to international agencies and grassroots advocacy groups, students of globalisation, and more specifically of globalisation's implications for local places, have laid a strong foundation for this multi-level view (see, for example Amin & Thrift, 1994; Swyngedouw, 2000; UNHCS, 2001; World Bank, 1999). It remains for us to sharpen connections between the macro and micro. Studies of local place effects rarely seek to grapple with globalisation in any meaningful way, a fact that makes it particularly difficult to determine how such effects may shift over time as places (contexts) are transformed around us. Moreover, significant gaps remain in the empirical evidence available to justify broad claims about how macro-level or global changes affect the relatively small areas in which human beings develop and actually lead their lives. That some effects are logical and even likely does not mean that they have been demonstrated, typed, or appropriately qualified.

The second meaning of 'global' stems from this first requirement, that views span multiple levels of analysis and intervention, from the very micro to the very macro. Beyond spanning levels, a global view of place and opportunity should be specific and accessible (non-abstruse) enough to speak to a wide audience yet broad and robust enough to offer explanatory power in a global age. That is, a global view should not merely address causal forces in the abstract but offer some purchase on how these macro-micro linkages combine and operate in a variety of settings around the globe.

Figure 1 offers a concise, although certainly not an exhaustive, model motivated by these requirements. Three elements of this basic model are of particular interest: the *levels* (the host of causes and effects likely to operate *within* each level, the spatial and other limits); the *linkages* among levels (including the nature of effects operating downward in the multi-level system, as well as the upward feedback effects); and the *relationships* between levels and linkages on the left side and interventions on the right. First, there will be a look at the levels and linkages among them, followed by what the interventions encompass and how they relate to the left side of the picture.

At the first and most macro level, forms and rates of global inequality have changed dramatically in recent decades thanks to pervasive, large-scale changes in the nature and organisation of work, exploitable technology and patterns of natural resource use, the scope of the sectors, the state, the market, and civil society, and the nature of relations across them, and the terms of global trade and investment. These changes have contributed to widening, and widely

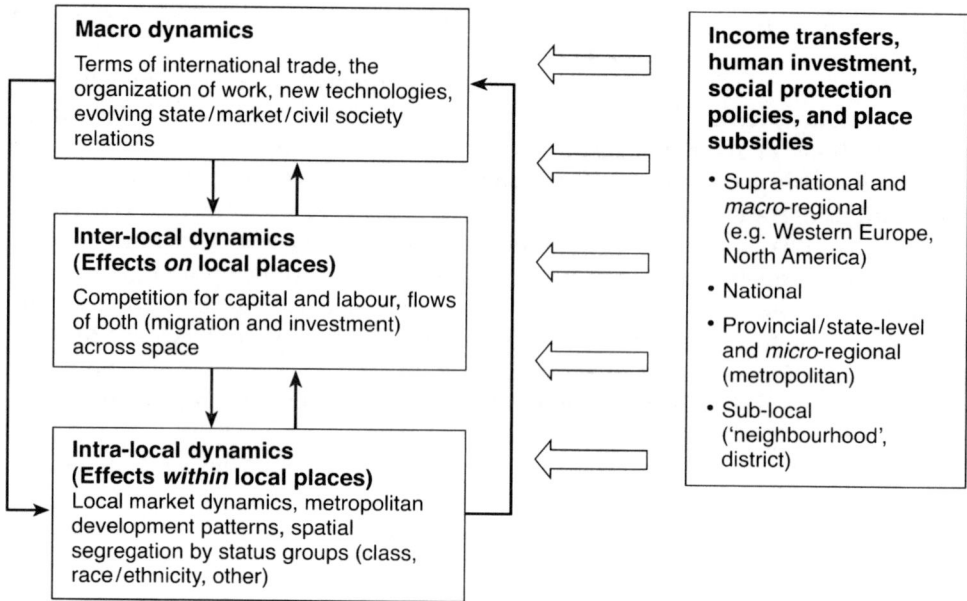

Figure 1. Place effects on inequality and opportunity, in global perspective.

documented, social and economic inequality, both within and among nations (Rodrik, 1999; Stiglitz, 2002; World Bank, 2000). From hunger to water scarcity to income poverty and more, 'global' changes clearly affect local places and depend on space to operate, but most such effects are probably indirect. They work through the second level in the model, that of inter-local dynamics, which will be looked at later.

Macro-level transformations, a focus for high-profile activism at World Trade Organisation (WTO), Genoa, and other anti-globalisation protests, have helped to renew and intensify important public debates, about how to reduce poverty and inequality overall, how to manage the tensions between growth (efficiency) and equity as societies change, and how, more specifically, to reform wage standards, working conditions, terms of trade, business regulation, and more, in technically promising and politically acceptable ways. Many advocates hope to accomplish these things on a global, defined as trans-national, scale. But rarely do these debates develop detailed, empirical diagnoses of local place effects on families and neighbourhoods that might be, in turn, shaped by the macro-level strains. That is, broad concerns about dislocation and exclusion do not, as a general rule, concern themselves with the details highlighted in this volume.

The second level of the model, which connects big changes 'beyond place' to particular local places, is defined by inter-local dynamics. These dynamics are not only about competitive pressures but about flows: rapid urbanisation in the global South owing to rural-urban migration, growth in suburban and metro-politan populations at the expense of rural ones in the industrialised North, and large flows of immigrant labour from South to North. The second level reflects labour, capital, and material flows among key urban economies, often across national borders. There is the race among cities for their place on a competitive, tiered global stage (Borja & Castells, 1997; Sassen, 2000; Savitch & Kantor, 2002). This local dimension involves a hierarchy of its own, not between owners and workers, members of distinct ethnic groups or technology 'have's' and 'have-not's' in general, but among localities as competing, live-work units. There are high-wage, high-tech 'knowledge economy' cities, cheap labour manufacturing cities (not the most desired niche), trade cities with elements of both, and other types.

In the global South, competitive strategic planning and regional economic development offer some logic of response while creating dilemmas of their own, about equity, efficiency, social and environmental sustainability, and more. In the wealthier North, and most visibly in the US, there is a new regionalism, part advocacy movement and part analytic label, employing broadly similar tools, sharing similar motives, and confronting many of the same complexities (Katz, 2000; Pastor *et al.*, 2000). To focus on the dominant, economic dimension of the new regionalism, metropolitan city-regions, to become competitive 'business units' it is said, and to promote the well-being of their residents, must consciously define their niches in a changing global marketplace (Porter, 2001). To secure and protect such niches, city-regions must marshal unprecedented co-operation among market, state and civil society actors to develop better skills, more attractive business climates, and more.

The second level of inequality thus defines a game in which, as part of global economic transformations and policy choices, the localities in which we work and live our lives face a wide variety of choices, and complicated fortunes, in the decades ahead. The choices have crucial political dimensions, of course, but the focus here is on the economic stakes: choices and outcomes in the inter-local game will help determine how large a pie will be available for local distribution or re-distribution. But those outcomes will also shape the spatial and occupational structure of cities, for example, channelling low-wage workers and the non-working poor toward some residential areas and middle- and upper-income workers to others. These effects are perhaps most widely documented London, New York, Tokyo, and other world cities, but they operate in all but the most isolated local economies (Sassen, 2000).

The structure and dynamics within local places (level three), and the nature of their effects on their residents, thus hinge in part on the stakes of the inter-local game (level two). Some debates at this second level centre on how the 're-scaling' of governance, at once downward toward local authorities and upward to nation-states and supra-national bodies, affects the choices likely to be made (Swyngedouw, 2000). The choices and their impacts have important implications for local markets in labour and land, community identity (self-image), economic redistribution, and other factors that shape space and local opportunity structures (Fainstein, 2001). But the material and political consequences of inter-local dynamics should operate upward in the model as well, feeding back into macro-level debates about how economies should be governed, who gains and who loses under given terms of trade, what industries and regions nation-states or supra-national institutions should target for special investment, and more.

At the third level in Figure 1, the one on which this special volume has focused, there is sorting and inequality within localities, whether town, city, or metropolitan areas (city-regions) are the focus. Effects within local places on individuals, families, and other actors take shape at this level. The study of local place effects on individuals, families, and sub-local units (neighbourhoods or other small areas) encompasses several overlapping traditions, some long-standing and others more recently developed, but each with distinct frames of reference and empirical emphases:

- *Studies of spatial (environmental) effects on human behaviour and attitudes*, including social interaction patterns inside and outside neighbourhoods of residence and neighbourhoods as ecologies of norms (e.g. Beckhoven & Van Kempen, this issue; Friedrichs & Blasius, this issue; review in Anderson, 1999; Briggs, 1998). These include studies focused on social organisation and collective traits (Sampson *et al.*, 1997), as well as studies that emphasise lifestyle or social 'type' differentiation within neighbourhoods or districts (Hannerz, 1969). Beckhoven & Van Kempen's study in this volume, like similar studies conducted in the US, reflects mixed intellectual origins, but these invariably include the Chicago School's concern for the distinctiveness of local social patterns or 'ways of life' (Gans, 1967; Wirth, 1964) and other branches of ecological thought.
- *Studies of social and residential mobility* as the intersection of two dynamic levels of analysis, changing neighbourhoods and changing household needs and opportunities (e.g. Kearns & Parkes, this issue; Musterd *et al.*, this issue; and see Fischer, 2002; Quillian, 1999; Taub *et al.*, 1984). Alternatively, this may be framed as the co-determination of choices about neighbourhood, employment, and other variables of interest (Galster, this issue).
- *Studies of cities and their neighbourhoods as ecological 'contexts' for human development*, wherein families mediate context effects on individuals. This tradition, with roots in the psychology of human development and sociology of the family, has dominated the past decade of research on place effects in the US (e.g. Brooks-Gunn *et al.*, 1997; Leventhal & Brooks-Gunn, 2000).
- *Studies of place as economic location, in which residential addresses offering differential access to economic opportunities in a metropolitan marketplace.* This domain includes research on the mismatch between residential concentrations of the unemployed or marginally employed and job locations—spatial mismatch (Ihlanfedlt, 1999)—as well as more complex efforts to show how spatial inequalities shape individual choices made under uncertainty and with imperfect information. For example, Galster & Killen (1995) argue that spatial differences in access to good jobs, schools and other opportunity mechanisms compound disadvantage, since some choices that appear functional and 'rational' in one's immediate social context (one of spatially concentrated deprivation) are in fact dysfunctional in the wider society, impairing functioning and mobility.

Rarely do these research traditions limit themselves to market processes, demographic change or other factors that define the left side of the model. Rather, analysts in these research traditions increasingly treat interventions as combining with the market to affect lives and life chances, to shape social interaction and economic exchanges in local places, and indeed to affect the fortunes of neighbourhoods or zones within cities. Place-based subsidies, for example for area-based upgrading (community revitalisation), do this directly. But so do decisions that affect capital flows across city space, 'fair lending' policies (to counter disparate treatment or impacts in capital markets), tax treatment of various classes of property, reforms in public school finance or enrolment (including voucher-based 'choice' schemes and desegregation) and more. The details of how we analysts treat interventions and markets as spatially organised are a matter for the next section, which will examine the issue of how we frame comparisons across national borders.

Before moving on, a note should be made of some of the most important ways by which forces at level three plausibly feed back into level two of the model: (a) by creating local labour market and sourcing/supplier failures that undermine the competitiveness of a local city-region in the global marketplace (e.g. by inefficiently matching workers and jobs, by inadequately linking local suppliers of goods and services to local demand by firms) or conversely, by creating local successes at these important linkage functions; (b) by creating a local reputation, e.g. for racial tension and exclusion or for co-existence and inclusion, that exerts signalling effects (attracting investment and human capital to particular localities and not others); and by shaping governance (collective action routines and effectiveness), influencing what actors in a local city-region can accomplish together in the inter-local game. In a recent comparative study of attempts at economic turnaround by US and Western European cities, for example, Savitch & Kantor (2002) analyse the interplay of local political behaviour, the reputations of local places in the global marketplace, reputations more malleable for some places than others, and dynamics of investment and labour flows. The list above outlines a few of the possible feedback effects (on level two of the Figure), all of them challenging to demonstrate directly, at least by traditional analytic standards.

Finally, not all macro-level (level one) effects on local places operate through inter-local competition and flows. This is true on the targeted intervention (right) side of the model, most obviously in the case of national social welfare policies (pensions, public assistance, health insurance) that directly affect individual households. But it is also true on the left side, e.g. where new technologies and new attitudes and mores (culture change) diffuse broadly across societies or, likewise, where national economic trends (contraction, expansion, re-structuring) register directly within local places.

To summarise this section and sharpen the argument that motivated it, what is most important is that those analysing fairly localised place effects not lose sight of how their work 'nests' in the bigger picture. This is true both for the analyses (which impose scoping conditions, such as ecological boundaries, on the contexts included versus those more or less ignored) and for the policy prescriptions that follow, too many of which divorce one or a handful of policy measures, such as area-based improvement schemes, from the larger package of interventions that aim to affect human welfare. It is not that any of us should seek to be comprehensive or exhaustive. The former will likely trade depth for breadth and false precision, and the latter is impossible. Rather, we should work harder to consider the proximate dynamics (left side of Figure 1) and interventions (right side) that are most likely to compromise our analytic conclusions and our prescriptions if ignored. With this as a general rule, one can imagine a number of enhancements to the highly localised studies of place effects that have been conducted to date, such as:

- Incorporating inter-local dynamics, e.g. significant immigration and capital flows, into the modelling of local or sub-local contexts and their effects, in effect, treating contexts, and not just context effects, as dynamic and porous; and
- Scaling apparent inter-neighbourhood differences in economic welfare and social well-being against city-wide and nationwide changes that reflect larger

social and economic patterns, in effect, nesting individual and local trajectories more carefully in national and supra-national (macro-regional) ones; and
• Mapping the key interventions for which residential location may have key effects on household access, use and outcomes.

Consider the example of a study of the effects of a court-ordered scattered-site public housing (subsidised development and relocation) programme on low-income families in Yonkers, New York. A team of social scientists, including this author, explored the role of education, personal networks, race, gender, neighbourhood poverty and other factors in the well-being of these families (whom I will call 'the movers'), most of them black and Latino, who left high-poverty, mostly minority inner-city neighbourhoods for mostly white, middle-income neighbourhoods across town (Briggs, 1998). The federal court found the local government and federal housing agency guilty of deliberate discrimination in the siting of public housing, which had been concentrated in Yonkers' lowest income, most racially segregated neighbourhoods over three decades. Beyond these most local and most visible factors of race, space, class and segregative public policy lay a set of challenging realities about how some of the mover families came to live in the city (at all) and, more specifically, in subsidised housing.

First, the team learned that a number of the immigrant families belonged to active transnational networks of Latin American workers and business owners for whom Yonkers was a site in the larger metro New York economy. Resources and threats important to these families' lives and life fortunes were thus a part of far-flung global structures that a navel-gazing focus on the immediate neighbourhood context could all too easily overlook. Second, Yonkers had for years been a declining industrial suburb of metro New York City (Harris, 1991), but a new phase of economic restructuring was beginning just as the low-income families at the heart of the study moved out of the city's compact, high-poverty ghetto in the early 1990s. Most relevant to these families was the start of a downtown renaissance tied to waterfront commercial development and new, market-rate housing. The latter boomed by the late 1990s as housing prices soared in adjacent New York City and households sought quality housing alternatives elsewhere in the metro area. New, high-wage entry-level jobs were created, and the first middle-income housing in downtown Yonkers in 30 years was developed, just as poor families departed for 'opportunity' elsewhere.

Third, relocation had mixed effects on the subject families' ('the movers') access to the public services and targeted interventions outlined on the right side of Figure 1. Some effects were quite basic, e.g. the courts had ordered the city-wide racial desegregation of Yonkers' public schools alongside the creation of scattered-site housing (a dual remedy that made the Yonkers case a landmark in US jurisprudence). This meant that changing neighbourhoods did not necessarily mean changing schools, to be more specific, did not ensure access to a 'better' school near one's new home. Other effects on service and subsidy access were more complex: as noted above, the movers' old neighbourhoods benefited from place subsidies for economic development, and the new neighbourhoods offered few health or human service institutions with experience meeting the needs of very low-income black and Latino families, no faith institutions that were familiar or seemed welcoming to the movers (organised religion is among the most racially segregated institutional sectors in the US), and few approachable civic associations as well.

The first insight above incorporated key inter-local dynamics, the second a scaling up in levels of analysis was considered—the larger, shifting geography of jobs could hardly be ignored as the effects of family relocation were sought—and the third some detailed knowledge of the spatial organisation of public services, targeted subsidies, and even accessible faith and civic groups. It is not that hypothesised micro-level effects were rendered intractable through a huge expansion of the targets of analysis. Rather, the major assumptions brought to the micro level, and the paths of effect that were considered for testing, were richer and more open-ended.

The long-run impacts of the Yonkers mobility programme on participating families are not yet clear, but the comments above underscore a simple and important notion: moves 'to opportunity' may involve quite uneven trade-offs (Briggs, 1997), and the nested (multi-level) view compels attention to be paid to this. On one hand, a stylised narrative about inner-city social and economic isolation may motivate societal response, particularly when combined with savvy legal advocacy and a willing judiciary. On average, a move away from high crime and high poverty areas within a city may indeed yield major benefits for movers, at negligible social cost to the movers, the neighbourhoods and the larger city. But the embeddedness of households, neighbourhoods and cities in larger regional and global dynamics requires a modicum of peripheral vision, not to mention a few specific, testable links, in this case, about immigration flows, dispersed networks, shifting economic patterns within and beyond the immediate city limits, and the spatial reach of institutions that focus on the needs of poor minorities. In lieu of such vision, formulaic and misleading assumptions about place effects may obtain.

Place–Opportunity Links Compared Across Places

Researchers have offered a range of insightful comparisons of the place-opportunity nexus in Europe and the US over the past decade. Ethnographic comparisons have explored differences in race and class relations in European and American cities (e.g. Wacquant, 1993). Broader comparisons have analysed markets, the welfare state and rates of social exclusion and material deprivation (e.g. Musterd & Ostendorf, 1998; Friedrichs, 2002). These studies, or commentaries, typically conclude that material poverty and other dimensions of social exclusion differ more in scale than form when European and American cities, neighbourhoods and households are compared with one another. Friedrichs (2002) observes, for example:

> European countries typically intervene earlier in declining areas … European governments pursue broader social welfare policies … There is no minority [in Europe] discriminated against like blacks in the US, neither Algerians in France, Surinamese in the Netherlands, West Indians in the UK, or Turks in Germany. Social integration is comparatively higher and spatial segregation lower than in US cities. Finally, crime rates and the corresponding fear of crime are much lower in Europe than in US distressed poverty neighbourhoods. (p. 101)

But he adds that poor neighbourhoods in Europe, like counterparts in the US, are typically quite heterogeneous. Only the most chronically poor and socially isolated individuals and families lead lives circumscribed distinctly by the poverty and spatial form of their immediate neighbourhoods. It would be useful to know how dynamic poor neighbourhoods are in Europe, since selective in and out-migration are known to play important roles in concentrating neighbourhood poverty and compounding household-level disadvantage in US cities (Quillian, 1999).

More encompassing comparisons of place-opportunity links in Europe and America (and elsewhere if possible) must address similarities and differences that cover markets, the welfare state, subtleties of perception (stigmas and more), and the circumstances in which individual choices are made by members of disadvantaged groups. Toward this more interactive analysis, for example, Galster (2002) proposes a three-part opportunity model that should be testable on both sides of the Atlantic and, indeed, in cities around the globe. It consists of:

1. An *opportunity structure*, defined as "the array of markets and institutions providing the potential means of social mobility with which the individual may interact, such as labour, housing and financial markets, schools, and the social welfare and criminal justice systems" (p. 6). Galster adds that the quality and practices promulgated by the elements of this structure can vary dramatically across localities within a given nation, and, it might be added, across nation-states as well.
2. *Individual characteristics*, some malleable (education, wealth, criminal record, residential location) and some not (race, gender, parents). Put differently, these constitute elements of status that are either *achieved* or *ascriptive*. The distinction is particularly important where potential place effects are potentially confounded by the fact that educational, residential, and other outcomes are co-determined (Galster, this issue).
3. *Individual 'perceptions' of the opportunity structure*: "what parts of it are feasible to access and what the potential payoffs are then likely to be" (Galster, 2002, p. 6). Including this choice dimension is much more than an acknowledgment of the agency of the poor or the disadvantaged. It has an analytic pay-off that is quite important, facilitating the consideration of: spatial variations in perceptions and the choices they motivate; spatial differences in the information to which the poor seem to have access (e.g. knowledge of the local housing and labour markets); and varied sources of local social influence (e.g. personal networks and civic groups) versus non-local influence (e.g. news and cultural media). These analyses, in turn, offer many leverage points for policies and practices that respond to poverty or other problems.

Assume that individual characteristics and perceptions indeed influence well-being and mobility beyond the direct effects of the 'opportunity structure'. Both empirical evidence and practical politics support the making of that big assumption, that living conditions and fortunes are a function of external supports, internal capabilities and choice. Assume further that both traits and perceptions can be analysed relatively well, subject to time, money, protection of human subjects, and other constraints. The distinctions among elements of the 'opportunity structure' remain to be analysed. Some elements plausibly exert direct effects on individual and household opportunity, while the primary function of other elements may be to mediate such effects, compounding negatives or reinforcing positives, in effect creating virtuous or vicious cycles.

Consider Table 1, which synthesises the US evidence on such direct and indirect effects. Some mechanisms operate through direct effects of spatial organisation–educational quality is higher in one jurisdiction or district than another, entry-level or professional/managerial jobs are growing here and not there, etc.—while other mechanisms are epiphenomena of those primary mechanisms—crime and its traumas are unevenly felt across space, local social ecologies (social resources and normative influence) are defined in part by spatial boundaries, and social stigmas map onto space (i.e. 'ghetto' becomes a place-associated social type, not just a stigmatised place). Interventions, as per Figure 1 above, may be benefit or burden in a given context, bridging spatial inequalities or tracking and reinforcing them. Subsidised (social) housing is a classic example, since it directly shapes locational choice. In the US, the geography of housing assistance is clear: subsidised housing for low and moderate income households is concentrated overwhelmingly in central-city areas and often in poor neighbourhoods specifically, while subsidies to middle- and upper-income households, primarily through favourable tax treatment of home ownership, disproportionately flow to more affluent suburban neighbourhoods (Newman & Schnare, 1997).

A programme of place-opportunity comparisons across places, whether within a nation or across many, may thus track the interaction, in a given context, of individual traits, individual perceptions of the opportunity structure and choices that follow thereon, and the direct and indirect effects of multiple elements of that structure. At the risk of belabouring the obvious, analysing place effects in the opportunity structure and individuals' relationships to that structure becomes a far more subtle and creative enterprise than the cataloguing of resource richness by place. The 'structure' is not just the aggregate structural traits of the formal systems, housing markets, education, criminal justice, and more, but is a resultant structure, a product of the formal and informal mechanisms interacting.

The next section applies some of these concepts to the studies in this volume, beginning with their analytic approaches and concluding with a discussion of action implications, i.e. for interventions that aim to change place effects on individuals or households.

Implications: Re-thinking and Re-shaping Place Effects

The European studies in this issue address residential mobility in relation to neighbourhood decline in the UK (Kearns & Parkes), effects of mixed-income neighbourhood restructuring in the Netherlands (Van Beckhoven & Van Kempen), potential links between neighbourhood traits and household social mobility in the Netherlands (Musterd *et al.*), and links among neighbourhood poverty, social networks, and reported norms in Germany (Friedrichs & Blasius). As the papers offer too much for comment to be made in detail, the main objective here is to offer synthesis and perspective and thereby to encourage richer comparative thinking.

Table 1. Place effect mechanisms: a framework for comparisons using US evidence

Primary mechanisms (formal)	Effects
1. Spatial organisation of metropolitan labour market opportunities.	Mismatch between job locations and housing concentrations of racial, income or other groups contributes to commuting barriers, job information loss, less proximate and less useful job networks to which minorities and the poor are connected (Hughes 1995; Ihlanfeldt, 1999; Kain, 1968; Kasinitz & Rosenberg, 1996; Ross, 2001).
2. Spatial organisation of universal-access public services, including education.	Variations in policy and funding by neighbourhood (within a political jurisdiction) and across jurisdictions within a metro area: provide residents of different locations unequal access to quality services (review in Galster & Killen, 1995).
3. Spatial organization (siting and management) of risk or opportunity-generating land uses.	Political decisions site environmental hazards and other risk producers and 'locally unwanted land uses' unequally across metro areasнthe focus of 'environmental justice' (Pastor *et al.*, 2001; Popper, 1991). Likewise, new job generators, parks and other positives are unevenly dispersed.

Mitigating or Compounding Mechanisms (informal) and their Effects

4. The benefits and costs of neighbourly ties.	While many social networks, influential norms and civic attachments develop beyond the immediate neighbourhood, proximate social forces can contribute significant burden as well as aid, including peer influences compounding or mitigating other effects of place (Briggs, 1998; Galster & Killen, 1995; Sampson *et al.*, 1997; Stack, 1974; Sullivan, 1989).
5. Space (place of residence) as a 'signal' of worth and intent.	Disadvantaged neighbourhoods and their residents obtain linked reputations or stigmas that act as signals, shaping perceptions and decisions of opportunity-brokering outsiders, such as employers (Kirschenman & Neckerman, 1991; Tilly *et al.*, 2001) and real estate professionals (Yinger, 1995). Residents of high-status ('cache') neighborhoods benefit from the opposite effect: people are thought better for living in the right places. In terms of economic decisions, race and space interact to perpetuate information failures.
6. Spatial concentrations of violent crime and other trauma-producing risks.	Trauma-inducing violent crime and other behaviours are highly concentrated physically, limiting healthy human development and social functioning (Fullilove *et al.*, 1998; Lawson, 1999), parental willingness to leave children at home and go to work, and even collective efficacy among neighbours to address shared problems (Morenoff *et al.*, 2001).

Mitigating or Compounding Mechanisms (formal) and their Effects

7. Spatial organisation of limited-access 'welfare state' services (by public, private, or non-governmental providers).	Specialty services for the disadvantaged (by racial minority, income, or other status) may relieve or exacerbate spatial inequalities. Subsidised housing, for example, may further concentrate the poor away from goods jobs, schools and services (Newman & Schnare, 1997), shaping where the disadvantaged live.
8. Presence and effectiveness of brokering ('bridging') institutions that compensate for spatial inequalities.	Workforce development (Harrison & Weiss, 1998), housing counseling (Turner, 1998), and other intermediaries, often not part of the formal welfare state, help mitigate spatial and other barriers.

Poor Places and Household Choices in the UK

Kearns & Parkes offer a helpful look at how place traits interact with household preferences and choices, and they discourage facile assumptions that the latter two vary neatly together. While the study does not clarify which pathways of effect are best supported by available data, the authors suggest that effects of neighbourhood decline on household mobility operate through perceptions and satisfaction on one hand ('will' to move) and ability to move ('way'). Thus, say the authors, neighbourhood decline "had the effect of *increasing* the odds that someone would wish to move home but *decreasing* the odds that they would actually do so" (emphasis added). Assuming that both in-migration to neighbourhoods and out-migration from them are selective, these results pose dilemmas for those trying to intervene: should society accelerate out-migration if those households most likely to move, controlling for tenure, represent important resources for neighbourhood revitalisation? If so, who should be targeted for assisted relocation? Does the right decision depend, as Galster *et al.* (2000) argue, on whether a neighbourhood has declined beyond a certain threshold or tipping point?

Future statistical estimates of these relationships should employ simultaneous equation models where possible. A key analytic risk is confounding selection effects with effects of context or other factors. If the same individual characteristics help shape (co-determine) decisions to move to or remain in a neighbourhood, (logically prior) assessments of neighbourhood quality, and ability to move if desired, what results is, at best, a multi-stage path or, more likely, a maze of simultaneity. Further, the complexity of these calculations for households make qualitative data invaluable as a complement to large, longitudinal datasets. Policy makers, community developers and service providers quite proximate to these households frequently need help targeting the diversity of respondents masked in broad statistical tabulations. Kearns & Parkes, for example, focus on broad description of perception and moving behaviour but do not yet explain what drives either.

These methodological challenges and hopes notwithstanding, Kearns & Parkes remind us of very straightforward risks to diverse household types living in, and in some cases apparently 'stuck', in declining neighbourhoods. One risk is to household wealth in the form of home owner equity. The action implications of this risk involve tricky questions of scale, and again, peripheral vision in policy making is crucial. For example, assistance programmes targeting home owners in older urban neighbourhoods have an important track record in the US, through the Congressionally chartered Neighbourhood Reinvestment Corporation's below market-rate capital and technical assistance, and through other mechanisms. But such programmes now struggle to compete with aggressive marketing from subprime lenders who target poor and minority households with credit problems. These lenders respond to national and international trends in capital markets (those larger, inter-local flows), and regulation has been slow to keep up (Apgar, forthcoming; U.S.HUD, 2000).

Urban Re-structuring and Localism in the Netherlands

Although their analytic aims are distinct, Van Beckhoven & Van Kempen confront methodological hurdles similar to those in the UK study. Whether the intervention triggering the research is mixed-income 'urban re-structuring' in the Netherlands or similar HOPE VI public housing revitalisation in the US, analyses must make an effort to distinguish class and life-stage effects from effects of place re-structuring *per se*. That is, prior evidence favours a powerful null hypothesis: that changes in attitude and behaviour following place re-structuring owe to selection effects and not to within-neighbourhood influences (changes in the context), i.e. that, as the authors themselves note, the key effect of the intervention was to change the composition of a neighbourhood. Once this is addressed, the study becomes, in effect, an updating of classic analyses of localism and 'way of life', with dimensions of psychological attachment (to place and neighbours), social networks and interaction habits, and the spatial organisation of households consumption and other activities (e.g. where shopping needs are met, where leisure happens). In general, the authors' appear to corroborate Gans' (1967) claim that class and life stage, two variables through which selection effects operate strongly, determine how localised everyday lives are. Like the builders of 'new towns' in the US, European decision makers have multiple levers with which to apply this knowledge, including occupancy policy (composition), urban design (layout, propinquity), and activity programming and institution building (retail, education and social services, recreation) tied to re-structured places.

Norms and Networks: Localism in Germany

Friedrichs & Blasius analyse localism in the reported norms and networks of residents in four Cologne neighbourhoods that vary in ethnicity, income and other compositional traits. They seek to test the possibility that neighbourhoods are in fact contexts for social learning, in effect, for 'norming', and that areas of comparatively concentrated deprivation are at greater risk of the influence of deviant norms. First, a bit of history: the authors are right to highlight William Julius Wilson's enormous influence on the recent spate of research and policy debate on effects of concentrated poverty. But in the US, specific concerns for the excessive social 'embeddedness' of disadvantaged persons in disadvantaged neighbourhoods precedes Wilson's seminal work by two decades. In the late 1960s and early 1970s, scholars defined and tested the idea that poor minorities in increasingly segregated inner-city neighbourhoods were 'ghetto bound', to use the term of that era (Wellman, 1971). But the empirical evidence suggested that the concern was largely unfounded, except perhaps for the very poorest minority households living among the concentrations of the same, such as in certain high-rise social housing projects (Rainwater, 1970; Wellman, 1971). These, of course, are the very hyper-concentrations, compounded and increased over 20 intervening years, that motivated Wilson's (1987) hotly debated arguments about the possible emergence of an urban 'underclass', an idea that resonated with the US public's understanding of ghetto life.

More generally stated, localism is the exception rather than the rule in social relations, and the key exception categories are these:

- *Life stage.* The social contacts (alters) and peer influences of the very young and very old tend to be more localised than those of other age groups (McPherson *et al.*, 2001).
- *Type of poverty.* The social lives of the chronically poor (not the short-term

poor) tend to be more constrained, due to constrained access to wider social milieus (Briggs, 1998). That said, ties to the most proximate neighbours may also be wary, owing to fears of exploitation by the chronically needy (Rainwater, 1970).

- *Geographic isolation.* Extreme physical isolation, such as living on a small island or remote peninsula, can localise social ties, in part by restricting alternative social options (Fischer, 1977). Such communities may also be comparatively more stable than others, i.e. minimally affected by in-migration that generates frequent encounters among strangers and perceived threats of displacement by 'newcomers'.

- *Pool effects.* A large local pool of socially similar persons may localise anyone's ties, particularly if the social world beyond that pool offers relatively fewer compatible alters (McPherson *et al.*, 2001). On the other hand, the scarcity of such alters locally makes it more likely that ties and interactions will be primarily extra-local, i.e. that persons will need to 'shop' further afield for contacts and affiliation (Gans, 1967).

These tendencies away from network localism notwithstanding, Friedrichs & Blasius focus on social influence and the development of recognisable norms among neighbours. The researchers recognise that the structure, localism and functions of networks should figure into the normative picture, but networks are not the primary interest. Friedrichs & Blasius consider competing theories of context effects on behaviour (a sub-category of context effects). They emphasise social contagion theories that allow for both 'cues' (behavioural influence through observation or what Tienda (1991) termed 'demonstration effects') and interaction (which may influence behaviour through persuasion, competition or other forces). The approach draws on and extends social disorganisation research, which focuses on norms and deviant behaviour and, increasingly, on joint capacity to exert informal social control, how and why 'collective efficacy' varies across neighbourhoods (Sampson *et al.*, 1997).

Friedrichs & Blasius' findings strongly corroborate the core of Wilson's concentration hypothesis, that high rates of spatially concentrated deprivation are associated with a greater incidence of deviant behaviours and less effective local social control, albeit primarily for areas of highly concentrated deprivation, as the authors warn. The implications for norming *per se* are less clear. The authors consider direct effects of neighbourhoods as well as those mediated by networks or other institutions. Several of the assumptions should be qualified, for example: neighbourhood traits probably help shape only the most localised elements of personal networks, not the networks as a whole (so networks cannot generally be treated as fully nested or embedded in spatial neighbourhoods); while it is true that neighbourhoods may act, particularly for the young, as an ecology of potential contacts (pools), the empirical evidence on social influence generally suggests that selection effects outweigh net peer influence, that is, that peers act in similar ways because they share similar individual traits more than because they emulate each other's attitudes and behaviours through 'contagion' (McPherson *et al.*, 2001); and finally, smaller networks tend to be more insular (less diverse in range and function), so it may be misleading to conclude that size of network, not localism per se, is associated with deviance and tolerance measures. This is particularly so where bivariate correlations are the only measures employed.

It seems possible, moreover, that studies of this type, regardless of the specific analytic models employed, track several interrelated, and perhaps confounded, phenomena, such as:

- 'Social types': that neighbourhoods are shared by those who are very residentially embedded (localised in social ties, normative perspective, and more) and those who are not (Yancey *et al.*, 1985). This is one dimension of the recurring theme of population homogeneity (on which more below). Residents of the most deprived neighbourhoods may be more alike than not on the crudest measures (income and education levels, ethnic identity, etc.) but quite diverse as social types. It is very helpful that Friedrichs & Blasius factor in within-neighbourhood 'exposure' and network localism as indicators of social embeddedness.
- Associations and individual organisers: secular, faith-based, and other local institutions that influence the emergence of norms and, in particular, of the capacity to exert social control. Since this is, in part, a collective action problem, civic associations and other social institutions can lower perceived risk, improve information flows, deepen social and psychological attachments (bonding) and more. Associational data are easier to come by in surveys than are data on the second set of actors, individual 'organisers' or social catalysts who frame issues, sharpen stakes and create useful relationships.

Whatever the nature of the underlying social structures and processes, Friedrichs & Blasius' results raise a series of intriguing questions about how proximate influence (localised learning) operates: is 'tolerance' (as the authors' define it using their survey) the same as permissiveness? Is an individual's resignation to some types of within-neighbourhood behaviour, even if the behaviour is objectionable to the person, an indicator of psychological make-up (and coping tendencies) as well as collective efficacy in the environment? That is, to what degree do survey respondents factor in expectations about neighbours' co-operation or non-co-operation to inhibit bad behaviour, a key to Sampson *et al.*'s collective efficacy construct? Acceptance is a many-faceted phenomenon, and this makes strong inferences from these survey data quite risky. Most of us routinely fail to respond to behaviour that we find objectionable, and some such 'failures', choosing among more and less objectionable behaviours, judging risk to ourselves, assessing the likely responses of neighbours, considering other facets of the situation, may be highly rational. The big questions in Europe, America, and elsewhere are when, why and what should be done? The study could be read as an endorsement of poverty deconcentration policies but also as support for effective community organising, particularly to overcome collective action problems in urban neighbourhoods.

Ecological Effects and Social Mobility in the Netherlands

Musterd *et al.* face perhaps the most serious empirical challenges, and again these relate most directly to selection effects of residential location. The researchers seek to determine effects of the spatial concentration of benefit-dependent households on households' shifts in/out of the labour force. That is, the study is fundamentally a risk analysis with two states (household has at least one employed member, household income is dependent on public benefits) and a single intervening period in which movement between states is possible. This is analogous to the Bane & Ellwood (1994) analysis of spells of benefits (welfare) receipt and predictors of transition between benefits and paid work in the US, except that Bane & Ellwood do not analyse ecological effects.

Having found relatively weak ecological effects, Musterd *et al.* propose that the critical variable may be strength of 'starting position' (what risk state the household is in at time 1), specifically that the effect of being in the benefit-dependent state may outweigh any ecological effects. This is certainly possible, although the claim is difficult to assess given potential selection effects. An alternative explanation is that employed households living in areas of concentrated benefit dependence are a quite select group of households primarily composed of the marginally employed or employable. Since the risk states under study do not include any state stronger than the starting positions of these households (e.g. higher income or more prestigious occupation), the results tend to emphasise downward mobility only. It may be that the study is picking up downward movement by the subgroup of employed households that is most vulnerable to downturns in the business cycle or to other shocks. The presence of such subgroups (population heterogeneity) is both the key analytic problem that risk analysis is meant to address and the bane of designing such analysis effectively (Stokey & Zeckhauser, 1978). Moreover, the US evidence on mobility into and out of poor neighbourhoods underscores the weaker labour market status and generally weaker employability (even where employed) of the households that are most likely to move into poor neighbourhoods and least likely to leave them (Quillian, 1999).

The policy utility of this study may lie in the very decision to emphasise risk states. Risk highlights the heterogeneity issue (what types, how much, what significance), the issue of entry as well as exit (between states), the importance of starting position (initial state), and the role of policy in affecting two things: (a) how households in a given state manage it (at least cost or greatest benefit to quality of life and future positive mobility); and (b) how to help households make positive shifts between states. Reviewing the evidence on wage earning and income dynamics in the UK, Hills (2002, p. 231) distinguishes these two as 'effects of' versus 'risk of', and identifies four types of policy intervention that may respond: (1) *prevention* (of entry into a negative state); (2) *promotion* (of exit or escape from a negative state); (3) *protection* (against negative effects of being in a negative state); and (4) *propulsion* (maximising effects of escaping a negative state toward a positive one). Musterd *et al.*'s results suggest that such thinking may fruitfully consider movement in and out of the workforce as well as in and out of poor neighbourhoods. But effects of the latter, whether 'net' of other factors or mediated by them too, remain unclear.

Conclusions: Enabling Better Comparisons and Better Outcomes

The European studies featured in this issue vary not only by context and types of data employed but by primary social concern: is the main 'problem' thought to be excessive concentrations of deprivation in urban space because of concentration effects on labour performance or control of deviant behaviour? Or the challenges of mixing population groups in 'deconcentrated' areas? Or place effects on economic risk, such as to household wealth, over and above the selection effects that segregate people by wealth into different areas?

From an analytic standpoint, the researchers' focus on specific contexts, and in some instances specific interventions, is a key strength. The models outlined here are to encourage more peripheral vision, specifically 'nesting' (Figure 1), and more careful distinctions among elements of an 'opportunity structure' thought to help shape place effects on human life (Table 1). But neither model emphasises a particular policy objective or clarifies how a particular objective should be pursued in a given context. It is hoped that these models leave room for the particular while encouraging more synthesis and learning across contexts.

From a policy perspective, though, there are several risks in having a conversation about poor neighbourhoods, or place and deprivation, that remains quite particular from context to context: confusion over what the specific, desired ends in fact are; reliance on inadequate 'theories of change' or logic models (Briggs, 2003; Chen, 1990; Weiss, 1995) to achieve chosen ends given available, or imaginable means; and competing ends for which no one has thought up ways to mitigate trade-offs. Analytic complexities, minutiae to the wider public but essential grist for the mill of scholarship, encourage a fairly narrow focus on which ends may in fact be desirable, let alone attainable, and a tendency to rely on existing policy rather than to imagine new possibilities. In the long run, this is a recipe for incrementalism both in the diagnoses we offer and defend and in the interventions we prescribe or seek to improve.

Where poverty of place is concerned, the public conversation has often ignored, and well-intended scholarly debates have muddled, a crucial distinction. Framed as a question of public strategy, the distinction is this: should we emphasise reducing place segregation (by race, poverty status, dependence on public benefits, or correlated factors) or reducing its social costs without trying to reduce the extent of segregation itself to any significant degree? Put differently, should we invest, often against the odds, in the US case, in changing where people are willing and able to reside or try to transform the factors that link a person's place of residence to well-being and opportunity, to living conditions and life chances?

Consider Table 2, the final model in this paper, wherein 'cure' strategies seek to reduce rates of segregation and 'mitigate' strategies seek to reduce the social costs. This distinction should not be confused with the one between people and place-based interventions. Assisting households or otherwise influencing their behaviour and social outcomes is classic 'people' policy, while area-based upgrading or neighbourhood-based political organising efforts undeniably target places. Note that, thus defined, both people and place-based interventions are logically useful under both the 'cure' and 'mitigate' strategies in Table 1 and that quite a few specific interventions target places as well as people (or households). Furthermore, 'place-based' often means 'targeting the behaviour and outcomes of groups of people in a place' rather than, more narrowly and literally, 'affecting a physical place' (e.g. through environmental design). The purpose of the model is to map a range of responses against corresponding problems. The problems range from exclusionary land use policies (large lot requirements, prohibitions against multi-family housing, etc.), which are pervasive in the US but visible in other countries as well, to stigmas associated with residence in low status neighbourhoods ('space as a signal'), all factors identified in research on place and opportunity. A given strategy may be prescribed for multiple problems; likewise, a given problem may require multiple strategies, well executed, at the appropriate scale. The studies and commentary in this issue

Table 2. Re-shaping the geography of opportunity: defining problems and strategies

Target problem/sub-problems	Responses
High rates of residential (place) segregation	*'Cure' strategies*
Exclusionary land use policies	'Fair share' housing policies, overrides of local land use decisions by higher authorities
Market discrimination by sellers, lenders, brokers	Regulatory (fair housing enforcement) and educational (sellers, consumers, real estate brokers, lenders)
Segregative residential choices by market-rate consumers (including neighbourhood avoidance)	Affirmative marketing (to minority and/or majority groups)
	Housing subsidies, relocation counseling and choice incentives ('housing mobility' interventions) for low-income households.
	Community development (area-based upgrading, including mixed-income and mixed-tenure housing development (e.g. U.S. HOPE VI programme), to attract diverse in-movers
Discrimination in subsidised (social) housing	Affirmative marketing (to minority and/or majority groups)
	Housing subsidies, counselling and choice incentives for low-income households
	Community development (upgrading) of social housing and environs to attract diverse in-movers
Segregative choices by subsidised consumers	Affirmative occupancy policy, housing mobility programmes
	Community development (upgrading) of social housing and environments
High costs of residential segregation	*'Mitigate' strategies*
Educational inequality across schools or school districts	School desegregation by mandatory busing or voluntary choice programmes and magnet schools
	Fiscal reform to reduce spatial inequality (equalise or affirmatively compensate)
Barriers to job access	Reverse commuting (transportation)
	Regional workforce development alliances or networks (intermediation, matching of workers and jobs)
	Equal employment opportunity (anti-discrimination) enforcement and education.
	Workforce development and 'job readiness' programmes (self-presentation, behavioural norms)
Spatially concentrated crime, lower quality housing and services, lack of amenities	Community development (upgrading) of neighbourhoods
	Public service reform and expansion (human services, health, policing, etc.)
Neighbourhood stigmas (space as a signal)	Community development (upgrading) of neighbourhoods

raise, but for the most part do not yet answer, questions about full policy intent and the logics of intervention.

If we believe that space is indeed an important contributor to inequality, deprivation and other measures of unacceptable social conditions and access-to-opportunity problems, not through simple 'addition' of a spatial barrier but as a mediator of varied factors, formal and informal, then the challenge becomes one of better specifying how place-opportunity links can be re-shaped. Helping households on housing assistance to relocate may be a fine strategy for many of those families, and encouraging mixed-income neighbourhoods preventatively will yield benefits even where interaction among the groups mixed is not evident (since many place effects do not depend on interacting with one's neighbours). But other types of intervention deserve our attention and our scrutiny as well, particularly where growing city-regions are able to mount multiple strategies and to head off the high rates of segregation found in many older cities.

In Europe and the US alike, defining official policy and having effective intervention strategies are two different things. Particular types of public and private action may be authorised but not adequately funded or, in the case of regulatory protections, enforced. Noble aims may rest on flimsy logics or action strategies, and the proverbial left and right 'hands' (multiple well-intended actors) may be working at cross purposes. The interest in neighbourhood poverty as a problem worthy of money, attention, political capital, and other precious resources is heartening, even where our progress is slow or a bit confused. But those of us who wish to support and expand this interest, and to encourage better public action, through our analyses can get better at both focusing our 'magnifying glasses' and stopping, from time to time, to survey the wider vistas before us.

Acknowledgments

Many thanks to the Annie E. Casey Foundation and The Rockefeller Foundation for supporting my research time and to MIT's Department of Urban Studies and Planning for hosting me as the Martin Luther King, Jr. Visiting Fellow (2002–2004). George Galster and David Varady provided helpful feedback on these ideas.

Correspondence

Xavier de Souza Briggs, Harvard University, John F. Kennedy School of Government, 79 JFK Street, Cambridge, MA, 02138, USA. Email: xavier_briggs@harvard.edu

References

Allen, J., Cars, G. & Mandanipour, A. (1998) *Social Exclusion in European Cities: Processes, Experiences, and Reponses* (London, Jessica Kingsley).
Amin, A. & Thrift, N. (Eds) (1994) *Globalisation, Institutions and Regional Development in Europe* (Oxford, OUP).
Anderson, E. (1999) *Code of the Street: Decency, Violence, and the Moral Life of the Inner City* (New York, W.W. Norton).

Apgar, W. C. (forthcoming) Second class capital: the racial geography of subprime lending, in: X. de S. Briggs (Ed.) *Housing Opportunity, Race, and the Regional Agenda*.

Bane, M. J. & Ellwood, D. T. (1994) *Welfare Reform: From Rhetoric to Reality* (Cambridge, MA, Harvard University Press).

Borja, J. & Castells, M. (1997) *Local and Global: The Management of Cities in the Information Age* (London, Earthscan).

Briggs, X. de S. (1997) Moving up versus moving out: neighborhood effects in housing mobility programs, *Housing Policy Debate*, 8, pp. 195–234.

Briggs, X. de S. (1998) Brown kids in white suburbs, *Housing Policy Debate*, 9, pp. 177–221.

Briggs, X. de S. (2003) Housing opportunity, desegregation strategy, and policy research, *Journal of Policy Analysis and Management*, 22, pp. 201–206.

Brooks-Gunn, J., Duncan, G. J & Aber, J. L. (1997) *Neighborhood Poverty: Context and Consequences for Children*, Volume 1 (New York, Russell Sage Foundation).

Chen, H. (1990) *Theory-Driven Evaluations* (Newbury Park, CA, Sage Publications).

Fainstein, S. (2001) Inequality in global city-regions, in: A. J. Scott (Ed.) *Global City-Regions* (New York, Oxford University Press).

Fischer, C. S. (1977) *Networks and Places: Social Relations in the Urban Setting* (New York, Free Press).

Fischer, C. S. (2002) Ever-more rooted Americans, *City & Community*, 1, pp. 175–193.

Friedrichs, J. (2002) Response: contrasting US and European findings on poverty neighborhoods, *Housing Studies*, 17, pp. 101–106.

Fullilove, M. T., Leon, V., Jimenez, W. & Parsons, C. (1998) Injury and anomie: effects of violence on an inner-city community, *American Journal of Public Health*, 88, pp. 924–927.

Galster, G.C. (2002) Editorial: trans-Atlantic perspectives on opportunity, deprivation, and the housing nexus, *Housing Studies*, 17, pp. 5–10.

Galster, G. C., & Killen, S. P. (1995) The geography of metropolitan opportunity: a reconnaissance and conceptual framework, *Housing Policy Debate*, 6, pp. 7–43.

Galster, G. C., Quercia, R. & Cortes, A. (2000) Identifying neighborhood thresholds: an empirical exploration, *Housing Policy Debate*, 11, pp. 701–732.

Gans, H. J. (1967) *The Levittowners: Ways of Life and Politics in a New Suburban Community* (New York, Columbia University Press).

Hannerz, U. (1969) *Soulside: Inquiries into Ghetto Culture and Community* (New York, Columbia).

Harris, R. (1991) The geography of employment and residence in New York since 1950, in: J. Mollenkopf & M. Castells (Eds) *Dual City: Restructuring New York* (New York, Russell Sage Foundation).

Harrison, B. & Weiss, M. (1998) *Workforce Development Networks: Community-based Organizations and Regional Alliances* (Thousand Oaks, CA, Sage Publications).

Hills, J. (2002) Does a focus on social exclusion change the policy response?, in: J. Hills, J. Le Grand & D. Piachaud (Eds) *Understanding Social Exclusion* (Oxford, OUP).

Hughes, M. A. (1995) A mobility strategy for improving opportunity, *Housing Policy Debate*, 6, pp. 271–297.

Ihlanfeldt, K. (1999) The geography of economic and social opportunity within metropolitan areas, in: A. Altshuler, W. Morrill, H. Wolman, & F. Mitchell (Eds) *Governance and Opportunity in Metropolitan America* (Washington, DC, National Academy Press).

Kain, J. (1968) Housing desegregation, negro employment, and metropolitan decentralization, *Quarterly Journal of Economics*, 32, pp. 175–197.

Kasinitz, P. & Rosenberg, J. (1996) Missing the connection: social isolation and employment on the Brooklyn Waterfront, *Social Forces*, 43, pp. 180–195.

Katz, B. (Ed.) (2000) *Reflections on Regionalism* (Washington, DC, Brookings Institution Press).

Kirschenman, J. & Neckerman, K. (1991) 'We'd love to hire them, but …': the meaning of race for employers, in: C. Jencks & P. E. Peterson *The Urban Underclass* (Washington, DC, Brookings Institution Press).

Lawson, A. (Ed.) (1999) *Disease Mapping and Risk Assessment for Public Health* (Chichester and New York, Wiley).

Leventhal, T. & Brooks-Gunn, J. (2000) The neighborhoods they live in: the effects of neighborhood residence on child and adolescent outcomes, *Psychological Bulletin*, 126, pp. 309–337.

McPherson, M., Smith-Lovin, L. & Cook, J. M. (2001) Birds of a feather: homophily in social networks, *Annual Review of Sociology* 27, pp. 415–444.

Morenoff, J. D., Sampson, R. J. & Raudenbush, S. W. (2001) *Neighborhood Inequality, Collective Efficacy, and the Spatial Dynamics of Urban Violence*. Report no.00–451 (Ann Arbor, Michigan, Population Studies Center at the Institute for Social Research, March).

Musterd, S. & Ostendorf, W. (1998) *Urban Segregation and the Welfare State: Inequality and Exclusion in Western Cities* (New York, Routledge).

Newman, S. J. & Schnare, A. B. (1997) 'And a suitable living environment': the failure of housing programs to deliver on neighborhood quality, *Housing Policy Debate*, 8, pp. 703–741.

Porter, M. (2001) Regions and the new economics of competition, in: A. J. Scott (Ed.) *Global City-Regions* (New York, Oxford University Press).

Pastor, M., Jr., Dreier, P., Grigsby, J. E. & Lopez-Garza, M. (2000) *Regions that Work: How Cities and Suburbs Can Grow Together* (Minneapolis, University of Minnesota Press).

Popper, F. J. (1991) LULUs and their blockage, in: J. Dimento & L. Graymer (Eds) *Confronting Regional Challenges* (Cambridge, MA, Lincoln Institute of Land Policy).

Quillian, L. (1999) Migration patterns and the growth of high-poverty neighborhoods, 1970–1990, *American Journal of Sociology*, 105, pp. 1–37.

Rainwater, L. (1970) *Behind Ghetto Walls* (Cambridge, MA, Harvard University Press).

Rodrik, D. (1999) *The New Global Economy and Developing Countries: Making Openness Work* (Baltimore, Johns Hopkins University Press).

Ross, S. L. (2001) *Employment access, neighborhood quality, and residential location choice*. Paper presented at the International Seminar on Segregation and the City, Lincoln Institute of Land Policy, Cambridge, Massachusetts, 25–28 July.

Sampson, R. J., Raudenbush, S. & Earls, F. (1997) Neighborhoods and violent crime: a multi-level study of collective efficacy, *Science*, 277, pp. 918–924.

Sassen, S. (2000) *Cities in a World Economy* (Thousand Oaks, CA, Pine Forge Press).

Savitch, H. V. & Kantor, P. (2002) *Cities in the International Marketplace: The Political Economy of Urban Development in North America and Western Europe* (Princeton, Princeton University Press).

Stack, C. (1974) *All Our Kin: Strategies for Survival in a Black Community* (New York, Harper and Row).

Stiglitz, J. E. (2002) *Globalization and Its Discontents* (New York, W.W. Norton).

Stokey, E. & Zeckhauser, R. (1978) *A Primer for Policy Analysis* (New York, W.W. Norton).

Sullivan, M. (1989) *Getting Paid: Youth Crime and Work in the Inner City* (Ithaca, NY, Cornell University Press).

Swyngedouw, E. (2000) Elite power, global forces and the political-economy of 'glocal' development, in: C. G. Feldman & M. Gertler (Eds) *A Handbook of Economic Geography* (Oxford, OUP).

Taub, R., Taylor, D. G. & Dunham, J. D. (1984) *Paths of Neighborhood Change: Race and Crime in Urban America* (Chicago, University of Chicago Press).

Tienda, M. (1991) Poor people and poor places: deciphering neighborhood effects on poverty outcomes, in: J. Huber (Ed.) *Macro-micro Linkages in Sociology* (Newbury Park, Sage Publications).

Tilly, C., Moss, P., Kirschenman, J. & Kennedy, I. (2001) Space as a signal: how employers perceive neighborhoods in four metropolitan labor markets, in: A. O'Connor, C. Tilly & L. D. Bobo *Urban Inequality: Evidence from Four Cities* (New York, Russell Sage Foundation).

Turner, M. A. (1998) Moving out of poverty: expanding mobility and choice through tenant-based housing assistance, *Housing Policy Debate*, 9, pp. 373–394.

United Nations Centre for Human Settlement (2001) *The State of the World's Cities 20001: Special Conference, Istanbul + 5* (Nairobi, UNHCS).

US Department of Housing and Urban Development (HUD) (2000) *Unequal Burden: Income and Racial Disparities in Subprime Lending in America* (Washington, DC, Author).

Wacquant, L. (1993) Urban outcasts: stigma and division in the black American ghetto and the French urban periphery, *International Journal of Urban and Regional Research*, 17, pp. 366–383.

Weiss, C. H. (1995) Nothing as practical as good theory: exploring theory-based evaluation for comprehensive community initiatives for children and families, in: J. Connell, A. Kubisch & L. Schorr (Eds) *New Approaches to Evaluating Community Initiatives: Concepts, Methods, and Contexts* (New York, Aspen Institute).

Wellman, B. (1971) Crossing social boundaries: cosmopolitanism among black and white adolescents, *Social Science Quarterly*, (December), pp. 602–624.

Wilson, W. J. (1987) *The Truly Disadvantaged: The Inner City, the Underclass, and Public Policy* (Chicago, University of Chicago Press).

Wirth, L. (1964) *Urbanism as a Way of Life* (Chicago, University of Chicago Press).

World Bank (1999) *Entering the 21st Century: The Changing Development Landscape: The World Development Report 1999/2000* (New York, OUP).

World Bank (2000) *Attacking Poverty: The World Development Report 1999/2000* (New York, OUP).

Yancey, W., Ericksen, E. P. & Leon, G. H. (1985) The structure of pluralism: 'We're all Italian around here, aren't we Mrs. O'Brien?' *Ethnic and Racial Studies*, 8, pp. 94–116.

Yinger, J. (1995) *Closed Doors, Opportunities Lost: The Continuing Costs of Housing Discrimination* (New York, Russell Sage Foundation).

INDEX

ability to move 32
academic perspectives 83
acceptance: complexity of construct
    134; deviant behaviour 11–28
age effects: benefit dependency 91,
    94; neighbourhood orientation 61;
    social contacts 132
agenda for research 7–8
America *see* United States
Amsterdam 64–75, 106–7
analysis: behavioural impacts 97–115;
    levels 120; non-linear principal
    components analysis 19–21
analysis of variance (ANOVA) 20
annoyance: deviant behaviour 19,
    26–7

behavioural impacts 97–118, 124
benefit dependency 89–95, 135
biases in research 4; *see also* selection
    biases
Big Cities Policy (Netherlands) 93, 95
bonding capital 59–60
bridging capital 59–60

CABE *see* Commission on
    Architecture and the Built
    Environment
Canada 103
capital volume 24
case studies 5–6
causation: absence 6;
    inter-relationships 7; poverty 84
challenges: statistical research 98
characteristics: individual 128
Chicago: deviant behaviour 12;
    intra-neighbourhood processes
    102, 103; mixed neighbourhood
    policies 84–5

child outcomes *see* behavioural
    impacts
children: neighbourhood orientation
    effects 60, 74
choice of housing: Netherlands 63,
    64; UK policy 32–3
choice processes 105
classification: household economic
    position 86–7; 'poor' areas 37;
    social environment 87–9
Cleveland 103
collective efficacy 100–1, 102, 134
Cologne 14–28, 132–4
Commission on Architecture and the
    Built Environment (CABE) 50
'communities without propinquity'
    (Webber) 60
compounding mechanisms 130
conformity pressures 105
contagion models: deviant behaviour
    13; non-linear effects 105; norm
    emergence 133; powerlessness
    25–7
context: research and policy 1–10
context effects 11–28, 124, 133
criminal activity: neighbourhood
    effects 7; owner occupation
    relationship 52
critical points *see* thresholds
criticisms: mixed neighbourhood
    policies 83–4
'cultures of poverty' 33–4, 53, 84
'cure' strategies 136, 137

delinquency *see* criminal activity
demand and supply: labour market 1
Denver 103
dependency: benefits 89–95
descriptions: poverty neighbourhoods
    65–7

judgements: deviant behaviour 18–19

labour market 1
levels of analysis 120
limitations of research 82
local authority housing:
    dissatisfaction 41; Netherlands 62;
    residential mobility 49; UK 33
local place effects 123–7
localism 132–4; see also
    neighbourhood orientation
location: residential (dis)satisfaction
    39–44
logistic regression modelling: actual
    mobility 37–8, 47–8; intention to
    move 37–8, 44–6, 49; limitations
    38; residential dissatisfaction 37–8,
    40–3
London: residential dissatisfaction 41
long-term poverty 132–3
long-term unemployment 8
longitudinal studies: residential
    mobility 31–53; social mobility
    81–96; statistical analysis 97–115;
    strengths and weaknesses 5–6

macro level dynamics 121–2, 125
measurement biases 4
Memorandum on Urban Renewal
    (Netherlands) 63–4
methodological approaches 5–6
migration: neighbourhood orientation
    effects 61–2; outward 33; poverty
    exacerbation 2; within
    neighbourhoods 73; see also
    residential mobility
'mitigate' strategies 136, 137
mitigating mechanisms 130
mixed neighbourhood policies 1–2;
    criticisms 51, 83–4; Netherlands
    57–75, 82, 83–5; see also
    heterogeneous populations
mobility see residential mobility;
    social mobility
model learning 6–7
Moving to Opportunity (MTO)
    programme 85, 108–9
multi-level models 5, 12, 121
municipal level policy 84

National Strategy for Neighbourhood
    Renewal 31–2, 33, 50

neighbourhood bonding 71–2
neighbourhood decline: future
    expectations 52; residential
    mobility 49–50, 131
'neighbourhood matters' model 84
neighbourhood orientation:
    influencing factors 60–2; isolation
    effects 58; old versus new
    inhabitants 69–71, 74
neighbourhood processes 101–4
Netherlands 57–79, 81–95, 131–2,
    134–5
networks see interpersonal networks
new inhabitants 68–74
New York 126–7
NLPCA see non-linear principal
    components analysis
non-experimental research 109–13
non-function of neighbourhoods 60,
    71
non-linear effects 104–8
non-linear principal components
    analysis (NLPCA) 19–21
norms: social 11–30, 33–4, 58
north-south divide 122–3
northern England 41

old inhabitants 68–74
omitted variables bias 108
operationalising variables 101–4
'opportunity structures' 14, 110, 128
outward migration 33
owner occupied housing: availability
    33; child outcome effects 100–1;
    crime relationship 52; 'mixed
    communities' 51–2; Netherlands
    62; social contacts 59

paid-job households 91–2
parental variables 114
parental wealth: child outcome
    effects 101; interrelated variables
    99
people-based interventions 136
perceptions: deviant behaviour 19,
    26–7; effects transmission 6–7;
    'opportunity structures' 128;
    residential mobility effects 31–53
perspectives on research 1
pessimism 52
physical environment: restructuring
    75

Lightning Source UK Ltd.
Milton Keynes UK
06 October 2009

144597UK00002B/42/P